DATE DUE			
JAN 0 2 1996			
JAN 2 5 1996			
FEB 1 2 1996			
APR 0 2 1996			
JUN 2 0 1996			
NOV 1 2 1996			

All-American Vegetarian

Other Cookbooks by Barbara Grunes

Kabobs on the Grill

The Heartland Food Society Cookbook

Classic Chocolate Cookbook

Skinny Chocolate

Skinny Potatoes

Skinny Seafood

Skinny Pizza

Roots

Appetizers on the Grill

Home and Grill Cookbook

Grill It In

Puddings and Pies

The Complete Fish Book

The Right Stuff (Meat on the Grill)

Poultry on the Grill

Gourmet Fish on the Grill

Shellfish on the Grill

Southwest Sampler

Chicago Epicure

Fish on the Grill

Joy of Baking

Soups and Stews

Chef's Kitchen Companion

Lunch and Brunch

Fish and Seafood

Cookie Cookbook

All-Holiday Cookbook

Food Processor Cookbook

Mexican Cookbook

Dining in Chicago, Volume II

Dining in Chicago, Volume III

Ultimate Food Processor Cookbook

Inside the Convection Oven

Oriental Express

All-American Vegetarian

A Regional Harvest of Low-Fat Recipes

Barbara Grunes and
Virginia Van Vynckt

HENRY HOLT AND COMPANY

NEW YORK

Henry Holt and Company, Inc.
Publishers since 1866
115 West 18th Street
New York, New York 10011

Henry Holt ® is a registered
trademark of Henry Holt and Company, Inc.

Published in Canada by Fitzhenry & Whiteside Ltd.,
195 Allstate Parkway, Markham, Ontario L3R 4T8.

Library of Congress Cataloging-in-Publication Data

Grunes, Barbara.
All-American vegetarian : a regional harvest of low-fat recipes /
Barbara Grunes and Virginia Van Vynckt.—1st ed.
p.   cm.
Includes bibliographical references and index.
1. Vegetarian cookery.   2. Low-fat diet — Recipes.   3. Cookery,
American.   I. Van Vynckt, Virginia.   II. Title.
TX837.G678   1995   94-238709
641.5'636—dc20   CIP
ISBN 0-8050-3509-5

Henry Holt books are available for special
promotions and premiums. For details contact:
Director, Special Markets.

First Edition—1995

Designed by Paula R. Szafranski
Illustrations by Laura Hartman Maestro

Printed in the United States of America
All first editions are printed on acid-free paper. ∞

1   3   5   7   9   10   8   6   4   2

To Marissa, Claire, and Suzanne,
the best granddaughters anyone could have,
and
to Marv and Lian, for their love and patience

Contents

Food Facts and Fancies xiii

Acknowledgments xv

Why Eat Vegetarian? 1

Ingredients and Techniques 10

1 The Northeast 19

2 The South 87

3 The Midwest and Heartland 143

4 The West 211

5 The Pacific Coast 271

Sources and Resources 329

Bibliography 335

Index 337

Food Facts and Fancies

Butter at Its Best 30

Saffron's Mystique 31

Amazing Grain. 36

Aromatics. 52

Crepe Magic 60

Herbal Alchemy. 73

Twisted History 78

Grunts, Bettys, and Fools. 82

Exotic Fruits 99

A Genius at Agriculture. 117

Quicker Risotto. 119

Grits Is (Are?) Good 124

Why Peel Tomatoes? 128

Glorious Greens. 134

Paint It Orange 178

A Seedy Lot. 178

Mad About Morels 187

Miso Magic 199

Snap and Crackle. 203

The Apple Man 207

Fruits of the Desert 221

Perfect Meringue 232

Packing Heat 238

Beans and Horses 242

The Perfect Baked Potato 255

Self-Starters 265

Nuts 302

Chile Dust 313

A Breath of Pungent Air 317

The Daily Grind 322

Acknowledgments

Thanks to our agent, Martha Casselman, for getting this show on the road and keeping us fueled up. And a big thank-you to our editor, Beth Crossman, for steering us in the right direction.

We also want to thank Bev Bennett for sharing ideas and casting a practiced eye on our prose.

We're grateful to our testers for their patience and good ideas: Michele Chroman, Sharon Sanders, Alan Magiera, and Lezli Bitterman. And we thank Roger St. Pierre for his practical wine suggestions.

We can't forget our corps of tasters, who praised the successful recipes, politely ate the less successful ones, and tossed us some good suggestions along the way: Jerry Grunes, the various Van Vynckts, the Ploenses, the Caves, and the Blackmans.

Why Eat Vegetarian?

We can give you five good reasons for enjoying a plant-based diet.

It's healthful. Everyone from the American Cancer Society to the U.S. Department of Agriculture is saying that in order to help prevent disease and feel your best you should replace the standard heavy-on-the-meat-and-dairy-products diet with one heavily weighted in favor of grains, fruits, and vegetables.

How you choose to interpret this advice is up to you. Some people become lacto-ovo vegetarians, eating no meat, fish, or poultry but enjoying low-fat dairy products and eggs. Others embrace a vegan diet and ditch all animal products. Still others eat a mostly vegetarian diet supplemented by fish.

Most of us who eat meatless meals these days could be best described as semi-vegetarian. That means we eat meat, fish, and poultry—but not every day, and not nearly as much of them as we once did. Vegetarian meals—once thought to be the fare of fanatics—show up on our tables with regularity.

It's simple to track. Tired of whipping out a pocket calculator to figure out how many fat grams you have left to consume? Wondering whether the beef in that stir-fry adds up to three ounces or four?

Relax. We have an easy recipe for better nutrition: Eat more plant foods, fewer animal foods, and smaller amounts of fat, especially saturated fats—fats such as shortening, butter, and margarine, which are solid at room temperature.

As at least one researcher has pointed out, the factors that seem to protect against disease—beta-carotene, vitamin E, vitamin C, fiber, folic acid—are found in abundance in plant foods. Substances shown to promote or aggravate disease—saturated fat, cholesterol, excess protein, and excess sodium—are found in abundance in animal foods.

This does not mean that you need to give up all animal foods (many experts would argue against shunning them completely) or that vegetarian fare is automatically low in fat. It does mean that if you eat plenty of grains, vegetables, and fruits, and fewer fats, dessert foods, and animal products, you do not need a calculator to figure out whether you're eating healthfully.

It's delicious. What would you like for dinner? Artichoke Pizza? Corn Chowder? Red Beans and Rice? Grilled Vegetables with Lemon-Sage Polenta? Swiss Cheese and Sauerkraut Sandwiches? Hot German-style Potato Salad? Mu Shu Vegetables? Chili? Sweet Potato–Peanut Soup?

When you cook with vegetables, fruits, and grains, you have dozens and dozens of combinations to experiment with and enjoy.

Vegetarian cooking celebrates the seasons and redefines eating. Forget the outdated idea that a meal consists of a main course, a starch, and a vegetable.

It's inexpensive. Surveys have shown that people tend to think of healthful diets as expensive—perhaps because they're used to buying boneless chicken breasts and thinking of vegetables and grains as side dishes rather than as the stars of the meal. As at least one study—and our own experience—has shown, eating "lower on the food chain" actually *saves* money.

If you usually eat meat, poultry, or fish several times a week, try this experiment: Eat vegetarian for a week, planning your menus around pasta, beans, rice, potatoes, and vegetables rather than chicken, red meat, and fish. Keep your grocery receipts. The difference in cost may shock you.

Of course, you can drive the cost of vegetarian dining sky-high if you insist on eating asparagus in December, building meals around radicchio and wild mushrooms, and buying boutique grains in tiny packages. But generally, giving up meat is kind to your budget.

It's American. This is the country that has reinvented the wheel dozens of times. Why not reinvent our standard diet? We have the biggest new wave of immigrants to arrive since the turn of the century, bringing with them lemongrass, miso, chiles, tomatillos, basmati rice, and in some cases centuries-old vegetarian cuisines. American cookbooks didn't even mention fresh coriander twenty years ago; now it shows up in supermarkets everywhere under its Spanish name, cilantro.

Meanwhile, American chefs and home cooks constantly rediscover and invent recipes for ingredients that formed the foundation of ancient American cooking: tomatoes, corn, squash, beans, potatoes, wild rice, avocados, cranberries, maple syrup, pecans, amaranth, quinoa, chocolate.

People are paying more attention to the environmental ravages of factory farming and overgrazing, and hearing more about preventive medicine. Folks who once swore they would never give up the thrice-weekly hamburgers are learning a million ways to serve pasta and vegetables.

You say barbecued tofu is not traditional American fare? It is now!

About Vegetarian Nutrition

One enduring myth about vegetarian eating is that you have to carefully combine plant foods with complementary proteins at any given meal to get the complete set of amino acids—building blocks of protein—that your body needs.

This idea dates back to the days when researchers were convinced nobody could live healthfully without plenty of animal protein. Frances Moore Lappé's 1971 classic *Diet for a Small Planet* brought the notion wider public attention.

In fact, as Moore Lappé pointed out in the 1982 anniversary edition of her book, most of us do not need to sit down with charts and studiously combine proteins. Although it's true that some plants do not have a complete set of the eight essential amino acids in forms readily available to the body, just eating a variety of healthful foods over the course of a couple of days will give you the complete protein you need. Of course, some plant proteins naturally combine deliciously—red beans and rice, for example.

If, for health or ethical reasons, you decide to give up animal foods completely, you may need to pay more attention to calcium, vitamin D, and vitamin B_{12}. Vitamin B_{12} occurs naturally in significant amounts only in animal foods, and a persistent deficiency in it can cause anemia. Fortunately, you don't need much B_{12}, and taking a supplement or eating a breakfast cereal fortified with the vitamin should be sufficient.

Calcium is a much more complex issue. Current research indicates that a good supply of dietary calcium may be important in staving off bone loss, high blood pressure, and other conditions. Some groups have aroused controversy by suggesting that dairy products are harmful and we would be better off without them. Others say dairy products are our best sources of calcium.

We believe in hedging our bets. For us, the current state of research suggests a commonsense approach:

Exercise regularly. Bone is like muscle; if you don't use it, you lose it. Exercise that requires your bones to bear weight—walking, weight lifting, dancing, jogging— thus forcing blood into the bone, is best.

Get a sufficient amount of dietary calcium from a variety of sources: low-fat dairy products (assuming you have no problem eating them), dark leafy greens, tofu made with calcium carbonate, almonds, beans, corn tortillas (because of the lime the corn flour is treated with), and calcium-fortified juice. If you think you might not be getting enough calcium, consult your doctor about taking supplements.

Eat a balanced diet lower in animal protein. Eating an overload of protein causes calcium to be excreted in the urine, perhaps to the extent that bones are threatened. In other words, vegetarians may need less calcium than meat-eaters.

Also, because vitamins and minerals work together, deficiencies or excesses of one can play havoc with another. An overdose of sodium, for example, abundant in processed foods, might interfere with calcium balance.

Vitamin D helps in calcium absorption. Our bodies manufacture vitamin D from sunlight. In northern climates in the winter, our bodies make much less vitamin D. The biggest dietary source of vitamin D in this country is fortified milk.

The good news for people who do not eat dairy products is that several soy milks are now fortified with vitamin D and calcium.

Of Cabbages and Phytochemicals

Nutraceuticals. Designer foods. Functional foods.

The names all refer to the same thing: foods that contain vitamins, minerals, or other chemicals that may help protect us against heart disease, cancer, and other illnesses. Recently, nutrition researchers have grown very interested in the potential healing powers of various vegetables, fruits, legumes, and grains. In other words, scientists are finally catching up to our great-grandparents.

Take garlic. Scientists have been exploring its potential for lowering cholesterol and blood pressure, preventing cancer, and acting as an antiseptic. People without access to laboratories have known all this for centuries. In cultures around the world, folks have used garlic to do everything from "cleanse the blood" to ward off vampires. Even babies know how valuable the stuff is. Studies have shown that infants really like Mom's breast milk when she has eaten garlic. Scientists are digging into the details. They have discovered dozens of potentially protective compounds in garlic. They're not sure exactly how they work.

Other foods that have shown great promise include cruciferous vegetables such as broccoli and cauliflower, and soy foods such as tofu and miso.

The "big three" protective elements for which there's the most evidence are vitamin A and its precursor, beta-carotene; vitamin E; and vitamin C. Beta-carotene is found in orange and yellow vegetables and dark leafy greens. Citrus fruits and their juices, berries, and the cabbage family are good sources of vitamin C. Whole grains and vegetable oils are the best sources of vitamin E.

Many people pop vitamins to get these nutrients. Most nutritionists agree there's nothing wrong with taking a well-balanced multivitamin and mineral supplement, but many draw the line at recommending large doses of specific vitamins or minerals. Others counter that to be truly therapeutic, vitamins such as C and E must be taken in amounts greater than what you can get in food.

Both sides agree that a good diet is the first defense. Relying too heavily on vitamin supplements or highly processed, low-fat foods is a simplistic approach to the intricate business of living and staying well. Plants are genetically far more complex than humans are and contain an enormous variety of substances that could be protective, neutral, or harmful, depending on the dosage or circumstances. Beta-carotene, for example, is just one of a group of substances called the carotenoids and may not have the same effect alone as it does in the company of its colleagues.

Good Fat, Bad Fat?

If you get the bulk of your nutrition education from headlines, you're probably thoroughly confused by now. First we were supposed to replace butter with margarine. Then TV stations and newspapers, responding to a doctor's commentary condemning trans fats—a category of fats formed when oils are hardened into margarine and shortening—implied that butter might actually be better for you than margarine.

Some doctors and food writers have been pushing the Mediterranean-style diet, which is low in meat and dairy products but very rich in olive oil. Still other doctors say we're poisoning ourselves with animal foods or added fats. They think people stay healthiest on an ultra-low-fat, strict vegetarian diet. No, no, retort more mainstream nutritionists: You should eat all foods in moderation.

Sexy headlines and differences of opinion aside, bottom-line dietary advice in the United States has not changed in nearly thirty years. Eat more vegetables. Eat more fruit. Eat more whole grains. Eat less fat, especially saturated fat.

Obviously, reducing fat and saturated fat means cutting back on the chief sources of them in our diets. They are red meat; full-fat and "low-fat" dairy products such as butter, cheese, and 2-percent milk; vegetable oils and margarines; poultry skin; and baked goods such as crackers, cakes, and cookies.

What about eating the "right" kinds of fats rather than worrying about total fat in the diet? Surveys indicate that about a third of the U.S. population is overweight. Butter, olive oil, and margarine are all fats, and all contain a whopping 100 calories or more per tablespoon. There's also evidence—still inconclusive—that eating a diet higher in fat, regardless of calories, encourages weight gain.

If you do want to sauté those onions in fat, however, your best bet probably is olive or canola oil. Both are rich in monounsaturated fats, which many researchers believe are neutral or even beneficial to heart health. Canola oil also is the lowest in saturated fat of all the vegetable oils.

Keep in mind that the nutritional messages you hear about fat or anything else are filtered through the biases of the person who did the study, the reporter telling you about it, and often the person paying for it. Cereal companies, margarine manufacturers, cattlemen's associations, dairy promoters, fast-food chains, olive oil traders, animal-rights groups, vitamin supplement manufacturers, and soybean growers are just a few of the self-interested organizations that have been more than happy to fund "educational" messages about nutrition.

Common sense is still your best ally in determining which fat to use or which food to eat.

Born to Shop

You've heard it said again and again, but it bears repeating: One of the biggest differences between an average cook and a good one is that the good cook knows how to shop.

Buy locally grown fruits and vegetables in season whenever possible. Determining what's local and what's in season does grow harder by the year. New Zealand apples arrive in the supermarket in March. Mangos, traditionally a summer fruit, are shipped nearly year-round now. And none of us in the North complain about being able to buy Florida oranges in the dead of winter.

But a peach that hasn't traveled two thousand miles stands a better chance of pleasing your palate. Farmers' markets and most supermarkets carry local produce at the peak of its season.

If you're lucky enough to live near a good health-food store (or natural-food store, as some prefer to call it), take advantage of it. It's likely to stock items that may not be readily available in the supermarket, such as exotic grains, beans in bulk, whole-grain pastas and couscous, sea vegetables, cold-pressed vegetable oils, various brands of tofu, and organically grown fruits and vegetables.

Wherever you shop, use your nose, your eyes, and your hands. A good tomato *smells* like a tomato. A fresh eggplant is firm and has a dark, glossy skin. Fresh broccoli is crisp. Ripe corn has dark brown silks and weighty ears. In the produce department, bigger is rarely better. The small Golden Delicious apples, strawberries, and tomatoes—often organically grown—usually taste better than their overlarge, cosmetically perfect counterparts.

We believe in cooking from scratch because we like good food and usually can't afford to pay some chef a fortune to make it for us. But we do not shun convenience products that can make our life easier. You won't find frozen dinners in our freezers, but you will find egg substitute in our refrigerators and canned beans on our shelves. We buy canned tomatoes in the winter because we see no reason to pay premium prices for fresh tomatoes that have been bioengineered, grown in water, or flown halfway around the world. We're just going to simmer them for hours in chili anyway.

Experimenting with low-fat cooking has become much easier in the last few years, thanks to the arrival of so many nonfat or reduced-fat items in the supermarket. Even tofu has slimmed down.

The quality of these items ranges from awful to amazingly good. We bought a light ricotta at the local health-food store that was fabulous. We bought one fat-free cream cheese that we tossed into the garbage and another that tasted fine mixed with other ingredients. We have yet to find a fat-free cheese we like, but we're still amazed that nonfat sour cream can taste as good as it does. It pays to buy different brands and "fat levels" of products and compare.

No matter where you buy your fresh produce and whether it has been organically grown or not, always wash fresh fruits and vegetables. This rinses off any surface sprays, dirt, and potentially harmful microorganisms such as salmonella. Although most food poisonings are traced back to animal foods such as chicken, meat, or eggs, vegetables are not exempt.

For the same reason, fruits and vegetables that have been cut into should be refrigerated if you're not going to use them within an hour.

How This Book Can Help

In *All-American Vegetarian* we have taken traditional American classics and some newer American favorites and updated them when necessary, making them vegetarian and lower in fat. We have also created some completely new recipes based on new or old American ingredients and inspired by recent cooking trends.

Our main criteria in developing and testing recipes were flavor and nutrition. We think the two go hand in hand. A blanket of cream (or oil) and a tablespoon of salt do nothing to enhance the sweetness of a good carrot or the toasted-nut flavor of wild rice. On the other hand, eating something just because it's low in fat or high in vitamins is no way to exercise your palate. If a small amount of butter or olive oil will elevate a dish from okay to excellent, we'll happily use it.

This book is for people like us who are eating much less meat but still yearn for the flavors that define our region of the country, our ethnic heritage, and what our families bring to reunions. We've divided the country into five broad regions, which overlap considerably. Mangos may grow in Florida and Hawaii, but they've become popular throughout the United States. Texas is "southern" for growing rice and pecans, but "southwestern" in its devotion to chiles and beans.

It would be silly to pretend that America evolved as a vegetarian nation or that a Thanksgiving "turkey" made of pressed tofu tastes like the real thing. But many American favorites are already vegetarian or can easily become so with simple omissions or substitutions. Other dishes in this book borrow flavors that have been associated with meat dishes. A sage-scented "unstuffing" doesn't need the turkey to make it taste good.

You'll find plenty of tomatoes, corn, and potatoes in this book because they're the most American of vegetables. You'll also find vegetables and grains that may be less familiar, such as quinoa, blood oranges, and seaweed, because we believe it's worth it to make their acquaintance.

Not all of the recipes in *All-American Vegetarian* are low-fat; sometimes a fair amount of fat carries the flavor, produces a pleasing texture, or adds to the comfort in a comfort food. We have not "banned" any particular fats because all fulfill particular functions. Thus, we put a bit of vegetable shortening into crusts and call for a small amount of butter or margarine when it will mellow the sharper flavors in a dish. Otherwise, we use canola and olive oils, which nutritionists believe are the most healthful—or at least neutral—of the vegetable oils.

All the dishes are as low in fat—and especially saturated fat—as we could make them without sacrificing flavor or mouth feel. Most of the recipes in the book get no more than 8 percent of their calories from saturated fat.

We use modest amounts of nuts, dairy products, sugar, and eggs to give recipes a lift. We have included plenty of recipes, however, that contain no animal products and little, if any, added fat or sugar.

Each recipe includes a per-serving nutritional analysis. The nutritional break-down does not include optional ingredients, the salt in the water used to boil pasta, nonstick cooking spray for greasing pans, or suggested garnishes that diners add at the table. When a recipe lists a range of amounts, it's analyzed for the larger amount. That is, a recipe that calls for 1 to 2 tablespoons of oil has been analyzed for 2 tablespoons. We figure "salt to taste" as ¼ teaspoon. The amount of fat listed includes saturated fat, which is also listed separately.

Many of the recipes call for vegetable stock, with canned vegetable broth as an alternative. The sodium content of those recipes reflects the use of canned broth from the supermarket.

We rounded gram numbers up or down to the nearest half, and milligrams up to the nearest whole.

Foods were analyzed using ESHA Research's Food Processor software, and nutrition analysis is computed per serving.

Ingredients and Techniques

Whenever possible we've included notes on ingredients and techniques with recipes they apply to. However, here are some miscellaneous notes about ingredients and techniques not covered elsewhere.

Beans and Dried Peas

Twelve ounces of pinto beans, Great Northern beans, lentils, black-eyed peas, or split peas equals roughly 2 cups. The exception is navy beans; 12 ounces is roughly 1½ cups. Pressure cookers are wonderful for cooking beans in no time flat. Use about 4 cups of water to 1 cup of beans, and add a little oil to prevent foaming. Bring up to high pressure. The cooking time for unsoaked beans will vary according to the type of bean and its age, but averages around 20 to 25 minutes.

You also can cook beans in the microwave, although you won't save a whole lot of time. Put them in a microwave-proof bowl, cover with an inch of cold water, and cover the bowl loosely with wax paper or plastic wrap. Cook them on high (100 percent) for 2 to 3 minutes, then on medium (50 percent) until tender. This will probably take at least 45 minutes.

Most cookbooks call for soaking dried beans overnight in cold water, draining them, covering them again with water, and cooking them. Soaking supposedly reduces both the cooking time and the beans' socially unpleasant side effects. On occasion we forgot to soak beans and went ahead and cooked them anyway. It didn't seem to make much difference in cooking time. Then we ran across an article that made a good case for not soaking beans. On average, it reported, soaking saves only about 30 minutes' cooking time, hardly a huge time savings for a food that simmers unattended. Not only that, but beans taste better when cooked without soaking.

As for the social question: Cold-soaking does little to help. The indigestible sugars in beans do cause flatulence, but you can get rid of them only by boiling the beans, then draining them. Unfortunately, you also pour nutrients down the drain. And sugars or no, beans have plenty of fiber that contributes to flatulence. Nearly all bean experts (yes, there are such folks) agree that the best way to make beans more digestible is to eat them more often, so your body adapts to their sugars and fiber. That makes sense to us.

Capers

The pickled buds of a Mediterranean flower, they come in small and large sizes and have a sharp, vinegary-olive flavor. They're sold near the olives in the supermarket aisle.

Citrus Fruits

Lemons, limes, and oranges will continue to ripen if left at room temperature for a day or two. They can be refrigerated, loose, for longer storage; keep them dry or they'll mold.

Before juicing lemons, limes, or oranges and grating the peel, roll them back and forth a few times to release the oils in the skin and the juices inside. Use the small holes of a grater or a citrus zester to remove the zest—the colored portion of the rind.

Egg Substitutes

Because they're labeled as substitutes for whole eggs, egg substitutes must be fortified with vitamins A and D and other nutrients found in the egg yolk. In that sense, they're superior to egg whites, which contain little nutritional value other than protein. Check the labels; the best egg substitutes are nothing more than egg whites, vitamins, and a little natural yellow coloring.

Egg substitutes also have been pasteurized, which means you can safely use them in recipes that call for lightly cooked or raw eggs. Using whole eggs in such recipes is not a good idea because of the risk of salmonella.

Whole eggs used in this book are "large."

Eggplants

In American supermarkets you're likely to find eggplant in three varieties: regular, averaging about ¾ to 1 pound each; Japanese, the long, slender type with lighter purple skin; and baby eggplants; the last two average three or four to a pound.

The Japanese and baby eggplants generally aren't bitter and don't need to be salted and drained. Larger eggplants, especially if they're seedy, should be sliced or diced, salted, and drained for 20 to 30 minutes.

Fats and Oils

"Butter" in this book means unsalted butter. Stick margarine may be substituted in most recipes that call for butter. Do not substitute tub or "diet" margarines and expect the same results, since most contain water.

Canola oil is a light, flavorless oil made from rapeseed. Canola has a low percentage of saturated fat (6 percent by weight) and a high percentage of monounsaturated fat, including beneficial omega-3 fatty acids.

A canola–corn oil blend is a little deeper in color and flavor. It can be used in place of canola oil in many of the recipes in this book.

Olive oil sold in this country is usually either pure or extra-virgin. Extra-virgin undergoes very little processing after being pressed from the olives. Pure (regular) olive oil is highly processed, like corn or vegetable oil, but then has some extra-virgin oil added back to it for color and flavor. If you can afford it, we recommend using extra-virgin olive oil for its flavor and purity.

Flours

All-purpose flour, whether bleached or unbleached, generally has a medium gluten (protein) content. For most purposes we prefer unbleached flour, which is not as chemically treated.

Bread flour is higher in protein and absorbs water differently; be sure to use it, not all-purpose flour, when the recipe calls for it.

Cake flour is heavily bleached and low in protein, and is used in cakes, biscuits, pastry, and wherever you want flaky or soft textures.

Whole wheat flour is the flour that still has the germ and bran. Whole wheat pastry flour is ground from softer wheat. Some whole wheat flours are stone-ground. When recipes were tested with stone-ground flour, which tends to absorb liquids differently, we mention it. Whole wheat flour goes rancid quickly and should be stored in the refrigerator or freezer if possible.

Be aware that of all the ingredients in recipes, flour is one of the most variable in how it absorbs moisture. Even if you consistently use the same type of flour and the same brand, you can get different results depending on where the wheat was grown and what weather it was subjected to, when the flour was milled, and the degree of humidity in your kitchen. That's why in bread recipes we try to describe the texture of the dough and give flour amounts in ranges.

Always measure flour by stirring it, scooping the cup into it, then leveling the top with a knife or the edge of the flour scoop.

Garlic

A bulb, or head, is the whole bunch, consisting of twelve to twenty individual cloves. An average clove of garlic will yield about ½ teaspoon minced.

Before chopping garlic, whack the clove with the flat side of the knife blade. This loosens the skin and flattens the clove for easier peeling and chopping.

Herbs and Spices

The quality of these makes a big difference in what you cook. Dried herbs and spices should not celebrate birthdays. Put a little label on the bottom of the jar with the date you bought it. If the spice is older than a year, replace it.

We think basil, cilantro, parsley, and dillweed lose too much flavor when dried and should be used fresh whenever possible. Other herbs such as thyme and rosemary can be used fresh or dried depending on what's available and what flavor you want.

To keep fresh herbs longer (if you buy them loose or have opened the container), stand them in a cup of cold water, like a bouquet, and refrigerate. Or put them in self-sealing plastic bags and squeeze as much air out as possible.

You can also finely chop them, put them in the compartments of an ice cube tray (1 to 2 tablespoons per compartment), top off with a bit of water, and freeze. When they're solid, transfer these herbal ice cubes to plastic freezer bags.

Cilantro is the Spanish name for fresh coriander; it's also sometimes called Chinese parsley.

Italian, or flat-leaf, parsley has a more robust flavor than the curly kind.

Nuts

Although they are very high in fat, nuts contain mostly unsaturated fat and make good additions to the diet in small amounts. Most are good sources of vitamin E and fiber. Almonds also contain some calcium. (See also page 302.)

Nuts should be refrigerated so they don't turn rancid. They freeze well up to six months in an airtight container.

To blanch almonds, drop them in boiling water for 1 minute. Drain, then let cool. Slip off the skins. Blanched almonds should always be toasted to crisp them.

Toasting helps intensify the flavors of nuts by bringing out their oils. To toast nuts, spread them in a single layer on a baking sheet and put in a 325-degree oven for 10 to 15 minutes, stirring once, until golden.

You can also toast sesame seeds this way; be careful because they burn easily.

You can toast nuts or sesame seeds in a dry frying pan, preferably cast iron, over medium heat. Shake the pan frequently and watch carefully so the nuts or seeds don't burn.

Peppers

For a rundown on hot chile peppers, see Packing Heat (page 238).

Roasting peppers serves three purposes: It enhances their sweetness, softens their texture, and rids them of their tough skin.

The best peppers for roasting are the ones with thick skin, sometimes called Holland peppers. You can roast the thinner-skinned varieties, such as Le Rouge Royale, but you may not be able to get every last bit of skin peeled off.

Roast peppers over an open flame, on a grill, in the oven, or under the broiler. We think the easiest way is to cut the peppers in half lengthwise (don't remove the cores or seeds), put them on a broiler pan, cut side down, and stick under the broiler (you can even use a toaster oven). Roast them for about 5 to 7 minutes, switching them from front to back once, until the skin is charred and blistered all over. You can also roast them whole by turning them often during the roasting. Stick them in a plastic bag and let them steam for 10 to 15 minutes. If they're still too hot to handle, run them under cold water. Pull off the skin with a paring knife, or scrape it off, and cut out the cores and seeds. You can cover the roasted peppers tightly with plastic wrap and refrigerate up to two days.

Or save the effort and buy roasted red peppers in a jar. Because they must contain acid or other preservatives, they're not as sweet and fresh-tasting as peppers you roast yourself, but they're wonderfully convenient. You'll find them in Italian groceries, specialty shops, and some supermarkets.

Potatoes

Although specialty stores carry all kinds of exotic varieties, including purple, most supermarkets carry three basic kinds. Russets have thick brown skins and flesh that's fluffy when cooked. They're best for baking, mashing, and frying.

Thin-skinned potatoes—red or white—have flesh that cooks up waxy and are best for salads. Small boiling potatoes are often labeled "new," but true new potatoes are the spring potatoes that are dug when tiny—usually no more than 1½ inches in diameter. They're wonderful cooked whole, in their jackets.

Yellow-fleshed potatoes fall somewhere between waxy and fluffy; they are often described as buttery textured and can be considered all-purpose potatoes.

Tofu or Bean Curd

Bean curd, better known in America as tofu, was invented in China centuries ago and has long been a staple in China, Korea, and Japan. It has the texture of well-baked custard and is cream-colored. Tofu's blandness (it should taste faintly beany) is one of its virtues; it picks up flavors like a sponge. It's also a good binder and can be used instead of eggs in baked goods.

Buying tofu can be confusing. It comes in three densities; soft, regular or firm, and extra-firm. Use firm or extra-firm for most cooking purposes; soft is good for sauces and desserts.

Tofu comes aseptically packaged or fresh, in tubs of water. You can use either kind in any of our recipes, but water-packed tofu tends to be a bit sturdier for frying, grilling, and stir-frying. If you buy the water-packed tofu, buy the freshest batch (check the expiration date), keep it refrigerated, and change the water every one or two days. If the tofu smells sour, throw it out.

Aseptically packaged tofu, which often is silken (extra-smooth) tofu, can be kept on the shelf in a cool place. We think it's best used in dishes where you're going to mash it, such as in cakes, dressings, sauces, and pasta fillings.

We've seen all sorts of torturous directions for pressing tofu, but we usually just sandwich it between paper towels and gently squeeze it between our palms. This firms up the tofu a bit and helps it absorb flavors more readily.

We also like to smoke tofu when we're using it in dishes that might normally be made with ham or bacon. To smoke it, first press it. If you like, marinate it in a mixture of molasses and soy sauce (2 parts molasses to 1 part soy sauce) to give it a more "bacony" flavor. Or sprinkle it lightly with salt and brown sugar just before smoking.

Prepare a stovetop smoker according to the manufacturer's directions and smoke tofu for 5 minutes. Do not smoke it longer than that or you'll think you're eating cigarettes.

You can also smoke it in a wok. Use a steamer rack or a bamboo steamer lined with cheesecloth. Put ½ cup of wood chips in the bottom of a foil-lined wok. Heat the wok over high heat until you see wisps of smoke rising from the chips. Set the steamer rack in the wok, cover tightly, and smoke for exactly 3 minutes. Turn off the heat and let the tofu sit another 5 minutes, then uncover and remove from the wok.

Tofu can be frozen in airtight bags for up to three months. Some people actually prefer it frozen and thawed because it has a chewier texture.

Tomatoes

Supermarket tomatoes have become better in the last few years, and it's now possible to get a decent-tasting tomato in February. You'll pay a hefty premium for it, however. For the most part, we use canned tomatoes in the winter when we're making slower-cooking dishes.

Plum tomatoes are best for sauces.

Dried tomatoes come plain or packed in oil; obviously, the plain ones have less fat. Reconstitute them by soaking in very hot or boiling water for a minute or two.

Vegetable Stock

There's absolutely no doubt about it: If you want a first-rate vegetable stock, you have to make it yourself. The canned vegetable broth sold in the supermarket tastes fine, if a little tinny, but it's very high in sodium. We tried a low-sodium vegetable broth from the health-food store, but it was more like pureed carrots than stock.

Making stock is a great way to use up those no-longer-crisp carrots, slightly wilted parsley, and potato peels. Anything that's not too strongly flavored can go into a vegetable stock. We would draw the line at broccoli, brussels sprouts, and cabbage, although kale works nicely. Dried mushrooms add a nice depth of flavor.

You can store vegetable scraps in a self-sealing plastic bag in the freezer until you have enough to make stock.

There are no real "rules" to stock-making as far as we're concerned, but we do recommend that you use several carrots (for color, sweetness, and their vitamin A), some greens (parsley, kale, celery), an onion or a couple of cloves of garlic, and a couple of dried mushrooms (we like shiitakes, which provide a deep flavor and some iron). If you have trimmings—tomato skins or fresh potato peels, for example—add them to the lineup.

We recently made a nice stock with 1½ cups of carrots and 2 cups of celery, each cut into 1-inch pieces; 3 green beans; 3 spears of asparagus (use this vegetable sparingly); a couple of sprigs of parsley; 4 cherry tomatoes; 3 dried shiitake mushrooms, a small onion; ½ red bell pepper; 12 peppercorns; a piece of fresh ginger; and 10 cups of water.

Put all the vegetables into a big pot and add just enough cold water to cover them—usually 8 to 10 cups. Toss in some peppercorns and a piece of ginger or lemon peel. You could also add a few coriander seeds.

Bring it to a boil, then reduce the heat as low as it will go and simmer for at least 2 hours and preferably 4 to 8 hours. Or cook in a pressure cooker for 30 minutes after bringing to high pressure. Strain the stock through cheesecloth or a coffee filter and taste it. If it seems weak, return it to the pot and boil it over high heat until it condenses to the strength you like.

Let the stock cool, then pour it into plastic freezer containers. Freeze for up to six months. You might also want to freeze some of the stock in ice cube trays for recipes where you need only a small amount of stock.

Wheat Germ

The nut-flavored embryo of the wheat berry, it is a good source of fiber and vitamin E. Like all whole wheat products, which become rancid easily, it's best refrigerated.

Adding Appeal Without Adding Fat

We use several techniques in this book to enhance the flavors of low-fat foods.

Putting fats up front: Fats carry flavor. Thus, we like to put the fats where you'll taste them first: in the frosting, in the brown crust of the sautéed food, in the filling.

Sautéing or frying in sprayed pans: A tablespoon or less of oil doesn't quite cover a large frying pan. On the other hand, simply coating it with nonstick cooking spray doesn't always allow foods to get brown or cooked enough without sticking. So in many recipes we combine the two, heating oil in a sprayed pan. This gives better coverage and makes it easier to brown foods. We consider nonstick cooking spray a staple of low-fat cooking. We recommend keeping two kinds on hand: a vegetable oil spray (corn, olive, or canola) and a butter-flavored spray.

Using yogurt and buttermilk: Acid cuts the gluten (protein) in flour and tenderizes the crumb. Buttermilk and yogurt also add a rich flavor.

Boosting the seasonings: A higher-fat cake might require only a teaspoon of vanilla; a lower-fat one might take a tablespoon. You'll find that we use spices and herbs generously for that reason.

I

The Northeast

Pennsylvania Dutch Sunday Dinner

Sweets and Sours Platter
(Pickled Mushrooms, Pepper Cabbage, Sweet-and-Sour Beets)
Whole Grain Icebox Rolls
Vegetable Potpie with Saffron Noodle Squares
Apple Upside-Down Gingerbread

A Tribute to the First Thanksgiving

White Corn Sticks and Yellow Corn Relish
Bean and Carrot Pâté with Watercress Sauce
Parsnip Fritters and Cranberry-Apple Relish
Hasty Pudding with Maple Syrup
Dark and Spicy Pumpkin Pie

North End Italian Dinner Party

Bruschetta with Tomatoes and Basil
Double-Spinach Crespelle (Manicotti)

Garlicky Sautéed Artichokes

Orange-Chocolate Biscotti

Appetizers, Salads, and Side Dishes

Two-Corn Succotash

Oscar's Waldorf Salad

Greengrocer's Cucumbers with Vegetable Shreds

Lemon-steamed Fiddleheads

Zucchini and Celery Sticks with Blue Cheese Dip

Soups

Italian Summer Vegetable Soup

Hot and Sour Soup

Chilled Blueberry Soup

Cold Beet Soup with Dill

Egg Lemon Soup with Endive and Orzo

Garlic-spiked Potato Soup

Entrées

Rye-Caraway Crepes with Glazed Onions

Whole Wheat Pasta with Eggplant and Toasted Pine Nuts

Buckwheat, Bows, and Mushrooms

Baked Beans with a Pumpernickel Crust

Soft Cornmeal Loaf (Mamaliga) Four Ways

New England Red Boiled Dinner with Honey-Mustard Sauce

Swiss and Sauerkraut Sandwich on Homemade Onion Rye

Savory Rice and Pigeon Peas

Mashed Potatoes with Kale

Tarragon-scented String Bean Salad, Shaker Style

Breads and Desserts

Baked Boston Brown Bread

Braided Egg Bread (Challah) with Wheat Germ

Soft Pretzels

Onion Rye Bread

Irish Soda Bread

Buckwheat Pancakes with Apple Cider Sauce

Strawberry Grunt

Four-Berry Summer Pudding

Peach and Nectarine Compote with Mango-Ginger Frozen Yogurt

For the Native Americans who lived there for centuries, as well as the explorers who came after them, the northeastern part of the continent was a heavily forested, rocky promise of a land. It was, in a word, unforgiving.

In a neck of the woods where winters could seemingly last forever and exact a brutal toll, seeds and cereals and beans played a crucial role in keeping people alive. So did root vegetables, which could be dug in the fall and stored for the winter to tide folks over until the fiddleheads, dandelions, and other welcome greens peeked through the mud. Preserved foods, such as dried berries and pickled vegetables, offered welcome diversion in the winter as well.

Summer brought one of the most prized gifts of the New World: corn. The residents of what became New England ate it fresh, ground it into meal, baked it into breads, and cooked it into coarse porridges. And summer brought berries, especially blueberries, that could be relished fresh or dried for winter use.

The settlers tapped maple syrup and used it to sweeten everything from puddings to pies. They baked humble beans into a dish far more sublime than the sum of its ingredients.

Through trade, they brought in spices from the islands to the south, along with rum and molasses. And, of course, some of the favorites of their homelands came with them: aged Cheddars and freshly churned butter, finely milled wheat flour, jams, ale, and whiskey.

As the new nation entered adolescence, waves of immigrants arrived, joining the lines at Ellis Island and bringing with them a taste for such foodstuffs as rye bread, garlic, broccoli, and caraway. Industrialization swept the nation, and soon many of the immigrants to the big coastal cities came from within the United States. They were escaping the rigors and uncertainties of farming for a steadier paycheck. People seeking their fortunes still pour into the big cities of the Northeast from all over the

United States and the rest of the world, although they're more likely to arrive by jet these days.

All of these immigrants have created in the Northeast one of the country's largest, most complex stews of ethnicity. Its ingredients originate from the gardens and pantries of Ireland, Italy, Portugal, the British Isles, France, China, Korea, Japan, the Philippines, Eastern Europe, Russia, India, Africa, Puerto Rico, Austria, and a world of other places.

Over the course of more than three centuries, settlers brought not only ideas and recipes from their native lands, but whipped up new creations with American ingredients or know-how, including maple pudding, cranberry relish, pumpkin pie, and aseptically packaged tofu. They opened delicatessens, groceries, and bakeries that transplanted the smells and languages of the old country to new soil. They introduced linguine to a country that barely knew macaroni. They stocked shelves with coconut milk and pigeon peas, and piled the greengrocer bins high with fat, white, crunchy radishes.

These days, "survival skills" refers more to finding a cab on a rainy afternoon than to foraging for wild foods. But the ingredients that built the foundation of Northeast cuisine still stand firm, even if today's chefs insist on calling cornmeal mush "polenta."

We present the ever-evolving foodstuffs and cooking styles of the Northeast in both traditional dishes and in new spins on old favorites. Here you'll find pretzels made with the aid of a bread machine, vegetarian hot and sour soup, rye-caraway crepes, green potatoes made with kale rather than cabbage, and brown bread that's baked, not steamed.

• PENNSYLVANIA DUTCH SUNDAY DINNER •

The Pennsylvania Dutch are not Dutch. Most claim German ancestry, by way of Germany, Alsace, or Switzerland ("Dutch" is probably a corruption of "Deutsch"). They're truly American in that they quickly settled in and took advantage of a classic opportunity in the rich, rolling hills of Pennsylvania.

Most were farmers, which means they sat down to big dinners, especially on Sundays. And their wives became famous for the kind of cooking that farm wives generally are known for, turning out hearty breads, pillowy rolls, preserves, pies, blue-ribbon cakes, pickles of all kinds, and hearty grain dishes.

Suggested Wines: A Sauvignon (or Chenin) Blanc is the right choice with the sweets and sours tray. The potpie would pair well with a sweeter-style Riesling or perhaps a buttery Chardonnay.

Sweets and Sours Platter

No Pennsylvania Dutch sitdown dinner is complete without "sweets and sours." The relish tray may include all kinds of preserved fruits and vegetables, such as bread-and-butter pickles, chow chow, coleslaw, pepper hash, candied cantaloupe, spiced apples, and sweet-and-sour beets.

In bygone eras, the Pennsylvania housewives picked all their produce in the summer and fall and sweated over huge boiling pots as they turned the surplus into pickles and preserves for the winter. With today's year-round supply of produce, there's less incentive to pack produce into jars and process it. All three of our "sweets and sours" are quick refrigerator pickles.

We've made the relishes a little more on the tart side because the main course in this menu is fairly sweet. Serve the relishes with the Whole Grain Icebox Rolls.

Each recipe makes 8 servings

PICKLED MUSHROOMS

1 pound white button mushrooms
¼ cup canola or olive oil
¼ cup white wine vinegar
Juice of 1 medium lemon
2 teaspoons sugar, or to taste

½ teaspoon salt
1 teaspoon minced fresh dillweed, or
  ½ teaspoon dried
2 tablespoons chopped fresh parsley

Wash mushrooms and pat dry; trim ends of stems. Place mushrooms in a glass bowl or a large, wide-mouthed jar. Whisk together oil, vinegar, lemon juice, sugar, and salt.

Stir in dill and parsley. Pour vinegar mixture over mushrooms and stir or shake well to coat.

Cover and refrigerate for several hours or overnight, stirring or shaking occasionally. Mushrooms will keep for up to 3 days.

54 calories, 4 g fat, 0.5 g saturated fat, no cholesterol, 1 g dietary fiber, 136 mg sodium

PEPPER CABBAGE

1 cup finely chopped green bell pepper
1 cup finely chopped red bell pepper
¼ cup finely chopped green onion
1¼ cups finely chopped cabbage
½ cup cider vinegar
4 to 5 tablespoons honey, to taste

2 tablespoons water
½ teaspoon salt
½ teaspoon celery seed
½ teaspoon mustard seed
Pinch of red pepper (optional)

Combine peppers, onion, and cabbage in a glass or ceramic bowl. Heat vinegar, honey, water, salt, celery seed, mustard seed, and red pepper in a small saucepan until mixture comes to a boil; simmer for 5 minutes. Pour over vegetables and stir well.

Cover and refrigerate, stirring occasionally, for several hours or up to 3 days.

26 calories, no fat, no saturated fat, no cholesterol, 1 g dietary fiber, 136 mg sodium

SWEET-AND-SOUR BEETS

1¼ pounds (7 to 8 medium) beets
½ cup orange juice
2½ tablespoons balsamic vinegar, or
  2 tablespoons red wine vinegar plus
  1½ teaspoons molasses

½ teaspoon sugar, or to taste
¼ teaspoon salt
½ teaspoon finely minced fresh
  tarragon, or pinch of dried tarragon

Trim greens from beets, leaving tail and some of the stem attached. Scrub beets but don't peel. Place beets in a saucepan with enough cold water to cover. Bring to a boil, then simmer over low heat for 35 to 45 minutes, or until beets can be easily pierced with a fork but are still firm. Drain. When cool enough to handle, peel beets, then slice or dice. Place beets in a glass bowl or large wide-mouthed jar.

Whisk together orange juice, vinegar, sugar, salt, and tarragon. Pour over beets. Refrigerate, stirring occasionally, for several hours or up to 3 days.

31 calories, no fat, no saturated fat, no cholesterol, 1 g dietary fiber, 105 mg sodium

Whole Grain Icebox Rolls

These nutritious rolls require no kneading and rise in the refrigerator while you sleep. Millet is available in some supermarkets and most health-food stores. It adds a pleasant crunch to these tender rolls.

Apple butter goes nicely with these.

Makes 12 rolls

1 cup skim milk
2 teaspoons unsalted butter
3 tablespoons canola oil
¼ cup honey
¾ teaspoon salt
1 package (2¼ teaspoons) active dry yeast

¼ cup warm water (110°)
2 cups whole wheat flour (preferably stone-ground)
½ cup cornmeal
¾ to 1¼ cups bread flour
2 tablespoons millet (optional)

Heat milk with butter just until butter melts. Stir in oil, honey, and salt.

Dissolve yeast in warm water. Stir into milk-oil mixture. With a wooden spoon, beat in whole wheat flour, cornmeal, and enough bread flour to make a soft dough. (If you use stone-ground flour, the dough may resemble a thick batter.) Stir in millet if using.

Cover bowl and refrigerate dough for several hours or overnight. Punch down.

Spray a muffin tin with nonstick cooking spray. Divide dough evenly among 12 muffin cups. Cover loosely with a towel and let rise in a warm place until very light, about 45 minutes to an hour.

Preheat the oven to 400°.

Bake rolls for 20 to 25 minutes, until golden. Let cool for 20 minutes, then run a knife around rolls and turn out of the tin.

240 calories, 4 g fat, 1 g saturated fat, 2 mg cholesterol, 3.5 g dietary fiber, 146 mg sodium

●━━━◆━━━●

Vegetable Potpie with Saffron Noodle Squares

To the Pennsylvania Dutch, a potpie traditionally rests on a bed of noodles, not under a flaky crust. This dish is fragrant with saffron, an unusual feature in American main dishes.

Because the noodle squares still have flour clinging to them, they create a gravy when added to the vegetable broth. Be sure they're well submerged in the liquid or they won't cook through.

This dish is on the sweet side, thanks to the squash. If you prefer a more savory main course, use a large regular onion (rather than pearl onions) cut into wedges, choose a smaller acorn squash, and toss in an extra potato.

Makes 8 servings

Saffron noodle squares:

*1¼ to 1½ cups flour, plus some for
   dusting noodles*

1 egg

2 egg whites, or ¼ cup egg substitute

¼ teaspoon salt

*Pinch of saffron threads softened in
   1 tablespoon hot water*

Vegetables:

1 medium (about 2½ pounds) acorn
 squash
½ pound pearl onions
1 pound boiling potatoes
1½ tablespoons browned unsalted
 butter, or regular unsalted butter
 (see Butter at Its Best,
 page 30)

4 cups vegetable stock (page 17) or
 3 cups canned vegetable broth
 diluted with 1 cup water
¼ cup chopped fresh parsley
1 teaspoon minced fresh tarragon, or
 ¼ teaspoon dried
¼ teaspoon salt
¼ teaspoon pepper

To make noodles: Place 1¼ cups flour in a small mixing bowl. Make a well in the center and put in egg, egg whites, salt, and saffron water. Mix with a fork to make a soft dough. Knead dough for 5 minutes, adding a little more flour if dough is too sticky.

Let dough rest for 10 minutes, then roll out on a floured board as thinly as possible (1/16 of an inch). Or put through a hand-cranked pasta machine, rolling on the second-thinnest setting. Cut dough into 2-inch squares. Dust noodle squares lightly with flour and set aside. (They may be refrigerated for up to 6 hours.)

To cook vegetables and noodles: Cut squash into quarters and scrape out seeds. Use a sharp paring knife to cut squash away from rind. Cut squash into bite-size chunks.

Blanch pearl onions in boiling water to cover for 2 minutes. When cool enough to handle, slip off skins.

Peel potatoes and cut into bite-size chunks.

Heat butter in a Dutch oven. Add squash, onions, and potatoes, and cook over medium-high heat about 10 minutes, until vegetables begin to brown. Stir in stock, parsley, tarragon, salt, and pepper. Bring to a simmer, then cook another 10 minutes, or until vegetables are tender but still firm. Use a slotted spoon to remove vegetables to a platter or bowl.

Add half of the noodle squares to liquid in pot, pushing them down gently to immerse in liquid. Simmer for 2 to 4 minutes, or until tender. Add the remaining noodle squares, push into liquid, and cook until tender. If necessary, add a little hot water to keep noodles submerged.

Spoon noodles out onto a large platter or into a big, shallow bowl. Top with vegetables.

252 calories, 4 g fat, 2 g saturated fat, 33 mg cholesterol, 6 g dietary fiber, 669 mg sodium

Butter at Its Best

In France, it's called *beurre noir,* or black butter. In Pennsylvania and elsewhere in America, it's just plain browned butter or burnt butter.

Whatever you call it, it's wonderful. Browned butter, made by reducing butter so the moisture in the milk fat burns off, leaving the essence of butter behind, has a nutty brown color and intensely rich flavor and aroma. It's a good solution for folks (like us) who can't tear themselves completely away from butter but would like to use less of it. You can brush a trace of browned butter on toast or vegetables, or use it in concert with oil in reduced-fat baked goods. Because it has a higher smoking point than regular butter, it's good for sautéing. It also lasts much longer than regular butter.

Making browned butter is easy. Cut a stick (or more) of butter into pieces and place in a shallow, heavy saucepan. Cook over medium heat. The butter will melt, then will begin foaming. If it splatters, turn heat to low. At this point, if you skim the foam and pour the butter off, leaving the white milk solids on the bottom of the pan, you'll have *clarified butter.*

Continue cooking until the crackling noise stops, the butter begins to foam again, and the particles on the bottom of the pan begin to brown. Watch carefully because the butter can quickly burn. At this point, when the milk solids are browned but the butter is still a deep yellow (after 6 to 7 minutes), you have *ghee,* used widely in Indian dishes.

As soon as the butter is a rich, nutty brown color, remove the pan from the heat; this is *browned butter.* The whole process, from melting the butter to browning it, will take about 8 to 10 minutes.

Let the butter cool for a couple of minutes, then strain through a double thickness of cheesecloth. Or skim any foam from the top, then carefully pour the liquid butter into a jar, being careful to leave the solids on the bottom of the pan.

Browned butter can be refrigerated for up to three months.

One stick of butter (½ cup) yields about 6 tablespoons of browned butter.

Saffron's Mystique

Saffron has a musty, medicinal aroma and bitter flavor, but what it does to a dish is magical. First, it dyes foods a lovely golden hue. Second, it imparts a flavor that is indescribable and indispensable. It's a key element in many classic rice dishes and desserts.

In the United States, saffron is favored among Italians (for risottos), Hispanics (paellas and other rice dishes), the Cornish (bread), and the Pennsylvania Dutch (soups, potpies, and baked goods). The Pennsylvania Dutch imported it from the Caribbean and were fond enough of it to grow their own, painstakingly harvesting the flower's stigmas each autumn.

At up to $250 an ounce, saffron ranks as the world's priciest spice. Saffron threads are the stigmas of an autumn crocus (*Crocus sativus*), a perennial with blue or purple flowers that grows across France, Spain, Italy, Germany, Iran, Turkey, Greece, Algeria, and Kashmir. It takes thousands of flowers to produce an ounce of saffron.

We recommend buying saffron as threads, not powder, because it's too easy for wholesalers or retailers to adulterate the powder or sell a lookalike such as turmeric as the real thing. Buy from a reputable merchant and look for thin, wispy, brittle threads that are a brilliant orange-red.

Although it is expensive (you can expect to pay $2 to $2.50 for one-fourth of a gram, or about a half teaspoon, of threads), a little bit of saffron goes a long, long way. A mere ¼ to ½ teaspoon can flavor a main dish for four to six people.

Hot liquid or acid releases saffron's color and flavor. Add the threads directly to hot foods or soften them in hot water or stock, wine, vinegar, or lemon juice.

When a friend tried to buy saffron in the supermarket, he was told it was behind the courtesy counter and not on the shelves because people liked to steal it. The clerks had none in stock, however, because hardly anyone bought it.

"It seems people would rather steal it than buy it," our friend mused.

Apple Upside-Down Gingerbread

The upside-down cake, baked in an iron skillet, has long been a popular American dessert. This version is made with gingerbread, a common treat among the Pennsylvania Dutch and anybody else of Germanic ancestry. You can substitute ripe but firm Bartlett pears for the apples.

Makes 8 servings

1 tablespoon unsalted butter

1 tablespoon brown sugar

3 medium Jonathan (or other tart) apples, peeled and sliced

1 tablespoon rum (optional)

1½ cups all-purpose flour

1 teaspoon baking soda

¾ teaspoon baking powder

¼ teaspoon salt

1 teaspoon ground cinnamon

2 teaspoons ground ginger

½ teaspoon ground allspice

¼ cup canola oil

½ cup unsweetened applesauce

⅔ cup unsulphured molasses

2 egg whites, or ¼ cup egg substitute

1 teaspoon vanilla extract

Preheat oven to 350°.

Heat butter in an ovenproof 10-inch skillet (cast iron is ideal) over medium heat. Stir in brown sugar. Add apples in a layer to cover bottom of skillet, overlapping as necessary. Sprinkle with rum if using. Cook over medium heat for 3 to 4 minutes, until apples begin to soften. Remove from heat. (If you do not have an ovenproof skillet, cook the apples to this point, then transfer them to an oiled 10-inch cake pan or baking dish.)

Sift flour with baking soda, baking powder, salt, cinnamon, ginger, and allspice. In a mixing bowl, beat oil with applesauce, molasses, egg whites, and vanilla until blended. Stir in dry ingredients just until mixed.

Pour batter over apple slices in skillet, being careful not to displace them. Bake about 35 minutes, or until a toothpick inserted in the center of the gingerbread comes out dry.

While still warm, place a plate over skillet and carefully unmold cake. If necessary, push apple slices back into place. Serve warm or at room temperature.

277 calories, 9 g fat, 1.5 g saturated fat, 4 mg cholesterol, 2 g dietary fiber, 252 mg sodium

• A TRIBUTE TO THE FIRST THANKSGIVING •

In December 1620, the Mayflower *anchored in Plymouth harbor. The 102 pilgrims aboard were filled with hope, a hope that may have begun evaporating as quickly as nice weather on that part of the coast. During that first winter, half of the settlers died.*

The survivors quickly learned a truth of American food: If you want to eat, let alone eat well, you borrow ideas from anybody who's willing to share them. In their case, they got ideas from Squanto (Tisquantum), who joined the Plymouth colony as a guide and interpreter. (His people had been wiped out by influenza.) He showed them how to grow corn; they gave him English cheese and biscuits. Squanto was so useful that William Bradford, later elected governor of the colony, called him "a special instrument sent of God for their good, beyond their expectation."

By the fall of 1621 the villagers had recovered their health and strength, and put in enough stores to hold them through another winter. Their English wheat and peas had failed, but the corn had thrived. In the autumn they celebrated with a feast of Thanksgiving, which they shared with Chief Massasoit and ninety of his men.

Not much description of that first Thanksgiving survives, but in addition to game and fish, we know the celebrants enjoyed corn, leeks, watercress and other salad greens, dried plums, wild berries, and wine. It seems likely that they would have had pumpkin or squash since it was the right time of year for it. The feasting and partying lasted for three days.

To this day Americans everywhere overeat on Thanksgiving and give thanks for one of the most abundant and varied food supplies on earth.

Suggested Wines: A "big," fairly fruity Chardonnay can stand up to the assertive flavors in this menu. The pâté would also go nicely with a rosé.

White Corn Sticks and Yellow Corn Relish

It seems only fitting to emphasize the wonders of corn by baking cornbread in the shape of its ears, then serving it with a country-style corn relish. Corn sticks freeze well if wrapped tightly. Reheat in a 300-degree oven before serving.

The relish can be prepared a day before serving. If fresh corn is not available, use frozen, defrosted corn.

The corn sticks and relish can, of course, be served separately.

Makes 8 servings

RELISH

3 large ears corn, or 2 cups frozen corn
   kernels
1 small red or green bell pepper, seeded
   and chopped
½ cup chopped celery
½ cup chopped green onion

⅓ cup sugar
⅔ cup white vinegar
⅓ cup water
½ teaspoon salt
1 teaspoon celery seed

Cut kernels from cobs and place kernels in a saucepan. Add remaining ingredients. Bring to a boil, reduce heat to simmer, and cook for 5 minutes, stirring often. Cool. Place relish in a serving bowl, cover, and refrigerate for at least 1 hour. Stir before serving.

Relish: 105 calories, 1 g fat, no saturated fat, no cholesterol, 4 g dietary fiber, 152 mg sodium

CORN STICKS

¾ cup white cornmeal

1 cup plus 2 tablespoons all-purpose
    flour

2 tablespoons baking powder

1 tablespoon minced fresh thyme

¼ teaspoon salt

3 tablespoons sugar

2 egg whites

1 cup buttermilk

3½ tablespoons canola oil or canola–
    corn oil blend

Preheat oven to 400°. Spray a corn stick pan with nonstick cooking spray, or use an 8-inch-square baking pan.

Mix cornmeal, flour, baking powder, thyme, salt, and sugar until combined. Mix in egg whites, buttermilk, and oil just until dry ingredients are moistened; do not overmix.

Pour batter into depressions in prepared pan, filling half full. (You may have to bake the batter in 2 batches.)

Bake on center rack for about 12 minutes (or 20 minutes if you are using a square baking pan), or until a cake tester inserted in one of the corn sticks comes out dry. They will be firm to the touch. Cool 5 minutes. Invert pan to release corn sticks. These taste best served warm.

Serve with corn relish.

Corn Sticks: 111 calories, 4 g fat, 0.5 g saturated fat, 1 mg cholesterol, 1 g dietary fiber, 262 mg sodium

Amazing Grain

Of all the foodstuffs the Plymouth colony gave thanks for, corn ranked at the top. It was the first real food they encountered in their new home. A scouting party from the *Mayflower* landed on Cape Cod in November 1620. Within a day or two they had stumbled onto a cache of corn the Native Americans had buried in sand for the winter. The men had never seen ears of corn in various colors and found it a "goodly sight."

They took part of the corn and reburied the rest. It was this corn that supplied the settlers with seeds for the following spring and kept the whole colony from starving. The colonists later made peace with the tribe whose corn they had taken and repaid them.

"Indian maize" continued to sustain the English settlers through brutal winters and failed crops, and they constantly sought ways to cultivate it more efficiently. They ate it fresh in the summer, then soaked dried corn to make hominy, ground it into meal to prepare breads, cakes, and puddings, and pounded it into a coarse porridge.

Bean and Carrot Pâté
with Watercress Sauce

Beans were one of the vegetables the Native Americans called "three sisters," a trinity of foods they considered indispensable. The other "sisters" were squash and corn. Native Americans often grew them together, letting the beans climb up the cornstalks and the squash vines sprawl on the ground around them.

Thanks to our increasing interest in health, beans have taken on a new sophistication. Try them in a low-fat pâté that's the star of the Thanksgiving table.

The sauce will take on some of the bitterness of the watercress if it sits too long. Make it just before serving the pâté. For a nondairy entrée, omit the sauce and serve the pâté on a bed of watercress lightly dressed with vinegar and oil.

Makes 8 servings

4 egg whites

1½ tablespoons olive oil

6 shallots, minced

4 large cloves garlic, minced

2¼ cups cooked white beans, drained

2 carrots, grated

½ cup plus 1 tablespoon whole wheat
   bread crumbs

⅓ cup vegetable stock

2 tablespoons lemon juice

2 teaspoons finely chopped fresh
   tarragon, or 1 teaspoon dried

¼ teaspoon salt

¼ teaspoon white pepper

1 tablespoon small capers, drained

Parsley or watercress sprigs for garnish

Sauce:

1 bunch watercress, stems removed

1 cup plain nonfat yogurt

½ cup reduced-fat mayonnaise

⅛ teaspoon salt

⅛ teaspoon pepper

¼ teaspoon finely chopped fresh
   tarragon, or ⅛ teaspoon dried

Spray an 8-by-4-inch loaf pan with nonstick cooking spray. Preheat oven to 375°.

Beat egg whites until they stand in glossy peaks. Set aside.

Heat oil in a nonstick frying pan. Sauté shallots and garlic until tender. Cool. Using a food processor, puree shallots, garlic, beans, carrots, bread crumbs, stock, lemon juice, tarragon, salt, and pepper. Fold in capers and beaten egg whites.

Spoon bean mixture into prepared pan. Cover with aluminum foil. Bake in the center of the oven for 45 to 50 minutes, or until a tester inserted in the center of the pâté comes out clean. The pâté will begin to brown around the edges. Cool 5 minutes, run a knife around the edges of the pâté, then unmold. Cover with foil and chill until serving time. Slice.

Make sauce shortly before serving. Wash and trim watercress. Using a food processor fitted with a steel blade, chop watercress. Add yogurt, mayonnaise, and seasonings, and puree until smooth.

Spoon watercress sauce onto individual small plates, top with a slice of pâté, and garnish with parsley or watercress.

196 calories, 8 g fat, 1.5 g saturated fat, 1 mg cholesterol, 4 g dietary fiber, 339 mg sodium

●━━◆━━●

Parsnip Fritters and Cranberry-Apple Relish

Creamy-colored parsnips, which are at their peak in the fall, have a flavor that's sweet, with a slightly pungent edge.

A cool cranberry-apple relish is a good partner for the warm fritters. Although cranberries probably did not show up on the table in 1621, they've become an important part of Thanksgiving feasts since then.

The cranberry-apple relish will keep, covered, for two to three days in the refrigerator. If you like, you can replace the orange juice with sweet red wine or cranberry juice cocktail.

Makes 8 servings

Relish:
2 cups unpeeled, chopped apples
⅓ cup orange juice
2 cups chopped fresh cranberries
½ cup chopped walnuts

1 teaspoon ground cinnamon
⅛ teaspoon ground nutmeg
¼ cup sugar

Fritters:

2 cups cooked, mashed parsnips, cooled

2 cups cooked, mashed potatoes, cooled

½ cup egg substitute, or 4 egg whites

1 tablespoon chopped fresh tarragon, or
1½ teaspoons dried

1 tablespoon chopped fresh chives or
green onion tops

½ teaspoon salt

¼ teaspoon white pepper

1 tablespoon canola oil

To make relish: In a bowl, toss chopped apples with orange juice. Add cranberries, nuts, cinnamon, nutmeg, and sugar.

Cover and refrigerate. Remove from refrigerator 15 to 20 minutes before serving time. Stir before serving.

To make the fritters: It's easiest if you cook and mash parsnips and potatoes the day before making the fritters. In a small bowl, mix mashed parsnips and potatoes. Stir in egg substitute, tarragon, chives, salt, and pepper.

Heat oil in a nonstick frying pan that has been sprayed with nonstick cooking spray. Drop potato mixture into pan in several mounds, using about 3 tablespoons batter for each, and smooth into patties with the back of a spoon. Fry until crisp on both sides. Place on a serving platter and keep warm in a 200° oven while you make the remaining fritters.

Serve with cranberry-apple relish.

221 calories, 9.5 g fat, 1 g saturated fat, no cholesterol, 4 g dietary fiber, 167 mg sodium

Hasty Pudding with Maple Syrup

Besides being the title for a sweet cornmeal creation, Hasty Pudding is famous as the name of the theatrical club at Harvard University and is referred to in the song "Yankee Doodle Dandy." Although the recipe may not seem as hasty to today's cooks as it did to Yankee cooks of yore, it is very easy to make. It is always served hot.

Use genuine maple syrup—not the mass-market imitations. Light or medium amber syrup is fine for this.

Makes 8 servings

1 teaspoon ground cinnamon	*4 cups water*
½ teaspoon salt	*⅔ cup cornmeal*
⅛ teaspoon ground nutmeg	*3 tablespoons maple syrup*

Mix cinnamon, salt, and nutmeg with water in a saucepan. Bring to a full boil over medium heat. Whisk in the cornmeal, crushing any lumps. Continue boiling for 1 minute, whisking continuously. Cover.

Fit a rack into a steamer or large pot and pour in an inch or two of water (it should not come up to the rack). Bring to a simmer. Set the covered saucepan containing the cornmeal mixture on the rack. Cover steamer. Steam pudding over low to medium heat for 25 minutes.

Uncover pudding. It will have a loose consistency. Spoon pudding into sauce dishes. Drizzle with syrup and serve hot.

57 calories, no fat, no cholesterol, 1 g dietary fiber, 137 mg sodium

Dark and Spicy Pumpkin Pie

For a marriage truly made in heaven, pair spicy pumpkin filling with the nutty goodness of whole wheat. This crust is crunchy rather than flaky. It's important to use whole wheat pastry flour, which is finer and softer than regular whole wheat flour. It is available in health-food stores, some specialty stores, and some supermarkets.

Makes 8 servings

Crust:

1½ cups whole wheat pastry flour	*4 to 5 tablespoons canola oil*
¼ teaspoon salt	*3 to 4 tablespoons cold water*
¼ teaspoon ground cinnamon	

Filling:

1 (16-ounce) can plain pumpkin

1 (12-ounce) can evaporated skim milk,
   or 1½ cups low-fat soy milk

¾ cup packed light brown sugar

2 teaspoons vanilla extract

1 egg

2 egg whites or ¼ cup egg substitute

2 teaspoons ground cinnamon

1¼ teaspoons ground ginger

¼ teaspoon ground allspice

¼ teaspoon salt

To make crust: Mix flour, salt, and cinnamon in a medium-size bowl. Stir in 4 tablespoons oil with a fork, then work in lightly with your fingertips. Dough should be moist and crumbly, and hold in clumps when pinched between your fingers. If necessary, add another tablespoon of oil. Stir in enough water to make a pliable dough. Don't overwork the dough.

Roll dough out on a lightly floured board or pastry cloth or between 2 sheets of wax paper to a 12-inch circle. Ease pastry into a 9-inch pie pan, pressing gently into pan. If it tears, patch it with your fingers. Trim excess pastry and crimp or flute edges.

Preheat oven to 425°.

To make filling: Combine all ingredients in a mixing bowl and whisk until smooth. Pour into pie shell (filling will come up to the top). Bake for 10 minutes, then reduce heat to 350° and bake another 35 to 45 minutes, until filling is set. Let cool completely before serving. If making more than a few hours ahead of time, cover pie loosely with foil and refrigerate.

Serve with light whipped cream, light ice cream, or frozen yogurt.

314 calories, 10 g fat, 1 g saturated fat, 28 mg cholesterol, 3 g dietary fiber, 328 mg sodium

• NORTH END ITALIAN DINNER PARTY •

The Italians have been settled in the Northeast long enough for the "old neighborhoods" such as Boston's North End to gentrify. The days of the vegetable-laden pushcarts have long faded, and small butcher shops and restaurants have turned into upscale temples of good dining and specialty ingredients. The streets are dotted with espresso bars, a sign that America has fallen in love with the morning pick-me-up the Italians thrive on.

In many ways the food has grown closer to its roots in Italy, with good ingredients, simply prepared. *"New" Italian-American cooking is heavy on pasta, fresh vegetables, and herbs, and lighter on meat-heavy sauces.*

This menu, suitable for spring or fall, takes advantage of fresh spinach and artichokes, prepared in ways to praise, rather than bury, their flavors.

Suggested Wines: *A lighter-styled Merlot, Chianti, or Burgundy would go nicely with the bruschetta, manicotti, and artichokes. If you choose to pair the biscotti with something besides coffee, try an orange liqueur or an Italian dessert wine.*

Bruschetta with Tomatoes and Basil

Bruschetta is a traditional Italian antipasto that celebrates the olive harvest. In its purest form, it consists of thickly sliced bread that is toasted, rubbed with fresh garlic, then drizzled with the season's first pressing of olive oil.

In this slightly more elaborate version, the bread is topped with tomato-basil salad, southern Italian style.

Be sure to use a really good bread, a top-quality olive oil, and good, ripe tomatoes.

Top the bruschetta with Asiago, a sharp-sweet Italian grating cheese, or with Parmesan.

Makes 8 servings

1 pound top-quality Italian or French bread, cut into 8 slices
1 large clove garlic, cut in half
3 medium tomatoes, or 18 cherry tomatoes
½ cup minced red onion

2 tablespoons chopped fresh basil
¼ teaspoon salt
¼ teaspoon pepper
2 tablespoons extra-virgin olive oil
2 tablespoons freshly grated Asiago or Parmesan cheese

Toast bread in oven (or on the grill) on both sides until just firm to the touch. Rub the cut side of garlic evenly over each bread slice. Set aside.

Cut tomatoes in half. Squeeze out seeds and coarsely chop. Mix with onion, basil, salt, and pepper.

Brush one side of each bread slice lightly with oil. Spoon tomato mixture on the toast and sprinkle with cheese.

Serve warm.

205 calories, 6 g fat, 1 g saturated fat, 1 mg cholesterol, 2 g dietary fiber, 431 mg sodium

Double-Spinach Crespelle (Manicotti)

Cooks of southern Italian ancestry often wrap light, thin crespelle (crepes) around fillings and bake them. Some Americans, Italian and otherwise, might prefer to call these manicotti.

It's easiest to make this dish if you prepare the spinach, crepes, and sauce ahead of time. Make the filling and assemble everything just before baking.

Makes 8 servings

3 bunches (about ¾ pound each) fresh spinach or 3 bags (10 ounces each) washed and trimmed fresh spinach

Crepes:

1 egg

*3 egg whites or 6 tablespoons egg
  substitute*

*Cooking liquid from spinach, plus
  enough cold water to equal 1 cup*

¼ teaspoon salt

⅔ cup plus 1 tablespoon flour

1 teaspoon olive oil

2 tablespoons reserved cooked spinach

Sauce:

1 teaspoon olive oil

2 cloves garlic, minced

*1 (28-ounce) can crushed tomatoes in
  puree*

*3 tablespoons coarsely chopped fresh
  basil*

Filling:

Cooked spinach

2½ cups light ricotta cheese

⅓ cup coarsely chopped fresh basil

⅛ teaspoon nutmeg

½ teaspoon salt

¼ teaspoon pepper

Wash spinach thoroughly; if using bagged spinach, just give it a quick rinse. Trim and discard large stems. Place spinach in a large pot and cook in just the water clinging to the leaves, over medium heat, until spinach wilts and turns dark. You may have to do this in 2 or 3 batches. Drain the spinach thoroughly by squeezing it, reserving the liquid. Finely chop spinach. (If not using immediately, refrigerate.) Set aside 2 tablespoons of spinach for crepes.

To make crepes: Place egg and egg whites, spinach liquid, and water in a small mixing bowl; whisk to blend. Add salt, flour, and oil, and whisk until smooth. Stir in reserved spinach. Let batter sit for 20 to 30 minutes.

Lightly coat a 6- to 7-inch nonstick skillet or crepe pan with nonstick cooking spray and heat over medium heat. Pour ⅛ cup (2 tablespoons) crepe batter into skillet, swirling skillet so batter thinly coats the bottom. Cook over medium heat for about 10 seconds per side, or until crepe is set. Place on a plate. Continue cooking crepes, stacking on top of one another, until batter is used up. You'll need to respray the pan now and again. When finished, you should have at least 16 crepes about 5½ to 6 inches in diameter. Refrigerate crepes until needed.

To make sauce: Heat oil in a heavy saucepan. Sauté garlic just until fragrant, then stir in tomatoes and basil. Cook over low heat for 10 minutes. Set aside (or refrigerate for later use).

To make filling: Just before assembling the dish, preheat oven to 350°. Combine spinach with remaining filling ingredients.

Spoon about ⅔ cup sauce evenly over bottom of a 13-by-9-inch baking dish. Place ⅓ cup filling down center of 1 crepe, then roll crepe around filling. Place crepe, seam side down, in baking dish. Repeat until filling is used up; you should have 16 filled crepes, with maybe a crepe or two left over.

Spoon remaining sauce evenly over filling. Bake about 30 minutes, or until bubbling hot. Serve immediately.

210 calories, 5.5 g fat, 0.5 g saturated fat, 27 mg cholesterol, 5 g dietary fiber, 733 mg sodium

Garlicky Sautéed Artichokes

Use the smallest artichokes you can find; they're more tender, and there's less waste when you prepare them. If they're available, use fresh baby artichokes. You may be able to find them in the spring or fall in specialty stores or some supermarkets.

Makes 8 servings

8 small fresh artichokes or 12 baby artichokes	**Leaves from 3 to 4 sprigs Italian (flat-leaf) parsley, minced**
Lemon juice	**¼ cup water**
1 tablespoon olive oil	**¼ teaspoon salt**
1 large clove garlic, minced	**Pepper to taste**
1 tablespoon drained capers	**1 teaspoon extra-virgin olive oil**

Trim stem of 1 artichoke and trim ½ inch from top. Pull off and discard outer leaves until you reach the point where at least half of the showing leaves are yellow. Using scissors, snip off the top green part of each leaf, working your way inward. Cut each artichoke in half lengthwise. Cut out the tough, innermost purplish leaves and scrape out fuzzy chokes (baby artichokes will not have fuzzy chokes). Place artichokes in a large bowl of cold water to which you've added the juice of ½ lemon.

Clean and soak remaining artichokes. When ready to cook, drain and pat dry.

Heat 1 tablespoon oil in a large frying pan that has been sprayed with nonstick cooking spray. Add artichokes, cut side down, and sauté over high heat about 5 minutes, until golden. Sprinkle with garlic, capers, and parsley; add water. Cover and cook over low heat for 10 to 15 minutes, or until artichoke bottoms can be pierced easily with a fork. It's fine if liquid evaporates, but if artichokes show signs of sticking or burning, add a bit more water.

Season with salt, pepper, extra-virgin olive oil, and a squeeze of lemon juice. Serve warm.

83 calories, 2.5 g fat, 0.5 g saturated fat, no cholesterol, 6.5 g dietary fiber, 207 mg sodium

Orange-Chocolate Biscotti

These hard, crunchy cookies are designed for dipping. True-blue Italians may dunk them in dessert wine—and they taste great that way—but we like them just fine with coffee or tea.

Makes 26 cookies

1½ cups whole wheat flour

1 cup all-purpose flour

1 teaspoon baking powder

½ teaspoon baking soda

½ teaspoon salt

¼ cup canola oil

1 cup sugar

1 egg

1 egg white or 2 tablespoons egg
 substitute

1 teaspoon vanilla extract

½ teaspoon orange extract

1 tablespoon grated orange zest

1 to 2 tablespoons water, if needed

¼ cup sliced blanched almonds

¼ cup semisweet chocolate mini-chips

Spray a 10-by-15-inch baking sheet lightly with nonstick cooking spray. Preheat oven to 350°.

Sift flours with baking powder, baking soda, and salt; set aside.

With a wooden spoon, beat oil, sugar, egg, egg white, vanilla and orange extracts, and orange zest until blended. Stir in dry ingredients and mix well. Dough should be stiff, but if it seems dry, stir in enough water to make it moist and workable. Stir in almonds and chocolate chips.

Divide dough into 2 parts. Place 1 part on wax paper. With floured hands, roll dough into a log about 10 inches long and 1½ inches wide. Place log on a baking sheet. Repeat with remaining dough.

Bake for 25 to 30 minutes, or until logs are firm, cracked on top, and light golden brown. Remove to a wire rack to cool for 15 minutes.

Turn oven heat down to 325°.

Using a serrated knife, carefully cut cooled logs on the diagonal into slices about ½ inch thick. Place on baking sheet that has been wiped clean and sprayed lightly with nonstick spray. Bake for 15 to 20 minutes, until golden and crisp.

Let cool completely, then store in airtight containers. Serve with coffee, tea, or a dessert wine.

106 calories, 3 g fat, 1 g saturated fat, 8 mg cholesterol, 1 g dietary fiber, 80 mg sodium

Appetizers, Salads, and Side Dishes

TWO-CORN SUCCOTASH

Succotash is another example of the New World foods and dishes the Native Americans introduced to European settlers. The word apparently is an English derivation of a Narragansett word, *msickquotash,* which referred to boiled ears of corn.

What dresses up this basic combination of beans and corn seems limited only by the cook's imagination. Colonial succotash recipes called for a combination of corn kernels and beans—white beans, lima beans, or even cranberries. Southern cooks used butter beans and green peppers from the West Indies in their succotash. The Pennsylvania Dutch enlivened the mixture with a combination of sautéed onions, green peppers, fresh tomatoes, and cubed potatoes.

For a different touch, we serve the corn and bean mixture on top of baby corn. These miniature ears, about 2½ to 3 inches long, come plain or pickled in cans or jars. Sometimes produce sections carry baby corn in plastic tubs (it is still processed, however, not fresh).

This colorful, sweet medley of vegetables often appeals to young children.

Makes 4 servings

1⅔ cups corn kernels, scraped from cob (frozen corn may be substituted)
1 cup cooked lima beans (fresh beans are best)
1 small red bell pepper, seeded and chopped
1 tablespoon unsalted butter or margarine at room temperature

⅔ cup evaporated skim milk
2 teaspoons cornstarch
4 teaspoons water
¼ teaspoon salt
¼ teaspoon white pepper
1 cup baby corn, drained and rinsed

Mix together corn kernels, beans, bell pepper, butter, and milk in a heavy saucepan. Bring to a boil. Reduce heat to simmer. Whisk cornstarch with water, then stir into vegetables. Cook for 5 minutes, or until vegetables are tender.

Season with salt and pepper. Sauce will be thin. Taste and adjust seasonings.

Arrange ears of baby corn in a circle around the edges of a plate. Spoon succotash in the center. Serve hot.

176 calories, 4 g fat, 2 g saturated fat, 9 mg cholesterol, 6 g dietary fiber, 199 mg sodium

OSCAR'S WALDORF SALAD

Waldorf Salad still appears on the menu at the Waldorf-Astoria Hotel in New York City. This is similar to the original salad, created by Oscar Tschirky, maître d' of the elegant hotel from 1893 to 1943. Originally it did not contain nuts; they were added later. If you like, you can toss the apple mixture with ¼ cup coarsely chopped walnuts.

Makes 4 servings

2 large ripe apples, such as McIntosh
4 teaspoons lemon juice
1 cup diced celery
¼ cup reduced-fat mayonnaise
¼ teaspoon salt
1 head Bibb lettuce, washed and dried

Toss apples with lemon juice to prevent apples from turning brown. Add celery, mayonnaise, and salt. Toss all ingredients to coat evenly.

Separate lettuce leaves and arrange on 4 salad plates. Spoon salad in center of lettuce. Serve chilled.

120 calories, 5.5 g fat, 1 g saturated fat, no cholesterol, 3 g dietary fiber, 270 mg sodium

GREENGROCER'S CUCUMBERS WITH VEGETABLE SHREDS

Given the abundance of fresh, seasonal vegetables in Korean cooking, it's no surprise that many of the greengrocers in New York are Korean. This pretty, whimsical summer appetizer is inspired by the stuffed vegetables that are popular in Korean cookery. On one of those scorched-asphalt August days, it could even serve as a light, refreshing lunch entrée.

Use toasted (dark) sesame oil in this dish. Some stores carry light, cold-pressed sesame oil, but it is not traditional to Asian cooking. The dark oil is much more intensely flavored.

A seedless cucumber, which is longer, thinner-skinned, and more flavorful than a regular cucumber, works best in this dish. You can substitute two small to medium regular cucumbers; they should be peeled and the seeds scraped out with the tip of a spoon. Cut them in half lengthwise just once.

Makes 4 servings

1 seedless cucumber, about 1 pound	*6 fresh shiitake mushrooms, caps only*
Salt	*1 medium carrot*
4 ounces firm tofu	*3 green onions, with about 1 inch of*
1 teaspoon minced garlic	*the green tops*
Soy sauce	*½ red bell pepper*
Pinch of red pepper	*Canola oil*
Sugar	*Freshly ground black pepper*
Toasted sesame oil	*2 teaspoons toasted sesame seeds*

Trim ends of cucumber and cut cucumber in half lengthwise. Use a melon baller or the tip of a spoon to scrape out the center of each cucumber half, creating a hollow the length of the cucumber. Cut each length of cucumber in half crosswise, to make 4 pieces in all.

Lightly salt cucumber pieces and place on a plate, hollowed side down. Let stand about 30 minutes while you prepare remaining ingredients. They should begin to soften and give off liquid.

Crumble tofu into a small bowl and mix with garlic, 2 teaspoons soy sauce, red pepper, 1 teaspoon sugar, and 1 teaspoon sesame oil. Let marinate while you prepare vegetables.

Wash mushroom caps and pat dry. Peel carrot. Trim green onions. Remove core and seeds from red pepper half. Cut vegetables into strips no more than ⅛ inch wide and 2½ to 3 inches long.

Heat ½ teaspoon canola oil in a medium-size nonstick frying pan. Add carrot and a pinch of sugar; stir-fry about a minute, just until carrot begins to soften. Remove to a plate. Do the same with the red pepper. Stir-fry the green onions and then the mushrooms the same way. Don't season the green onions but season the mushrooms with a splash of soy sauce and a little black pepper.

Add tofu to frying pan and stir-fry over high heat until golden. Remove to a bowl or plate.

Drain off any liquid from cucumber slices and pat them dry.

Wipe out frying pan and add 2 teaspoons sesame oil. Add cucumber pieces and stir-fry over medium-low heat just until heated through. Don't brown them.

Arrange cucumber pieces on a plate, hollowed sides up. Divide tofu evenly among hollows and top with strips of stir-fried mushrooms, green onions, red pepper, and carrot.

Sprinkle with toasted sesame seeds. Serve warm or at room temperature within an hour of assembling.

116 calories, 7 g fat, 1 g saturated fat, no cholesterol, 3 g dietary fiber, 450 mg sodium

LEMON-STEAMED FIDDLEHEADS

Cooks in northern New England mark spring's arrival by the sight of fiddlehead ferns. The unopened, tightly coiled fronds have a texture and flavor similar to that of asparagus. They're available fresh in some gourmet food stores. (Don't pick your own unless you're experienced in identifying wild plants.)

Makes 4 servings

1 pound fiddlehead ferns or asparagus
1 long strip fresh lemon peel
1 teaspoon unsalted butter or margarine
½ teaspoon minced fresh tarragon

½ teaspoon salt
⅛ teaspoon pepper
2 tablespoons chopped fresh chives

Clean fiddlehead ferns. Arrange in a steamer and set over boiling water to which you've added the strip of lemon peel. Reduce water to simmer and steam fiddleheads, covered, about 10 minutes, or just until fork tender. If using asparagus, break into 2-inch pieces and steam for 5 minutes.

Arrange ferns or asparagus in a serving dish. Toss with butter, tarragon, salt, and pepper. Sprinkle with chopped chives. Garnish with the lemon peel if desired.

35 calories, 1 g fat, 1 g saturated fat, 3 mg cholesterol, 2 g dietary fiber, 269 mg sodium

Aromatics

When you're steaming vegetables, create a whisper of extra flavor by adding "aromatics" to the steaming water. Some of our favorites are orange, lemon, or lime peel; lemongrass; a smashed clove of garlic; a piece of fresh gingerroot; a green onion; a dried red chile pepper; a tablespoon of soy sauce; or a sprig of basil, tarragon, rosemary, or cilantro.

ZUCCHINI AND CELERY STICKS WITH BLUE CHEESE DIP

This is our vegetarian alternative to the spicy chicken wings with blue cheese dip that are so popular in Buffalo, New York. This makes a tasty appetizer or snack for a party.

Makes 4 servings

4 medium-small zucchini, trimmed

2 tablespoons canola oil

1 teaspoon chili powder

½ teaspoon paprika

½ teaspoon garlic powder

½ teaspoon dried basil

4 stalks celery, trimmed and cut into
3- or 4-inch celery sticks

Blue Cheese Dip:

1 cup low-fat (1-percent) cottage cheese

2 tablespoons crumbled blue cheese

½ cup plain nonfat yogurt

⅛ teaspoon garlic powder, or to taste

Slice zucchini lengthwise into quarters. Set aside. In a nonstick frying pan, mix the oil with chili powder, paprika, garlic powder, and basil.

Heat spicy oil until very hot. Fry zucchini sticks, cut side down, a few minutes on each side, until brown.

In a small bowl or in a food processor, blend cottage cheese, blue cheese, yogurt, and garlic powder.

Fan out zucchini sticks decoratively on 4 small plates. Divide dip and spoon near zucchini; set celery sticks near dip. Serve immediately.

161 calories, 9 g fat, 2 g saturated fat, 6 mg cholesterol, 3 g dietary fiber, 357 mg sodium

Soups

ITALIAN SUMMER VEGETABLE SOUP

This soup is a meal in a bowl. It mellows well and tastes best the next day. Whole wheat bread makes an excellent accompaniment.

Some farmers' markets carry fresh shelling beans in late summer or early fall. If you find some, cook fresh beans for this soup. Remove them from the pods, then simmer them in unsalted water to cover for 15 to 25 minutes, or until tender.

Fresh herbs give this soup a wonderful, summer-fresh flavor. Use dried herbs in an emergency.

Makes 8 servings

1 tablespoon olive oil

1 cup sliced onion

2 cloves garlic, minced

2 quarts water or vegetable stock
   (page 17)

1 cup sliced cabbage

2 cups chopped fresh tomatoes (peel
   first if desired)

2 medium-small zucchini, sliced

2 carrots, sliced

1 (14½-ounce) can crushed tomatoes,
   including juice

1 teaspoon salt

½ teaspoon pepper

1 cup cooked white beans or chick-peas
   (if using canned beans, drain and
   rinse well)

1 cup cooked penne or other pasta

1½ to 2 tablespoons chopped fresh basil
   or 2 teaspoons dried

2 teaspoons chopped fresh marjoram,
   or 1 teaspoon dried

Heat oil in a soup pot or large saucepan. Sauté onion and garlic over medium heat until soft. Add water or stock, cabbage, fresh tomatoes, zucchini, carrots, and canned tomatoes and their juice. Stir in salt, pepper, and dried herbs if using.

Bring soup to a boil, reduce heat to medium-low, and cook for 1¼ hours, partially covered. Add beans, pasta, and fresh herbs; cook another 10 minutes.

Adjust seasonings. Ladle into bowls and serve hot.

107 calories, 2 g fat, 0.5 g saturated fat, no cholesterol, 4 g dietary fiber, 364 mg sodium

HOT AND SOUR SOUP

Where would America be without Chinese takeout? Countless urban householders have grown to rely on fried rice, Sichuan broccoli, stir-fried vegetables, and egg rolls to provide dinner on nights when cooking is out of the question.

It's fun to recreate some of these Chinese favorites at home. This spicy, thick, and warming soup, a longtime carryout favorite, is guaranteed to soothe body and soul, especially on a winter night. Vinegar provides the "sour" and pepper is the "hot." The ingredients are available at Asian food markets and some large supermarkets.

Makes 4 servings

6 dried shiitake mushrooms,
  reconstituted in hot water
  15 minutes and drained
2 tablespoons dried tiger lily buds,
  reconstituted in hot water
  15 minutes and drained
2 tablespoons dried cloud ear
  mushrooms, reconstituted in hot
  water 15 minutes and drained
5 ounces firm tofu
1 quart vegetable stock (page 17) or
  3 cups canned vegetable broth diluted
  with 1 cup water

3 green onions, minced
½ cup sliced, drained bamboo shoots
2 tablespoons cornstarch mixed with
  1 tablespoon stock
½ teaspoon sugar
3 tablespoons red wine vinegar
½ teaspoon salt (omit if using canned
  broth)
½ teaspoon freshly ground pepper
1 teaspoon dark sesame oil
1 egg, beaten

Discard stems of shiitakes and thinly slice caps. Set aside. Chop tiger lily buds and cloud ears; set aside. Cut tofu into ½-inch pieces.

In a soup pot or large saucepan, bring stock to a simmer. Gently stir in shiitakes, tiger lily buds, cloud ears, tofu, onions, and bamboo shoots. Continue simmering for 5 minutes.

Mix in cornstarch, sugar, vinegar, salt, pepper, and sesame oil. Bring soup to a boil. Drizzle in beaten egg. Turn heat off immediately. Egg drops will form.

Ladle hot soup into bowls and serve.

113 calories, 5 g fat, 0.8 g saturated fat, 53 mg cholesterol, 2 g dietary fiber, 527 mg sodium

CHILLED BLUEBERRY SOUP

Like most cold-weather areas, New England yields an abundance of berries, which go into everything from muffins to cobblers to salads. If you can lay hands on some of the intensely wild blueberries or huckleberries, use them in this refreshing summer soup. This can be served for breakfast, lunch, dessert—or even as a light entrée for supper if you're in a sweet mood.

Makes 4 servings

*2½ cups fresh blueberries, washed and
　picked over*
2 tablespoons lemon juice
1 stick cinnamon
2 cups water
⅓ cup sugar, or to taste

½ cup red wine
1½ tablespoons cornstarch
*½ cup plain nonfat yogurt or light sour
　cream (optional)*
Whole berries for garnish

Simmer the berries, lemon juice, cinnamon, and water for 10 minutes. Discard cinnamon stick. Mix in sugar and wine. Bring mixture to a boil.

Meanwhile, whisk cornstarch with a few tablespoons of soup, then return mixture to pan. Cook over medium heat, stirring continuously, until soup is clear, about 1 to 2 minutes.

Cool and then refrigerate soup until ready to serve. Stir and, if desired, garnish with yogurt or sour cream. Top with a few fresh whole berries.

168 calories, negligible fat, no saturated fat, no cholesterol, 2 g dietary fiber, 31 mg sodium

COLD BEET SOUP WITH DILL

The citrusy, grassy notes of dill complement the sweetness of beets in this favorite root vegetable soup. Serve it in late summer or early autumn as a main dish or a first course. For a pleasing contrast, serve it with warm mashed potatoes on the side.

Makes 8 servings

2 pounds beets, peeled and thinly sliced
1 potato, peeled and thinly sliced
2 bay leaves
3 tablespoons lemon juice

¼ cup sugar
½ teaspoon salt
1 cup plain nonfat yogurt (optional)
¼ cup chopped fresh dillweed

Place beet and potato slices and bay leaves in a large kettle; add water to cover. Heat to boiling. Cover, reduce heat to medium, and cook until vegetables are tender, about 40 to 45 minutes. Discard bay leaves.

Stir in lemon juice, sugar, and salt.

Puree soup and return to pot. Taste and adjust seasonings. Cover and refrigerate. Serve cold. Top with a dollop of yogurt, if desired, and sprinkle with dill.

135 calories, 0.5 g fat, no saturated fat, 1 mg cholesterol, 4 g dietary fiber, 248 mg sodium

EGG LEMON SOUP WITH ENDIVE AND ORZO

Barbara learned how to make escarole in egg lemon sauce from her daughter's Greek mother-in-law. We like to use curly endive and add more liquid to make a lovely soup. Serve with plenty of good bread. You can substitute escarole or beet greens for the endive.

Makes 4 servings

2 large bunches curly endive or escarole
1½ tablespoons olive oil
¾ cup chopped green onion
2 cloves garlic, minced
5 cups water
¾ teaspoon salt
½ teaspoon pepper

1 cup cooked orzo
1 egg yolk
2 egg whites, beaten until frothy
½ cup freshly squeezed lemon juice
1 lemon, sliced thin, to float on soup,
    or 2 lemons, cut in wedges, to pass
    at the table

Wash and trim endive. Cut into 2-inch pieces.

Heat oil in a large pot. Add onion and garlic, and sauté until soft, about 5 minutes. Add water and bring to a boil. Add endive, salt, and pepper. Cook about 6 minutes, until endive is cooked through and softened. With the back of a spoon, push endive into water so it is submerged. Add cooked orzo.

While soup is cooking, whisk egg yolk and beaten whites in a bowl until fluffy. Add lemon juice and continue beating. Slowly beat in ½ cup of the hot soup.

Remove soup from the heat. Beat egg mixture slowly into soup. Let stand about 3 minutes, then stir and serve. Float a lemon slice in each bowl of soup or pass lemon wedges at the table.

168 calories, 7 g fat, 1 g saturated fat, 53 mg cholesterol, 4.5 g dietary fiber, 489 mg sodium

GARLIC-SPIKED POTATO SOUP

Originally attracted by the lure of jobs in the whaling industry, many Portuguese immigrated to New England, particularly Massachusetts and Rhode Island, in the nineteenth century. This soup pays tribute to New England's fine boiling potatoes and a heady duo of ingredients commonly found in Portuguese cooking: garlic and cilantro (or Italian parsley). We like to eat it in late September, with a side salad of tomatoes, bell peppers, and cucumbers.

Makes 4 servings

2 teaspoons olive oil
3 to 4 cloves garlic, chopped
1 cup diced onion
4 medium red boiling potatoes, peeled
*   and cubed*
4 cups water

½ teaspoon salt, or to taste
½ cup loosely packed fresh cilantro or
*   Italian parsley leaves*
2 teaspoons extra-virgin olive oil
Freshly ground black pepper

Heat olive oil in a large saucepan. Add garlic and sauté a few seconds, just until it begins to turn golden. Stir in onion, turn heat to low, and cook for 8 to 10 minutes, until onion is soft. Add potatoes, water, and salt. Bring to a boil over high heat, then turn heat to low, cover, and simmer for 30 minutes, or until potatoes are tender. Stir in cilantro or parsley.

Puree soup in a food processor or blender in 2 or 3 batches. Stir in extra-virgin olive oil and pepper to taste.

176 calories, 5 g fat, 1 g saturated fat, no cholesterol, 3 g dietary fiber, 275 mg sodium

Entrées

RYE-CARAWAY CREPES WITH GLAZED ONIONS

Who says crepes are French? Here we've given them a "deli" flair with rye, caraway, and onions, and stuffed them with potatoes to make a hearty winter entrée. Let crepe batter sit for a while before cooking it, so the flour has a chance to relax.

Makes 4 servings, with crepes left over

Batter:

2 eggs

2 egg whites

1 cup skim milk

1¼ cups water

2 tablespoons canola oil

½ cup rye flour

½ cup all-purpose flour

½ teaspoon salt

1 teaspoon caraway seeds

Canola oil to cook crepes

Filling:

2 cups plain mashed potatoes, at room temperature

¼ cup plain nonfat yogurt

2 green onions, minced

⅛ teaspoon salt

⅛ teaspoon pepper

Topping:

1 tablespoon olive oil

3 cups thinly sliced onions

1 clove garlic, minced

1 teaspoon caraway seeds

Crepe batter can be made in a blender, food processor, or by hand. If preparing crepes by hand, sift flour and use a whisk. Otherwise, place all batter ingredients except seeds in a food processor or blender. Blend only a few seconds until batter is smooth. Mix in seeds. Let batter stand for 20 minutes before using. Mixture should be smooth.

Heat a nonstick 6-inch crepe pan and brush lightly with oil. Pour about 2½ to 3 tablespoons of batter into pan. Tilt pan so batter thinly covers the bottom; pour off any excess batter.

Crepe is ready when it is set and firm around edges. Loosen edges with a knife. Flip crepe and cook only a few seconds on the other side. Stack crepes between sheets of aluminum foil or wax paper.

Make the filling: In a bowl, mix together potatoes, yogurt, onions, salt, and pepper until creamy and smooth.

Spoon 2 to 3 tablespoons filling down center of each crepe, then roll up crepes. You will have some crepes left over; stack between sheets of aluminum foil or wax paper and freeze for later use.

Place filled crepes, seam side down, on warmed serving plates, allowing 2 crepes per serving.

Make the topping: Heat oil in a nonstick pan. Sauté onions and garlic until tender, about 5 minutes. Stir in caraway seeds.

Top crepes with hot onion mixture. Serve immediately.

If you prefer crepes hotter, top them with onion mixture, then bake in a preheated 375° oven for 10 minutes.

311 calories, 11 g fat, 1.5 g saturated fat, 62 mg cholesterol, 4.5 g dietary fiber, 291 mg sodium

Crepe Magic

Crepes enjoyed a heyday in the '70s when a knowledge of French cooking was *de rigueur* for any serious cook.

We think it's time these charming, ultrathin pancakes made a comeback. We like to think of crepes as faster alternatives to homemade pasta. Instead of kneading, rolling, and cutting dough, you pour batter into a skillet, cook for a few seconds, and—voila!—you have a lovely round noodle you can wrap around almost anything: ricotta cheese, mashed potatoes, spinach, ratatouille, mushrooms, and on and on. Such versatility is a real prize for the vegetarian cook.

We enjoy taking crepes beyond the ordinary plain egg pancake. You can flavor them with anything you'd put into pasta, and then some. We've even made one delectable batch with rye flour and caraway seed.

Cooking crepes can intimidate a cook who's not used to it. Actually, it's an easy process if you keep a few rules in mind:

- Batter for crepes should be thin, about the consistency of whipping cream (or buttermilk, for the more health-conscious types among you). For best results let the batter stand 20 minutes before using. This allows the proteins in the flour to "relax" and absorb the liquid, making for a tender crepe. If crepes fall apart when you cook them, add another tablespoon or two of flour.

- Use a nonstick crepe pan (skillet) with sloping rather than straight sides.

- Add just a small amount of fat—nonstick cooking spray is ideal. You want the crepe to set, not fry.

- The pan should be hot, but not too hot or the batter won't flow smoothly. We suggest heating the skillet over a medium flame, then holding it away from the heat for 2 or 3 seconds before pouring in the batter. Quickly twirl the skillet so the batter evenly films the bottom of it.

- Cook the crepe on the first side just until set. This should not take more than 10 to 20 seconds.

- To turn, lift one edge of the crepe with a butter knife, drape the crepe over a thin, flexible spatula, and carefully flip. Or slide the crepe out onto a paper plate, then invert the plate over the skillet.

- Cook the second side for just a few seconds, until the crepe is set and moves freely in the pan. Slide out onto a plate.

Crepes freeze well. Stack them between sheets of wax paper or aluminum foil, then seal in a plastic bag.

To defrost, remove the crepes from the plastic bag and place the stack in a 350-degree oven about 10 minutes. The crepes will separate easily. If they're stacked between wax paper, you can defrost them in the microwave. (Do not use the microwave if they're stacked between foil.) Remove from the plastic bag and defrost the stack of crepes on medium (50 percent) just until they can be easily separated.

WHOLE WHEAT PASTA WITH EGGPLANT AND TOASTED PINE NUTS

With its "meaty" texture and bland mushroomy flavor that adapts well to many seasonings, eggplant has long been a friend of vegetarians everywhere. Here, it makes a hearty sauce for pasta.

Toasting the pine nuts mutes their resiny notes somewhat and emphasizes their richness.

Makes 4 servings

2 large eggplants, peeled and diced
Salt
2 tablespoons olive or canola oil
1½ cups chopped onions
3 cloves garlic
1 medium bulb fennel, cored and diced
1 red bell pepper, cored, seeded, and
* diced*

1 can (14½ ounces) stewed tomatoes,
* including liquid*
2 tablespoons chopped fresh oregano or
* 1 teaspoon dried*
¼ teaspoon pepper
8 ounces whole wheat pasta
¼ cup pine nuts

Layer diced eggplant in a large colander or on a double thickness of paper towels. Sprinkle lightly with salt. Let stand for 45 minutes, rinse well, and drain.

Heat oil in a large pan that has been sprayed with nonstick cooking spray. Add onions and garlic, and sauté for 3 minutes. Add eggplant and fennel, and cook for 10 minutes over medium heat. Stir only occasionally so eggplant browns. After 6 or 7 minutes, add red pepper. Continue cooking until eggplant is soft. Add tomatoes with their liquid, oregano, pepper, and a pinch of salt. Cook until sauce is heated.

Cook pasta according to package directions. While pasta is cooking, toast pine nuts in a nonstick frying pan, stirring often, until lightly browned. Divide pasta among 4 plates. Top with sauce and pine nuts.

231 calories, 13 g fat, 2 g saturated fat, no cholesterol, 9.5 g dietary fiber, 565 mg sodium

BUCKWHEAT, BOWS, AND MUSHROOMS

Barbara's mother-in-law, who lived on New York's Lower East Side, would sweeten cooked buckwheat groats (kasha) and serve them as cereal. The earthy-flavored cracked kernels of buckwheat are available in some supermarkets, kosher markets, and health-food stores, and also taste wonderful in a savory dish with mushrooms.

The egg white coating helps keep the kernels of buckwheat separate so they don't get mushy.

Makes 4 servings

*1 cup medium-grain buckwheat groats
   (kasha)*
2 egg whites
2 cups boiling water
6 ounces bow-shaped egg noodles
½ teaspoon salt

¼ teaspoon pepper
1½ tablespoons canola oil
1 cup chopped onion
*⅓ pound fresh brown, shiitake or white
   mushrooms*

Cook groats in a dry nonstick skillet over medium heat until toasted, about 2 to 3 minutes. Stir in egg whites until groats are coated. Stir in boiling water. Cover skillet. Cook over medium heat, stirring occasionally, about 10 minutes or until all the liquid is absorbed.

While groats are cooking, cook bows in salted water according to package directions. Drain.

Add bows to groats. Season with salt and pepper.

Heat oil in a nonstick pan. Fry onion and mushrooms over medium heat, stirring occasionally, until soft. Toss with buckwheat and bows. Serve hot.

388 calories, 9 g fat, 1 g saturated fat, 40 mg cholesterol, 8 g dietary fiber, 306 mg sodium

BAKED BEANS WITH
A PUMPERNICKEL CRUST

One of the most characteristic dishes of New England, Boston baked beans became a standard meal or side dish wherever Yankees settled throughout the country. Boston women traditionally prepared baked beans on Saturday to serve that night, with leftovers for Sunday.

The cooking time of beans can vary considerably depending on how long they've been in storage, so just cook until they reach the desired tenderness.

Makes 10 servings

1 pound dried navy or pea beans	*½ cup ketchup*
3 tablespoons canola oil	*½ teaspoon salt*
¼ cup packed dark brown sugar	*¼ teaspoon pepper*
3 to 4 tablespoons dark molasses	*1 cup pumpernickel or whole wheat*
1 teaspoon dry mustard	*bread crumbs*
1 tablespoon powdered ginger	

Check over beans and rinse thoroughly. Place beans in a large saucepan with water to cover. Bring to a boil, then reduce to a simmer and cook for 1 hour. Drain.

Preheat oven to 300°.

Put beans in a bean pot or other deep ovenproof dish. Add water to cover. Stir in oil, sugar, molasses, mustard, ginger, and ketchup.

Bake in the center of oven for 3 to 4 hours, or until beans are tender. Check beans every hour, adding water as necessary to keep them covered. Season with salt and pepper. When beans are nearly tender (about a half hour before you expect them to be done), sprinkle crumbs over beans, patting them in place with the back of a spoon. Continue baking, uncovered, until beans are tender and top is crusty. Stir beans slightly, mixing in the bread crumb crust. Serve beans with brown bread.

Leftovers are good reheated and can be mashed.

263 calories, 5 g fat, 0.5 g saturated fat, no cholesterol, 9 g dietary fiber, 339 mg sodium

SOFT CORNMEAL LOAF (MAMALIGA)
FOUR WAYS

Long before trendy chefs began playing around with polenta, Eastern European immigrants on New York's Lower East Side were serving cornmeal loaf for breakfast, lunch, or dinner. In Romanian, this comfort food is called mamaliga.

It is important to mix the cornmeal with cold water before cooking. This prevents lumps.

Makes 12 slices; 6 servings

1 cup cold water
2 cups yellow cornmeal
3 cups boiling water
½ teaspoon salt
¼ teaspoon white pepper
3 tablespoons unsalted butter or
    margarine

½ cup fat-free cottage cheese
¼ cup nonfat sour cream
¼ cup sugar
1 teaspoon ground cinnamon
⅛ teaspoon ground nutmeg

Pour cold water into a saucepan. Using a wooden spoon or whisk, mix in cornmeal. Add boiling water, salt, and pepper. Bring mixture to a boil. Reduce heat to medium and continue cooking, stirring often, until mixture pulls away from the sides of the pan, about 5 to 10 minutes.

Mix in butter. Continue cooking 3 to 5 minutes, or until mixture again pulls away from sides of pan. Cool for 5 minutes.

Stir in cottage cheese and sour cream, mixing thoroughly.

Serve in a soup bowl. Mix together sugar, cinnamon, and nutmeg, and sprinkle over mamaliga.

VARIATION: Mamaliga No. 2. Pour cooked cornmeal mixture into a nonstick 9-by-5-inch loaf pan. Cool, unmold, and slice. (Loaf can be refrigerated for up to 2 days.) Eat plain or pan-fry mamaliga in a small amount of oil until golden.

VARIATION: Mamaliga No. 3. Mix 1 teaspoon fennel seeds into the cooked batter and shape into a loaf as directed for Mamaliga No. 2. Heat 1 tablespoon canola oil or unsalted butter in a nonstick frying pan and heat. (If necessary to coat pan, spray first with cooking spray.) Sauté mamaliga slices on both sides until golden and heated through. Serve plain or with a dollop of nonfat sour cream.

VARIATION: Mamaliga No. 4. Prepare Mamaliga No. 3. Serve it with Shiitake Sauce (recipe follows).

SHIITAKE SAUCE

Makes 6 servings

1 cup dried shiitake mushroom pieces
1 tablespoon unsalted butter or
  margarine
½ cup pink Zinfandel or rosé

1 cup evaporated skim milk
¼ teaspoon sugar
¼ teaspoon salt

Reconstitute mushrooms in boiling water for 30 minutes, then drain and coarsely chop.

Sauté mushrooms in butter in nonstick frying pan for 3 minutes over medium heat. Stir in wine and cook until wine is reduced to about 3 tablespoons liquid. Stir in milk, sugar, and salt. Heat through and serve. Or prepare ahead of time and reheat before serving.

With sugar and cinnamon: 275 calories, 7 g fat, 4 g saturated fat, 16 mg cholesterol, 5 g dietary fiber, 263 mg sodium

With shiitake sauce: 320 calories, 9 g fat, 5 g saturated fat, 23 mg cholesterol, 5 g dietary fiber, 403 mg sodium

NEW ENGLAND RED BOILED DINNER WITH HONEY-MUSTARD SAUCE

This hearty, thrifty winter main dish represents New England cooking at its most traditional. Rutabaga, potatoes, carrots, turnips, and red cabbage are simmered to form a one-dish meal that's topped with a spicy honey-mustard sauce. The cabbage and beets give this a rosy hue.

Makes 4 servings

8 new red potatoes, unpeeled and
    scrubbed

2 large carrots, peeled and sliced

2 turnips, peeled and quartered

1 large rutabaga, peeled and cubed

1 small head (about 1⅓ pounds) red
    cabbage, cored and cut into 8 wedges

2 tablespoons whole allspice, wrapped
    securely in cheesecloth

½ teaspoon salt

½ teaspoon pepper

2 large beets, unpeeled and scrubbed;
    leave tail and 2 inches of stem intact

Sauce:

1 cup plain nonfat yogurt

¼ cup reduced-fat mayonnaise

2 tablespoons stone-ground mustard

½ teaspoon honey

Place potatoes, carrots, turnips, rutabaga, and cabbage wedges in a large pot; add water to cover. Add allspice pouch, salt, and pepper. Bring to a boil over medium heat. Reduce heat to low. Partially cover pot and continue cooking for 45 minutes, or until all vegetables are tender. Drain vegetables and discard spice packet.

Meanwhile, cook beets separately. Place them in a pan with water to cover. Bring to a boil, reduce heat to medium, and cook about 45 minutes, or until beets are tender. Drain and let cool. Trim stems and tails, peel, and slice.

While vegetables cook, whisk together yogurt, mayonnaise, mustard, and honey. Cover and refrigerate until ready to serve. Stir sauce before serving.

Divide hot vegetables, including beets, among individual plates or serve on a large platter. Drizzle sauce over vegetables or pass it separately at the table.

325 calories, 6 g fat, 1 g saturated fat, 1 mg cholesterol, 10.5 g dietary fiber, 507 mg sodium

SWISS AND SAUERKRAUT SANDWICH ON HOMEMADE ONION RYE

Swiss cheese with sauerkraut and Thousand Island dressing is a classic combination that evokes visions of the quintessential New York delicatessen—complete with worn floors and indifferent service.

To really lift this sandwich out of the ordinary, serve it on bread you made yourself. For an open-faced sandwich, use just one slice of bread per person.

Makes 4 servings

Light Thousand Island dressing:

½ cup reduced-fat mayonnaise
2½ tablespoons ketchup or chili sauce
1 teaspoon minced pimiento-stuffed
  olives

2 teaspoons minced green onion
2 hard-cooked egg whites, chopped

Sandwiches:

8 slices Onion Rye Bread (page 78) or
  a top-quality bakery rye or
  sourdough rye bread

1 cup sauerkraut
4 (1-ounce) slices reduced-fat Swiss
  cheese

To make dressing: Mix all ingredients together until well blended. Pour into a jar and refrigerate until needed.

For each sandwich, spread about 1 tablespoon of dressing over 1 slice of bread. Drain and rinse sauerkraut and arrange ¼ cup on the bread. Top with a slice of cheese and another slice of bread.

Spray a large nonstick frying pan with butter-flavored nonstick cooking spray. Add sandwiches, two at a time, and heat, turning once, until they just begin to brown. Remove sandwiches with spatula, cut in half, and serve hot with lengthwise slices of sour pickle.

You'll have about ½ cup of Thousand Island dressing left over; use it on sandwiches or lettuce salads.

471 calories, 12 g fat, 4 g saturated fat, 21 mg cholesterol, 6 g dietary fiber, 499 mg sodium

Dressing (per tablespoon): 40 calories, 3.5 g fat, 1 g saturated fat, no cholesterol, no dietary fiber, 128 mg sodium

SAVORY RICE AND PIGEON PEAS

Rice with pigeon peas is a standard on Puerto Rican tables—which means the dish is almost as popular in New York City as it is in the islands. Savory Puerto Rican dishes are often seasoned with a mixture of sautéed vegetables and seasonings called *sofrito*. The seasoning varies from cook to cook but usually includes garlic, onions, and peppers.

Medium-grain rice is available in many supermarkets, but you can use long-grain rice in this. You may need to add ¼ cup more water.

Pigeon peas are available dried or canned in stores that carry Caribbean ingredients. Crowder peas, a close relative, come canned or frozen and can be found in many supermarkets.

Gravelly pink annatto seeds, called *achiote* in Spanish, give the rice a beautiful yellow hue. They're available in any grocery that carries a good stock of Hispanic ingredients.

Makes 4 servings

2 tablespoons canola oil

2 teaspoons annatto seed (achiote)
(optional)

1 cup finely diced green bell pepper

½ cup finely diced mild chile pepper

3 cloves garlic, minced

1 cup finely chopped onion

½ cup finely diced fresh or canned
tomato

¼ cup chopped green pimiento-stuffed
olives

½ teaspoon dried oregano

1 cup medium-grain rice

2 cups cooked pigeon peas or crowder
peas

1½ cups water

½ teaspoon salt

2 tablespoons chopped fresh cilantro
(optional)

Heat oil in a large heavy-bottomed saucepan. Add annatto seeds if using and cook over medium heat for 1 minute, until oil is orange-red and fragrant. Remove from heat. Use a spoon to scoop seeds from oil and discard them.

Add peppers, garlic, onion, tomato, olives, and oregano to oil in pan. Cook over medium heat, stirring, for 3 to 4 minutes, until onion softens. Add rice and stir to coat. Stir in peas (if using canned peas, rinse well and drain), water, and salt. Bring to a simmer. Reduce heat to low, tightly cover pan, and cook for 18 to 20 minutes, or until liquid is absorbed and rice is tender. Stir in cilantro and serve.

386 calories, 9 g fat, 1 g saturated fat, no cholesterol, 7 g dietary fiber, 462 mg sodium

MASHED POTATOES WITH KALE

Propelled by a potato famine in their native land, huge numbers of Irish people, many of them young women, came to America's East Coast in the nineteenth century. To this day New York City and Boston throw a grand party on Saint Patrick's Day.

This dish is inspired by colcannon, a traditional Irish mixture of greens and potatoes. It's often made with cabbage, but it's a lot greener if you use kale, a bluish-green, frilly cousin of cabbage that is packed with calcium, beta-carotene, and other nutrients. Kale is available year-round but is at its peak in the fall and winter months.

Makes 4 servings

2 pounds potatoes, baked or boiled
    until tender
¾ pound kale or cabbage
1 tablespoon unsalted butter or
    margarine

1 tablespoon canola oil
1 cup chopped leeks (white parts only)
½ cup water
½ teaspoon salt
Pepper to taste

Peel cooked potatoes and mash with a fork.

Strip kale leaves from stems and discard stems. Finely chop leaves. (If using cabbage, core it and cut the cabbage into thin strips.)

Heat butter and oil in a large frying pan. Add leeks and sauté until softened. Add kale and water. Cover and cook over medium heat, stirring once, for 3 to 5 minutes, or until kale softens and turns bright green. Stir in potatoes and mash well with the kale. Season with salt and pepper. Serve warm.

287 calories, 6.5 g fat, 4 g saturated fat, 16 mg cholesterol, 7 g dietary fiber, 306 mg sodium

TARRAGON-SCENTED STRING BEAN SALAD, SHAKER STYLE

One of the Shakers' welcome contributions to American culture was their extensive cultivation and use of kitchen herbs. Hancock Village in Hancock, western Massachusetts, still offers an incredible display of herbs in its well-tended Shaker gardens.

This salad is our nod to the simple but delicious salads and other dishes that came out of Shaker kitchens. Enjoy it as a light summer main course, with whole wheat bread as an accompaniment.

Note that if you make your own tarragon vinegar, it needs to mellow for four weeks before using.

Makes 4 servings

*¾ pound string beans, trimmed and cut
  into 1- or 1½-inch pieces*
*4 tablespoons tarragon vinegar (use
  store-bought vinegar or following
  recipe; see also Herbal Alchemy,
  page 73)*
3 tablespoons olive oil
½ teaspoon dry mustard
*1½ teaspoons minced fresh thyme or
  ½ teaspoon dried*

*1½ teaspoons minced fresh basil or
  ½ teaspoon dried*
½ teaspoon salt
2 large tomatoes, chopped
½ cup chopped red onion
*4 heads Bibb lettuce, washed, dried,
  and torn into bite-size pieces*
⅓ cup minced fresh parsley

Cook beans in lightly salted boiling water to cover just until tender, about 4 to 5 minutes. Rinse under cold water. Drain.

Mix vinegar and oil with mustard, thyme, basil, and salt. If using dried herbs, let dressing stand for at least 15 minutes. Toss beans with dressing in a serving bowl. Add tomatoes, onion, lettuce, and parsley. Taste and adjust seasonings. Serve chilled.

147 calories, 11 g fat, 1.5 g saturated fat, no cholesterol, 5 g dietary fiber, 284 mg sodium

TARRAGON VINEGAR

Makes 1 pint

¼ cup fresh tarragon leaves   *1 pint white vinegar*

Wash leaves and pat dry with paper towels.

Heat vinegar to simmering. Pour into a sterilized jar and add tarragon. Cover jar securely.

Let vinegar steep for 4 weeks in a cool, dark area before using. Vinegar mellows as it ages. Place in refrigerator after opening.

Herbal Alchemy

Every summer Barbara makes batches of scented vinegar from the beautiful tarragon her husband grows. In fact, herbal vinegars wonderfully capture the flavor of summer herbs for winter use.

Wash a couple of sprigs of your favorite herb or herbs and pat dry. Put the herbs in a sterile bottle (an old vinegar bottle, boiled in water to cover for 10 minutes, is ideal). Heat the vinegar to simmering, then pour it over the herb. Seal and let sit for at least a month, shaking the bottle now and then. Strain out the herbs and store the vinegar in a cool, dry place. For more visual appeal you can leave a sprig of herb in the bottle.

You can also flavor vinegar with other spices, such as dried hot peppers, garlic, coriander seeds, or mustard seed.

If you're tempted to infuse your olive oil with fresh rosemary or basil—don't. The U.S. Department of Agriculture cautions against adding any fresh food—herbs, garlic, or dried tomatoes—to oil that's stored at room temperature. Garlic and herbs can carry botulism spores from the soil. Normally harmless, the spores can release toxins when kept at room temperature in an oxygen-free environment—which smothering them in oil creates.

The USDA recommends using dried supermarket herbs to infuse oils and keeping the oil refrigerated. If you must use fresh herbs, wash and dry them well, refrigerate the oil, and use it within two weeks.

If you want to give herb-infused concoctions as gifts, stick to vinegars.

Breads and Desserts

BAKED BOSTON BROWN BREAD

Loaves of Boston brown bread, made from rye, wheat, and corn flours and sweetened with molasses, traditionally accompany baked beans. The batter usually is poured into cans and steamed, but like most modern cooks, we'd rather spend our time and labor elsewhere. So we adapted the recipe to a quickbread and baked it in a loaf pan, with fine results.

Slice and toast any leftover bread. For a comforting dessert, mix toasted, crumbled brown bread into softened low-fat vanilla ice cream or frozen yogurt.

Makes 1 loaf; 10 servings

2 cups yellow or white cornmeal
1 cup rye-wheat flour or ½ cup all-
 purpose flour and ½ cup rye flour
2 teaspoons baking soda
¾ teaspoon baking powder

½ teaspoon salt
⅔ cup molasses
2 cups buttermilk
¼ teaspoon ground ginger
1 cup currants or dark raisins

Preheat oven to 350°. Grease a 9-by-5-inch loaf pan.

Stir together cornmeal, rye-wheat flour, baking soda, baking powder, and salt in a mixing bowl. Stir in molasses, buttermilk, ginger, and currants just until mixed.

Pour batter into prepared loaf pan. Bake on the center rack of the oven for 55 minutes, or until a tester inserted in the center comes out dry.

Cool in pan for 5 minutes, then turn out onto a wire rack.

245 calories, 2 g fat, 0.5 g saturated fat, 2 mg cholesterol, 5 g dietary fiber, 374 mg sodium

BRAIDED EGG BREAD (CHALLAH) WITH WHEAT GERM

This beautiful braided loaf, often served for Jewish holidays, has universal appeal. If you'd like the bread to have a deeper golden color, add a pinch of saffron to the liquid mixture (in higher-fat versions of challah, egg yolks give it a golden color). A small amount of saffron goes a long way; only a few threads will give the loaf a rich color.

Makes 1 loaf; about 10 servings

1 package (2¼ teaspoons) active dry
   yeast
¾ cup warm water (105° to 115°)
3 tablespoons sugar
½ teaspoon salt
3 tablespoons melted unsalted butter or
   margarine, cooled

¾ cup egg substitute, at room
   temperature
3½ to 4¼ cups bread flour
½ cup wheat germ
1 egg white, slightly beaten
2 teaspoons poppy seeds

Dissolve yeast in warm water in the bowl of a heavy-duty electric mixer. Mix in sugar and salt. Add butter, egg substitute, 3 cups of flour, and wheat germ. With dough hook attachment, mix until blended. Knead, adding remaining flour as needed, until dough is smooth and elastic. Let dough rest for 5 minutes, then knead by hand a minute or two on a lightly floured pastry cloth or board.

Place dough in a large bowl and cover with a damp towel. Let dough rise in a warm area until doubled in bulk, about 1½ to 2 hours.

Punch dough down and knead again for 2 to 3 minutes.

To braid bread, divide it into 3 equal pieces. Roll each piece into a long rope. Attach the 3 ropes by pinching together at one end. Braid the 3 ropes together and secure the ends by pinching them together.

Grease an 8-inch-round baking pan. Coil dough into pan. Let dough rise for 1 hour, or until doubled in bulk.

Preheat oven to 375°. Brush bread with slightly beaten egg white, and sprinkle with poppy seeds.

Bake in the center of the oven for 25 to 30 minutes, until bread is golden and sounds hollow when tapped. Cool in pan for 5 minutes, then turn out onto a wire rack.

271 calories, 5.5 g fat, 2.5 g saturated fat, 10 mg cholesterol, 2.5 g dietary fiber, 140 mg sodium

SOFT PRETZELS

A pretzel maker in Pennsylvania once told us that real pretzels barely exist west of the Mississippi. Certainly the mass-produced lacquered items sold in most supermarkets bear little resemblance to the delicious twisted breads, hard and soft, that come out of the East, especially Pennsylvania.

Because it kneads so thoroughly, the bread machine is ideal for chewier breads— such as pretzels—that require more gluten development. We tested this recipe by hand and with a kneading and first rise in a Zojirushi S15 machine, with fine results.

Serve these warm from the oven with mustard. Or let cool, then keep in storage bags for up to a day, or freeze them for up to two months. The crust will soften; reheat pretzels in a 300-degree oven until crisp.

Pretzels can be sliced in half lengthwise for sandwiches. Smear with a bit of hot mustard, then slap a thin slice of reduced-fat Swiss cheese between the halves.

Makes 12 pretzels

1 package (2¼ teaspoons) active dry yeast
1 cup warm water (105° to 115°)
3 cups bread flour, plus more if needed
1 tablespoon malted milk powder or 2 teaspoons molasses
1 tablespoon gluten flour (optional; but it gives the pretzels a chewier texture)

1 teaspoon salt
Cornmeal
1 quart water
2 tablespoons baking soda
Coarse (kosher) salt (optional)

Sprinkle yeast on warm water in the bowl of a heavy-duty mixer. Stir in bread flour, malted milk powder, gluten flour if using, and salt. Knead dough with the dough hook, adding a little more flour if necessary, until smooth and springy. Let dough rest for a minute, then turn out onto a floured board and knead by hand for another minute or two. (Or mix and knead bread completely by hand.)

Place in an oiled bowl and let rise, covered, in a warm place for 1 to 2 hours, until doubled.

Punch dough down and divide into 12 equal-size pieces. With your palms, roll each piece into a rope about 16 inches long and the thickness of a pencil (dough will be very springy, so you may have to exert some pressure). Bring the ends of the dough rope up and twist around each other, then bring them down across the loop that's formed, so you have a pretzel shape. Place on a greased baking sheet.

Repeat with remaining pieces of dough. Let rise in a warm place for 40 to 60 minutes, or until light.

Preheat oven to 425°. Sprinkle cornmeal evenly over a clean baking sheet.

Bring the quart of water and baking soda to a simmer in a nonaluminum saucepan. Add pretzels, 2 or 3 at a time, and cook for 1 minute, turning after 30 seconds. Place on the baking sheet and sprinkle lightly with coarse salt.

Bake for 10 to 15 minutes, or until a dark golden brown.

Serve warm.

VARIATION: Bread machine (1½ to 2 pounds): Put ingredients in bread machine in order recommended by manufacturer. Set to Dough or Manual (if your machine does not have a manual setting for dough, put it on a basic bread setting, then reset or turn off the machine after first rising).

After first rising, remove dough from machine and shape, let rise, simmer, and bake as directed above.

120 calories, no fat, no saturated fat, no cholesterol, 1 g dietary fiber, 536 mg sodium

Twisted History

The Sturgis Pretzel House in Lititz, Pennsylvania, boasts of being the oldest commercial pretzel bakery in the United States—it began making pretzels in 1861—but the twisted breads go back much farther in history.

Supposedly, medieval monks baked the breads into shapes suggesting prayer (supplicants used to cross their arms and place their hands on their shoulders) and gave them as rewards to children who learned their prayers. Pretzels became a popular street food in fifteenth-century Germany.

Today, both soft and hard pretzels (which are just soft pretzels left to dry out in a low oven) are very popular in the East. Pennsylvanians not only eat pretzels as is, but crumble the hard variety into everything from pie crusts to salads.

One common ingredient in a good Pennsylvania-style pretzel is malt, which gives the dough a hint of grain-fed sweetness. In a true connoisseur's book, mass-produced pretzels sweetened with corn syrup don't have a prayer.

Dipping the bread in a soda water bath before baking is essential. It gives the pretzel its distinctive dark brown, crackly-crisp crust.

ONION RYE BREAD

This recipe produces a dense, European-style bread. Rye bread doughs tend to be sticky. They need the extra liquid to create more steam, which helps heavy flours like rye to rise. Don't work in too much flour.

Makes 1 loaf; about 12 servings

1 package (2¼ teaspoons) active dry
    yeast
¼ cup warm water (105° to 115°)
1 cup skim milk, warmed
2 tablespoons honey
1 tablespoon canola oil
2⅔ cups bread flour

1 cup stone-ground rye flour or rye-
    wheat flour
3 teaspoons caraway seeds
¼ cup dry onion flakes
½ teaspoon salt
1 egg white

Dissolve yeast in warm water in the bowl of a heavy-duty electric mixer fitted with a dough hook. Mix in warm milk, honey, and oil. Add flours, 2 teaspoons caraway seeds, onion flakes, and salt. Knead until elastic and pliable; dough will be somewhat sticky. (Or mix and knead by hand on a floured board.)

Place dough in a bowl, cover, and let rise in a warm draft-free place for 1½ hours, or until doubled in bulk. Punch dough down. Knead 2 to 4 minutes on a lightly floured surface.

Set dough in a greased 9-by-5-inch loaf pan. Let rise for 45 minutes, or until light. Preheat oven to 375°.

Brush top of loaf with egg white and sprinkle with remaining 1 teaspoon caraway seeds.

Bake bread about 40 minutes, or until it is golden brown and sounds hollow when tapped.

Let stand for 5 minutes, then turn out onto a wire rack. Cool before slicing.

167 calories, 2 g fat, 0.5 g saturated fat, no cholesterol, 2 g dietary fiber, 103 mg sodium

IRISH SODA BREAD

Traditional Irish soda bread is a simple proposition. Just mix flour, salt, soda, and buttermilk. This hearty quickbread, essentially a giant scone, is good for breakfast (add the currants or raisins) or as an accompaniment to various main dishes.

Makes 1 loaf; about 10 servings

3 cups all-purpose flour

1 cup whole wheat flour

1¼ teaspoons salt

1 teaspoon baking soda

2 cups buttermilk

½ cup raisins or currants (optional)

Melted unsalted butter (optional)

Preheat oven to 375°. Spray an 8-inch cake pan with nonstick cooking spray.

Mix flours, salt, and baking soda together thoroughly in a mixing bowl. Add buttermilk to make a soft, somewhat sticky dough. Stir in raisins or currants if using.

Pat into a cake pan. With a small, very sharp knife or a razor blade, slash the top of the loaf in the shape of an **X**. The cuts should be about ½ inch deep.

Bake for 45 to 55 minutes, or until loaf is golden brown all over. Brush top with melted butter if you like. Let cool before slicing.

197 calories, 1 g fat, 0.5 g saturated fat, 2 mg cholesterol, 2.5 g dietary fiber, 401 mg sodium

BUCKWHEAT PANCAKES WITH APPLE CIDER SAUCE

Buckwheat is actually an herb, not a grain, and is related to rhubarb and sorrel. Native to Russia, it grows just about anywhere, but is especially popular in the East. Buckwheat has an earthy, love-it-or-leave-it flavor. We love it in pancakes, with a sweet topping as a foil.

If you like, you can serve these pancakes with maple syrup instead of apples.

Makes 4 servings

Sauce:
2 cups apple cider

1 cup peeled and chopped apples

1 stick cinnamon

Pancakes:
1¼ cups sifted all-purpose flour

½ cup buckwheat flour

¼ cup sugar

2 teaspoons baking powder

¼ teaspoon salt

½ cup egg substitute

2 tablespoons melted unsalted butter or margarine, cooled

1½ cups skim milk

Put cider, apples, and cinnamon stick in a saucepan. Bring mixture to a boil, reduce heat to simmer, and cook for 10 to 15 minutes. Liquid should have reduced to about 1½ cups, and apples should be tender. Remove from heat and let sauce cool. Discard cinnamon stick and mash or puree apples. Set aside.

To make pancakes: In a large mixing bowl, mix flours, sugar, baking powder, and salt. Stir in egg substitute, melted butter, and milk until batter is smooth.

Spray a large nonstick frying pan or griddle with butter-flavored nonstick cooking spray and heat. Pour pancake batter, using a ¼-cup measure, into pan or onto griddle, being careful not to crowd pancakes. Cook until bubbles begin to form and edges begin to look firm and cooked.

Turn pancakes over and cook until golden. Repeat with remaining batter.

Serve buckwheat cakes with cider sauce, which should be at room temperature or warmed slightly.

423 calories, 8 g fat, 4 g saturated fat, 18 mg cholesterol, 3 g dietary fiber, 471 mg sodium

STRAWBERRY GRUNT

If you like a slightly tarter filling in this spring fruit pudding, replace 1 cup of the strawberries with a cup of peeled and diced rhubarb.

Makes 8 servings

Filling:
6 cups hulled, sliced strawberries
½ cup sugar
¼ cup fresh orange juice

Dumplings:
¾ cup cake flour
2 tablespoons sugar
1 teaspoon baking powder
¼ teaspoon ground nutmeg
¼ teaspoon salt
3 tablespoons unsalted butter or margarine
About ¼ cup skim milk

To make filling: In a large saucepan or Dutch oven, stir together strawberries, sugar, and orange juice. Heat berries to boiling, reduce heat to low, and simmer for 5 minutes.

To make dumplings: In a mixing bowl or the bowl of a food processor, mix flour, sugar, baking powder, nutmeg, and salt. Cut in butter or margarine to make a crumbly mixture. Add enough milk to make a soft dough.

Drop dough from a tablespoon into strawberries, using another spoon to push dough off the tablespoon. Cook, uncovered, for 10 minutes. Cover pan and simmer 10 minutes longer, until dumplings are cooked through.

To serve, spoon into dessert dishes, allowing dumplings to rest on top of berries. Serve warm.

174 calories, 6 g fat, 3 g saturated fat, 12 mg cholesterol, 3 g dietary fiber, 163 mg sodium

Grunts, Bettys, and Fools

Whether inspired by their English forebears or rendered giddy by the oh-so-brief northern summers, New Englanders came up with all sorts of colorful names to tell their numerous fruit puddings apart.

A grunt is cooked on top of the stove and topped with dumplings. It supposedly got its name because of the grunting sounds the fruit makes as it cooks. Buckles and slumps seem to be similar, except that they're baked.

A betty is fruit layered with buttered bread crumbs and baked.

A cobbler is baked fruit with a biscuit topping. It becomes a dowdy when the topping is pie pastry.

A crisp or crunch is baked fruit with a crunchy, crumbly topping that is made with flour, butter, and plenty of sugar to give it the crunch. If the person making it is of German ancestry, it's a streusel. Sometimes oats or other grains are used in crisps.

A fool, which supposedly got the name because it's a trifling afterthought, is pureed fruit with cream swirled through it. To make a quick, low-fat fool, use a food processor to puree berries or peeled fruits such as mangos, rhubarb, peaches, or pears, add a bit of lemon juice and sugar if desired, place the puree in a dessert dish, and swirl softened vanilla frozen yogurt through it.

FOUR-BERRY SUMMER PUDDING

This is one of the prettiest desserts we've seen. It's adapted from a recipe given to us by Rick Moonen, chef at Oceana in New York City. He recalls that when he was a child, his mother always let him choose the dessert for his birthday. His favorite was angel cake, with the top removed, insides scooped out and stuffed with berries, and the top replaced.

Most summer puddings are made with bread, but pillowy angel food absorbs the fruit juices even better. This pudding slices beautifully, and the fruits glisten like jewels.

Makes 8 servings

Cake:

1 cup egg whites, at room temperature
1 teaspoon cream of tartar
¼ teaspoon salt
1¼ cups sugar

1 cup cake flour, sifted
1 teaspoon vanilla extract
½ teaspoon almond extract

Filling:

1 quart strawberries, washed, hulled,
  and quartered
1 quart blueberries, washed
1½ cups raspberries, washed

1½ cups blackberries, washed
½ cup sugar
Juice of ½ lemon

To make the cake: Preheat oven to 350°.

Beat egg whites in the large bowl of an electric mixer on high speed until foamy. Sprinkle cream of tartar and salt over egg whites. Continue beating until soft peaks form. Sprinkle sugar, a few tablespoons at a time, over egg whites and continue beating until all the sugar has been incorporated and the whites form firm, glossy peaks.

Sprinkle flour over egg whites and fold in gently with a rubber spatula or balloon whisk. Sprinkle vanilla and almond extracts over batter and fold in gently.

Spoon batter into an ungreased 10-inch tube pan. Bake cake on lowest rack in the oven for 45 minutes, or until cake springs back when lightly touched. Invert cake pan onto a can or other object to cool. When completely cool, remove from pan. Cake may be made up to 2 days in advance, wrapped tightly, and stored at room temperature.

Cut cake into ¼-inch slices. Line a 9-by-5-inch loaf pan with overlapping sheets of plastic wrap. Line the bottom and sides of the pan with slices of cake, trimming and adjusting to fit. Reserve any leftover cake for another use.

To make filling: Cook berries, sugar, and lemon juice in a large pan over medium heat just until the juices begin to flow. Cool.

Fill cake-lined loaf pan with one-third of the fruit. Cover fruit with a layer of cake, pressing it down as you cover the fruit. Continue in this manner until all the fruit is used up. Top with a layer of cake. Bring up the sides of plastic wrap to cover the top of the pudding. To weight the cake, lay unopened cans of food on their side to cover the top. Refrigerate overnight.

When ready to serve, remove cans, pull aside the plastic, and invert pudding onto a serving plate. Pull off and discard remaining plastic wrap. Slice and serve.

330 calories, 2.5 g fat, 0.5 g saturated fat, no cholesterol, 6.5 g dietary fiber, 172 mg sodium

PEACH AND NECTARINE COMPOTE WITH MANGO-GINGER FROZEN YOGURT

Bistro fare that pays homage to America's rich ethnic and cultural diversity is the specialty of the house at New Rivers in Providence, Rhode Island. Co-owner and dessert chef Pat Tillinghast shared the recipe for this compote that overlays traditional New England favorites with the alluring perfume of mangos and ginger.

Makes 6 servings

1 pint nonfat vanilla-flavored frozen
   yogurt
2 fresh, ripe mangos, peeled, sliced
   from the pit, and chopped
2 tablespoons ginger marmalade or
   finely chopped candied ginger
¼ cup sugar, or to taste
¼ to ½ teaspoon ground cinnamon

3 fresh, ripe peaches
3 fresh, ripe nectarines
Juice of 1 lemon
1 to 2 tablespoons dark rum or
   Benedictine
½ cup blueberries, washed and picked
   over
6 sprigs fresh mint for garnish

Let frozen yogurt soften at room temperature for 10 minutes. In the food processor, puree mangos until smooth. Add ginger marmalade and softened yogurt. Pulse 3 or 4 times to mix well. Spoon the mango yogurt into a nonaluminum container and freeze several hours, until firm enough to scoop.

About an hour before serving, mix sugar and cinnamon in a large bowl. Wash, peel, pit, and slice peaches into bowl. Wash and slice unpeeled, pitted nectarines into bowl. Toss to coat with cinnamon sugar. Add lemon juice, rum or liqueur, and blueberries, and toss again. Cover and let stand until ready to serve.

Spoon fruits into dessert bowls, scoop yogurt on top, and drizzle liquid from fruit over all. Garnish with mint.

228 calories, 1 g fat, no saturated fat, 1 mg cholesterol, 4 g dietary fiber, 49 mg sodium

2

The South

A Taste of the Tropics

Plantain Chips or Fu Fu (Crispy Plantain Cakes)

Lemon-scented Black Bean Soup

Jerk Sweet Potato Slices with Vidalia Onion Conserve

Key Lime Ice and Assorted Tropical Fruits

Jazz Brunch

Green and Red Gumbo

Artichoke and Spinach Frittata

Orange and Grapefruit Salad with Pecans

Silky Bread Pudding with Bourbon Sauce

A Jeffersonian Fourth

Pasta Torte with Goat Cheese, Tomatoes, and Olives

Grilled Medley of Garden Vegetables

Light Strawberry Ice Cream

Appetizers, Salads, and Side Dishes

White Cornmeal and Grits Spoonbread

"Barbecued" Baby Limas

Savory Stuffed Mirlitons

Shimmering Gazpacho

Soups

Bisque of Fresh Peas

Sweet Potato–Peanut Soup

Entrées

Broccoli and Roasted Pepper Risotto

Louisiana Rice and Eggplant

Red Beans and Rice

Hoppin' John Bake (Black-eyed Peas and Rice)

Souffléd Grits with Red Peppers

Fried Grits and Cheese Finger Sandwiches

Ratatouille-filled Corn Crepes with Dill

Tofu Sandwiches with Barbecue Sauce and Tangy Slaw

Spice-crusted Tofu with Green and Red Tomatoes

Boiled New Potatoes and Cucumbers with Sour Orange Sauce

Wilted Kale and Beet Salad

Slow-roasted Vidalia Onions with Collard Greens

Gratin of String Beans and Yellow Squash

Breads and Desserts

Fluffy Buns

French Bread

Whole Wheat Biscuits

Sweet Potato–Pecan Bread with Sherried Fig Spread

Benne Wafers

Peach Custard Rice Pudding

In the beginning, the South was the agricultural capital of the nation. It still is. And why not? The South has a growing season that most of the rest of the country can only dream about. Tomatoes, eggplant, sweet and hot peppers, melons, okra, cucumbers, tropical fruits—if it requires long days and heat to grow, it'll grow well in the South.

The Native American, British, and French influences that marked early American fare traveled south from New England where, in large part because of the slave trade, they were joined by African and Caribbean ingredients and cooking styles. Alongside the soufflés and cream puddings, the South developed a spicy, down-home cuisine incorporating such ingredients and dishes as cornbread, garlic, hot peppers, peanuts, sesame seeds, beans and rice, watermelon, dark leafy greens, and tropical fruits.

The Acadians came from the north to the swamps of Louisiana, where they renamed themselves Cajuns, and the islanders and Latin Americans came from the south to Florida. In true American fashion, they were joined by the French, Spanish, Greeks, Italians, Chinese, and others.

The South is home to cosmopolitan capitals such as Atlanta, which shows off southern cooking and African cuisines at their finest; Miami, a fascinating stew of Cubans, Nicaraguans, Vietnamese, northern escapees, and young chefs who love to experiment; Memphis, where barbecue is king; and New Orleans, home to an utterly fascinating blend of Creole, Cajun, French, and southern cooking that residents like to brag is the only original American cuisine.

More than anything, the cooking we think of as traditional southern is African-American. Whether they were eking out their slave rations with produce from their gardens or turning out lavish feasts in a plantation kitchen, many of the good southern cooks were, and still are, African by ancestry.

After the Civil War and during the droughts of the 1930s, the South suffered poverty that cut like a knife across class and racial lines. In the kitchen, poverty can give birth to creativity, as cooks put the best spin on the raw ingredients that are readily available. And what magic was created. The ice tea is sweet, the whiskey is smoky, the green beans dance with flavor, the biscuits melt in the mouth, the barbecue sauces sing on the tongue.

Corn, America's most enduring staple grain, goes soft in the South, in moist cornbreads of every description, spoonbread (which is really more a pudding than a bread), and grits, a coarse cracked corn that is made into an infinite variety of dishes, from soufflés to breakfast porridge.

But the star attraction is all those fruits and vegetables. Southerners boil them, fry them, bake them, cream them, and mash them into pies. They turn them into casseroles and even desserts. Only a southerner (or a Yankee whose family hailed from the South) can cook okra so it's just right.

Florida supplies us with most of our oranges, most of our tomatoes, nearly all of our eggplant, and a growing number of exotic tropical fruits such as passion fruit and carambola (starfruit). Our sweet potatoes come from the South. Our peanuts come from the South. Our rice comes from the South and Southwest.

Even though we're Yankees, we love southern food with an abiding passion. How can you argue with feather-light breads and vegetables that just don't quit?

• A TASTE OF THE TROPICS •

The South, especially Florida, is home to a large number of people who claim Caribbean ancestry, whether Jamaican, Cuban, Haitian, Puerto Rican, Bahamian, or Trinidadian.

Their contributions to southern cooking include plenty of starches. Beans and rice, together or separate, are eaten throughout the Caribbean, and the plantain, a starchier cousin of the banana, is widely used. The cuisine also embraces plenty of spices, including allspice and the fruity-flavored habañero or Scotch bonnet, a lumpy little chile pepper that aficionados rate the most scorching on earth.

Of course, any Caribbean-inspired menu must feature fruit: bananas of all colors and sizes, mangos dripping with juice, mouth-puckering little limes. Then there's the passion fruit, whose haunting perfume and intense flavor, reminiscent of citrus crossed with papaya and jasmine, have made it a favorite among the "exotic" fruits.

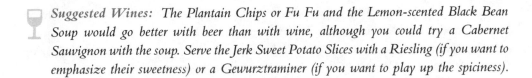

Suggested Wines: The Plantain Chips or Fu Fu and the Lemon-scented Black Bean Soup would go better with beer than with wine, although you could try a Cabernet Sauvignon with the soup. Serve the Jerk Sweet Potato Slices with a Riesling (if you want to emphasize their sweetness) or a Gewurztraminer (if you want to play up the spiciness).

Plantain Chips or Fu Fu (Crispy Plantain Cakes)

Plantains look like bananas, but they are starchier, harder, and not as sweet. They must be cooked before eating. They are available at Caribbean food markets and many large supermarkets. Plantains are used when they're green or when they're ripe, when the skin turns yellowish.

We offer two plantain recipes, one using a green plantain and one using a ripe one. You must use plantains to make the chips. A barely ripe banana could be used for the Fu Fu (plantain fritters).

Unlike bananas, plantains are difficult to peel. Trim the ends and cut the plantain into 2-inch segments. Using a small, sharp knife, slit open the peel and lift it off.

PLANTAIN CHIPS

Makes 8 servings

4 large ripe plantains
2 tablespoons unsalted butter or
  margarine

½ teaspoon salt, or to taste

Peel plantains and cut on the diagonal into thin slices.

Spray a large nonstick frying pan with butter-flavored cooking spray and melt butter over medium heat. Fry the plantain chips until golden brown, about 1 to 2 minutes on each side. Turn chips as they cook, using a slotted spoon. They tend to brown easily so watch them carefully.

Drain chips on paper towels. Sprinkle with salt and serve hot as an appetizer or side dish.

164 calories, 3 g fat, 2 g saturated fat, 8 mg cholesterol, 3 g dietary fiber, 138 mg sodium

FU FU

Makes 8 servings

4 large green plantains
1 egg
1 egg white
¼ cup skim milk
4 cloves garlic, minced
½ teaspoon dried oregano

½ teaspoon dried thyme
½ teaspoon salt
Pepper to taste
1 tablespoon olive oil
Nonfat sour cream and snipped chives
  (optional)

Peel plantains and cut into 1½-inch pieces. Cook in lightly salted boiling water for 45 minutes, or until fork tender but not mushy. Drain and mash. Mix in egg, egg white, milk, garlic, oregano, thyme, salt, and pepper.

Spray a large nonstick frying pan and heat oil over medium heat. Shape plantains into patties and fry on both sides until firm and lightly browned.

Serve crispy cakes hot, topped with sour cream and chives if desired.

170 calories, 3 g fat, 1 g saturated fat, 27 mg cholesterol, 3 g dietary fiber, 157 mg sodium

Lemon-scented Black Bean Soup

Black bean soup, served as is or ladled over white rice, Cuban style, is a longtime favorite of Floridians. Lemon provides a sprightly counterpoint to the beans' earthy, almost smoky flavor.

Makes 8 servings

12 ounces (about 1¾ cups) black beans
4 large bay leaves
2 tablespoons grated lemon zest
4 cups vegetable stock (page 17) or
   3 cups canned vegetable broth
   diluted with 1 cup water
1 tablespoon olive oil
1 cup chopped onion
4 cloves garlic, minced
1 cup chopped celery
1 green bell pepper, diced

1 cup chopped fresh or canned tomatoes
2 teaspoons fresh thyme or 1 teaspoon
   dried
1½ teaspoons ground cumin
1 teaspoon salt (¼ teaspoon if using
   canned broth)
½ teaspoon pepper
2 to 3 tablespoons lemon juice, to taste
Hot cooked rice (optional)
Lemon wedges

Check over beans and rinse thoroughly. Place in a pot and cover with 3 inches of hot water. Bring to a boil and cook for 2 minutes. Add bay leaves and lemon zest. Reduce heat to medium and continue cooking until beans are tender, 1½ to 2½ hours. Add hot water as necessary to keep beans covered. Cool beans slightly. Discard bay leaves. In a blender or food processor, puree beans and their cooking liquid with vegetable stock in 2 or 3 batches. Return to clean pot.

    Heat oil in a nonstick frying pan that has been sprayed with nonstick cooking spray. Add onion, garlic, and celery, and sauté for 5 minutes, covered, over medium heat, stirring occasionally. Mix in green pepper, tomatoes, thyme, cumin, salt, pepper, and lemon juice. Cook for 2 minutes. Stir vegetables into beans. Cook until soup is heated through.

If desired, place a scoop of cooked rice in each bowl and ladle soup over it. Serve soup hot, with lemon wedges on the side.

160 calories, 3 g fat, 0.5 g saturated fat, no cholesterol, 6 g dietary fiber, 464 mg sodium

Jerk Sweet Potato Slices with Vidalia Onion Conserve

"Jerk" refers to an island rub that's used to marinate grilled foods. Its splashy citrus-allspice perfume goes well with sweet potatoes. You can use an outdoor grill or a stovetop grill for this recipe.

The Vidalia onion is named for a town in east-central Georgia where the climate and soil produce the unusually sweet and easily digestible onion. Vidalias spoil more readily than regular onions. Store them in a cool, dry place and use soon after buying them.

Makes 8 servings

Jerk marinade:

3 tablespoons whole allspice

4 green onions, minced

3 cloves garlic, minced

½ teaspoon minced Scotch Bonnet pepper or ¼ teaspoon Caribbean hot pepper sauce

3 tablespoons lime juice

1 teaspoon dried thyme

½ teaspoon ground cinnamon

¼ teaspoon salt

¼ teaspoon ground nutmeg

2 tablespoons canola oil

For sweet potatoes:

4 large sweet potatoes, boiled until tender but still firm, cooled and peeled

Vidalia Onion Conserve (recipe follows)

To prepare marinade: Preheat oven to 350°. Place allspice in a shallow pan and heat in oven about 3 minutes, or until fragrant. Grind allspice, using a small food processor or coffee grinder or a mortar and pestle, or crush with a rolling pin. Mix in remaining jerk ingredients.

Cut sweet potatoes lengthwise into ½-inch slices. Brush on jerk marinade. Set sweet potatoes on a plate and marinate for 1 hour.

Grill sweet potatoes on an outdoor grill (spray the rack with nonstick cooking spray) or on a sprayed indoor grill according to manufacturer's directions. Cook a few minutes per side, or until warmed through.

Serve hot, with onion conserve.

209 calories, 9.5 g fat, 1.5 g saturated fat, 4 mg cholesterol, 4 g dietary fiber, 145 mg sodium

VIDALIA ONION CONSERVE

Makes 8 servings

1½ tablespoons canola oil

1½ teaspoons unsalted butter or margarine

3 cloves garlic, minced

3 large Vidalia onions, thinly sliced

¼ cup firmly packed light brown sugar

½ teaspoon tarragon

½ teaspoon grated fresh gingerroot

¼ teaspoon salt

¼ teaspoon pepper

Heat oil and butter in a large nonstick frying pan over medium heat. Add garlic and onions and sauté, stirring occasionally, until soft but not brown, about 5 minutes. Mix in remaining ingredients. Simmer, stirring occasionally, until onions are soft and glazed, about 4 minutes. Serve warm.

81 calories, 3.5 g fat, 0.5 g saturated fat, 2 mg cholesterol, 1.5 g dietary fiber, 72 mg sodium

Key Lime Ice and Assorted Tropical Fruits

This ice is based on the small, invigorating key limes. If key limes or their bottled juice are not available, substitute 3 regular limes.

Serve this ice with a platter of tropical fruits such as cubed mangos, passion fruit, baby bananas, carambola, and papayas. For an extra treat, pour 1 tablespoon of orange liqueur into each dessert dish before adding lime ice.

Makes 1 quart; 8 servings

1½ cups sugar
3 cups water
Zest of 1 lime, cut into strips

½ cup key lime or regular lime juice
(you will need 8 to 10 key limes to
make ½ cup)

Boil the sugar, water, and lime zest in a heavy saucepan, uncovered, for 8 minutes, stirring often. Cool, then strain. Mix in juice.

Freeze mixture in an ice cream maker according to manufacturer's directions or pour into a metal cake pan and freeze until almost solid, about 5 hours. Remove pan from freezer, break lime ice into chunks, and place in a food processor fitted with the steel blade. Let stand for 10 minutes, then process until smooth. Pour mixture into a freezer container, cover, and freeze for 1 hour, until firm. Let stand in refrigerator for 20 minutes before serving. This freezes well for up to about 5 days.

149 calories, no fat, no cholesterol, no dietary fiber, 1 mg sodium

Exotic Fruits

Beginning in the 1980s, Florida's exotic-fruit business began expanding well beyond the familiar mango and papaya. Here are three of our favorite "new" Florida fruits.

Passion fruit: The ripe fruit, about 2½ to 3 inches long, comes in different varieties. The dark purplish kind is ripe when the skin is leathery and wrinkled, but not too soft. The lighter red kind stays smooth but will have some give when it's ripe. Passion fruit's flavor is a wonderfully complex blend of citrus, honey, jasmine, melon, and pineapple. The Florida crop is in season from August through January.

Buy passion fruit that's heavy for its size. If it's not completely ripe, let it sit at room temperature for a few days. Once ripe, passion fruit can be refrigerated for about a week, or put in plastic bags and frozen.

To eat, cut the fruit in half crosswise over a bowl and use a spoon to scoop out the juicy orange pulp and edible crunchy black seeds. To juice a passion fruit, push the pulp through a strainer. You'll get only a couple of teaspoons of juice from one fruit, but a very small amount will flavor drinks (try it with rum), salad dressings, and desserts.

Carambola: This yellow, waxy-skinned fruit is 3 to 6 inches long and has five fleshy ribs along its length. It's also called starfruit because when sliced crosswise it produces five-point stars, which make pretty garnishes for just about anything. In flavor and texture, carambolas remind us of crisp, tart white grapes. Florida starfruit is in season from August through March.

Look for fruits that are smooth and not too bruised, although a tinge of brown along the ribbing is no problem. Carambolas will keep at room temperature for a day or two and in the refrigerator for up to two weeks.

To eat, slice crosswise and pick out and discard the small black seeds.

Lychee: Native to China, this 1- to 1½-inch-long fruit has a rough, bumpy shell that's either brown or a gorgeous rose, depending on variety. The translucent grayish white flesh is crisp-juicy, like a grape. The flavor is slightly grapey as well, but with floral notes. Florida lychees are in season during the summer.

Buy lychees that are heavy for their size. Store them in a plastic bag in the refrigerator and use within a few days, or freeze them.

To eat a lychee, crack the crisp peel with a fingernail, your teeth, or a knife, then peel the lychee as though it were a hard-cooked egg. Lychees have pits, which is no problem if you know how to eat an olive. To serve the fruit pitted, it's easiest to cut it in half and twist or pry out the seed.

• JAZZ BRUNCH •

The cooking of southern Louisiana is a soul-warming blend of African, Spanish, American, and French influences. It's spicy. It's rich. It's at home in moss-draped swamps and crystal-decorated dining rooms.

It's no wonder that in New Orleans, brunch is not just brunch, it's an experience.

Jazz, unfortunately an increasingly scarcer commodity these days in the city's nightclubs, still plays well at brunch. Wrapped in the haunting call of a clarinet, you can decide whether to have the champagne or the bourbon-spiked milk punch (this is in the morning, mind you). Then waiters bring out eggs bathed in hollandaise, spicy gumbos, potatoes with garlic butter, maybe a baked apple or some berries with cream. How about topping it all off with some bread pudding in whiskey sauce?

By the time brunch is over, it's maybe noon at best, and you're lucky if you can still walk.

Here we offer a modernist version of the jazz brunch, a composition that's scaled down to remove much of the fat but none of the mood.

Put on your favorite jazz CD. And don't forget the champagne.

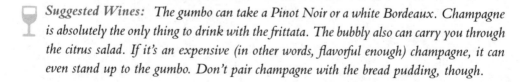 *Suggested Wines: The gumbo can take a Pinot Noir or a white Bordeaux. Champagne is absolutely the only thing to drink with the frittata. The bubbly also can carry you through the citrus salad. If it's an expensive (in other words, flavorful enough) champagne, it can even stand up to the gumbo. Don't pair champagne with the bread pudding, though.*

Green and Red Gumbo

A gumbo is a spicy Creole soup that often begins with the flour-oil paste called roux. It's usually thickened with either okra (in fact, the word *gumbo* derives from African words for okra) or filé, the ground leaves of sassafras.

Making a good roux requires patience; it must be stirred continually to keep it from burning. The roux should be cooked until it is a deep, dark reddish brown, like mahogany.

Makes 8 servings

2 tablespoons canola oil

4 tablespoons all-purpose flour

3 cloves garlic, minced

2 cups minced onions

1½ cups sliced celery

2 red bell peppers, seeded and sliced

1 can (16 ounces) tomatoes, crushed, including liquid

1½ quarts vegetable stock (page 17) or 4 cups canned vegetable broth diluted with 2 cups water

¾ teaspoon dried thyme

4 bay leaves

¾ teaspoon salt (omit if using canned broth)

¼ teaspoon pepper

⅛ teaspoon Tabasco

1 pound okra, trimmed and sliced

2 cups cooked brown or white rice

Heat oil with flour in a large, heavy pot over medium heat. Stir often, scraping up and including any brown bits from the bottom of the pan. In about 5 to 10 minutes, the roux will turn a golden brown and then a rich brown color. Stir in garlic and onions. Stir and cook another 5 minutes. Stir in celery, peppers, and crushed tomatoes and their liquid. Continue cooking for 10 minutes, stirring often. Add vegetable stock, thyme, bay leaves, salt, pepper, Tabasco, and okra. Simmer, uncovered, for 1 hour. Taste and adjust seasonings. Remove soup from heat. Discard bay leaves.

To serve, put a scoop of hot rice in the center of each soup bowl and ladle soup around the rice. Serve hot.

177 calories, 4.5 g fat, 0.5 g saturated fat, no cholesterol, 4 g dietary fiber, 623 mg sodium

Artichoke and Spinach Frittata

The classic New Orleans pairing of poached eggs and artichoke bottoms inspired this recipe.

We like this served with garlic toast sticks. To make them, cut eight thin slices of French bread into ¾-inch strips. Melt 1 tablespoon unsalted butter or margarine with 4 cloves minced garlic in a frying pan. Pan-fry bread slices until toasted and flavored with garlic. Serve hot.

If you are serving this frittata on its own rather than as part of a menu, it will serve four to six people.

Makes 8 servings

2 teaspoons canola oil
½ cup minced onion
1 clove garlic, minced
¾ pound fresh spinach, trimmed,
washed, and roughly chopped
½ teaspoon salt
¼ teaspoon pepper

¼ teaspoon ground nutmeg
1 cup chopped frozen artichoke
bottoms, defrosted
4 egg whites
4 eggs, lightly beaten, or 1 cup egg
substitute
1 teaspoon grated Parmesan cheese

Heat oil in a 10-inch ovenproof nonstick frying pan (well-seasoned cast iron is ideal). Sauté onion and garlic for 4 minutes over medium heat. Stir occasionally. Add spinach and cook just until limp. Sprinkle with salt, pepper, and nutmeg. Add chopped artichoke bottoms. Remove from heat.

Preheat the broiler.

Beat egg whites until glossy peaks form. Fold in eggs or egg substitute. Pour egg mixture over vegetables, then gently stir to mix vegetables into eggs. Cook frittata over low heat about 10 to 15 minutes, or until eggs are set and slightly moist on top and a golden brown on the bottom. Sprinkle with Parmesan.

Place frying pan under the broiler for a minute, or until frittata is lightly browned on top.

Let cool for 5 minutes before cutting into wedges. It is good warm or cold.

With whole eggs: 80 calories, 4 g fat, 1 g saturated fat, 102 mg cholesterol, 2.5 g dietary fiber, 242 mg sodium

Orange and Grapefruit Salad with Pecans

Although native to southern Asia, oranges these days are grown mostly in the Americas. Florida produces the most oranges in the United States; worldwide, it ranks second only to Brazil in orange production.

Navel oranges, which are easy to peel and usually seedless, are best for this salad.

Makes 8 servings

Salad:
4 navel oranges, peeled
2 red grapefruits, peeled
1 cup cooked chick-peas (if canned, drain and rinse)

1 medium Vidalia or other sweet onion, thinly sliced
2 cups chopped celery
8 lettuce leaves

Dressing:
1 cup orange-flavored low-fat yogurt
¼ cup chopped fresh cilantro

¼ cup chopped pecans

Remove any strings or pith from oranges and grapefruit. Chop fruit and put in a bowl. Toss with chick-peas, onion, and celery.

Put a lettuce leaf on each chilled salad plate. Spoon salad on lettuce leaf.

Put yogurt in a bowl and stir in cilantro. Spoon dressing on top of salad, then sprinkle with pecans. Serve chilled.

152 calories, 4 g fat, 0.5 g saturated fat, 1 mg cholesterol, 5 g dietary fiber, 181 mg sodium

Silky Bread Pudding with Bourbon Sauce

We can't think of a better way to use up day-old French bread than to make a bourbon-kissed pudding with it. If you don't have day-old bread, cut fresh bread into cubes and toast them in a 300-degree oven for 20 to 30 minutes, until they're dry.

Makes 8 servings

Pudding:
7 cups cubed day-old French bread
½ cup dark raisins
1¼ cups hot water
2 eggs, slightly beaten
2 egg whites, slightly beaten
½ cup sugar

2 cups evaporated skim milk
1 teaspoon vanilla extract
¾ teaspoon ground cinnamon
¼ teaspoon ground nutmeg
¼ teaspoon salt

Bourbon Sauce:
1 can (12 ounces) evaporated skim milk
2 tablespoons light brown sugar

3 tablespoons bourbon, or to taste

Lightly butter a 2-quart baking dish. Preheat oven to 350°.

Put cubed bread and raisins in a bowl. Pour in hot water. Set aside. In a large mixing bowl, mix beaten eggs and egg whites with sugar, milk, vanilla extract, cinnamon, nutmeg, and salt. Toss mixture with bread cubes and raisins. Spoon into baking dish.

Bake for 45 minutes, or until a tester inserted in the center comes out clean.

To make sauce: Pour milk into a bowl. Stir in sugar and bourbon. Taste and adjust sugar and bourbon if needed. Cover and refrigerate until serving time.

Spoon warm bread pudding into a dessert dish. Spoon sauce over pudding.

296 calories, 2.5 g fat, 1 g saturated fat, 57 mg cholesterol, 1.5 g dietary fiber, 426 mg sodium

• A JEFFERSONIAN FOURTH •

In addition to his other extraordinary virtues, Thomas Jefferson, author of the Declaration of Independence, third president of the United States, and lord of the stately manor of Monticello in the Virginia hills, was a connoisseur and gourmet. His dinner parties, which drew heavily on his southern hospitality and on his wallet, were famous—or infamous, in some quarters—for their abundance of dishes and wines. Good cooking was so important to him that he freed one of his slave cooks, James Hemings, only after the man promised to train a replacement.

In true eighteenth- and nineteenth-century fashion, Jefferson served his guests tons of meat, cream, and rich puddings. But he personally followed a more Mediterranean-style diet that was rich in vegetables, salads, and wine, and light in animal foods.

"I fancy it must be the quantity of animal food eaten by the English which renders their character insusceptible of civilization," he once wrote Abigail Adams.

Jefferson, who had traveled widely in France and Italy, absorbed another Mediterranean trait: a passion for wine. He thought nations would be far better off if they were to forgo hard liquor for the grape.

"Like my friend [physician Benjamin Rush] I have lived temperately, eating little animal food," Jefferson wrote at the age of seventy-six. "I double, however, the doctor's glass and a half of wine."

Patrick Henry once scornfully remarked that Jefferson had become so "Frenchified" he thumbed his nose at American foods, but that wasn't true. Although Jefferson introduced Americans to French-style ice cream and crème brûlée and Italian macaroni, he never lost his love for such native foodstuffs as sweet potatoes, black-eyed peas, and corn on the cob, which he introduced to the Parisians.

Jefferson found peace in gardening and grew an enormous number and variety of vegetables.

He especially liked peas and used to "race" neighboring gardeners to see who could harvest the first batch each spring. He kept careful notes of all the vegetables and their harvest dates.

What better way to celebrate the Fourth than to commemorate a man who not only helped to forge our nation, but had enough taste and vision to know, long before nutritional science was even a dream, which diet was most healthful?

Incidentally, Jefferson died on July 4, 1826—even as the celebrations were under way to mark the fiftieth anniversary of the signing of the Declaration of Independence. He was eighty-three.

Suggested Wines: Because of the goat cheese and olives, the macaroni pie really needs a light red, such as a Merlot or Pinot Noir. The vegetables, on the other hand, require a crisp white such as a Sauvignon Blanc or Chenin Blanc.

But then, legend has it that Jefferson wrote the Declaration over a glass of ale. So you could forgo wine for a good American beer. We'd suggest Samuel Adams Boston Ale, named for another Revolutionary War patriot who was second cousin to John Adams, Jefferson's longtime friend and sometime adversary.

Pasta Torte with Goat Cheese, Tomatoes, and Olives

Jefferson introduced macaroni and Parmesan cheese to the United States (although his cooks' recipes for "macaroni" actually were egg noodles). One of the recipes from his kitchen was for a macaroni pie, made with butter, cheese, and pasta, and baked like polenta. That idea inspired us to create a lower-fat pasta torte, essentially an upscale version of macaroni and cheese.

Given Jefferson's great love of olives, we thought it fitting to top the pie with them. Use good, cured ripe (black or purple) olives from France or Italy—or from California, if you can find honest-to-gosh cured black olives. (The typical canned olives from California are not cured and taste like the water they sit in.) If you can't get top-quality ripe olives, use good green ones.

Makes 8 servings

1 pound thin macaroni-type pasta
(such as penne, mostaccioli, or
gemelli)
5 ounces (1 cup) goat cheese, crumbled
6 tablespoons freshly grated Parmesan
cheese
1 cup buttermilk
4 egg whites, or ½ cup egg substitute
Pinch of ground nutmeg
Pinch of cayenne
¼ teaspoon salt
¼ teaspoon freshly ground black
pepper
2 to 3 medium, very ripe tomatoes or 5
to 6 ripe plum tomatoes
½ cup flavorful Italian, French, or
Greek olives (ripe or green, or
both), pitted and coarsely chopped
3 tablespoons dry bread crumbs
2 teaspoons olive oil, plus some for pan

Preheat oven to 350°. Lightly oil a 10-inch cake pan or a 13-by-9-inch rectangular baking dish.

Cook pasta in boiling water until al dente, about 10 minutes. Drain, then return to pan.

Whisk together goat cheese, Parmesan, buttermilk, egg whites, nutmeg, cayenne, salt, and pepper. Add to hot pasta and stir until evenly coated with sauce. Spread evenly over bottom of prepared baking pan.

Slice tomatoes and remove seeds; place tomato slices on top of macaroni in overlapping circles or rows. Scatter olives over top.

Mix bread crumbs and oil. Sprinkle over top.

Bake for 20 to 25 minutes, or until topping is golden. Serve warm or at room temperature.

336 calories, 9 g fat, 4 g saturated fat, 13 mg cholesterol, 2 g dietary fiber, 538 mg sodium

Grilled Medley of Garden Vegetables

If you're not serving this as part of a menu with the pasta torte, you could top the vegetables with a few slices of goat cheese just before serving.

If possible, grill these over hardwood charcoal. It burns better than briquets and is made without the use of petroleum, resulting in cleaner flavors for grilled foods. For a source of hardwood charcoal, see Sources and Resources.

Makes 8 servings

Vegetables:

2 medium yellow summer squash, trimmed

2 medium zucchini, trimmed

2 long, thin Japanese eggplants, trimmed

1 medium red bell pepper

1 medium yellow bell pepper

1 bulb fresh fennel, feathery tops trimmed

1 chayote squash

8 whole okra, or 12 sugar snap peas

4 green onions, trimmed

4 fresh shiitake mushrooms, stems removed and discarded

1½ tablespoons olive oil

Vinaigrette:

1½ tablespoons balsamic vinegar

1½ tablespoons rice wine vinegar

3 tablespoons olive oil

Cut squash, zucchini, and eggplants in half horizontally. Quarter peppers and remove veins and seeds. Cut fennel into ¼-inch slices, leaving core intact. Peel chayote and cut into ¼-inch slices.

Put all vegetables in a bowl and toss with oil.

Put vegetables on an oiled grill screen, about 6 inches from ashen coals. Cook about 3 to 4 minutes on each side, until tender-crisp and nicely browned. Some vegetables cook faster than others, so watch carefully and remove them as necessary.

When vegetables are cooked, remove to a platter.

Combine balsamic vinegar, rice vinegar, and oil. Drizzle vinaigrette over hot vegetables and serve immediately.

122 calories, 8 g fat, 1 g saturated fat, no cholesterol, 4 g dietary fiber, 7 mg sodium

Light Strawberry Ice Cream

Although Jefferson did not introduce ice cream to the United States, he reportedly had the first written recipe for a French-style (custard-based) ice cream, and his cooks made dozens of different kinds of ices and frozen creams.

This delicious cross between a sorbet and an ice cream uses plenty of strawberries and only a little light cream (half-and-half). Make sure the berries are as fresh and sweet as can be.

Makes 1 generous quart; 8 servings

**2 quarts (about 3 pounds) fresh
    strawberries
¾ cup half-and-half
¾ cup sugar**

**½ cup egg substitute
1 tablespoon vanilla extract
Pinch of salt**

Place berries in a food processor and process to make a chunky puree. Pour into a large glass or ceramic bowl. (Or put strawberries in a bowl and mash coarsely with a potato masher.)

Whisk together half-and-half, sugar, and egg substitute in a heavy-bottomed saucepan. Cook over very low heat, stirring constantly, until custard thickens enough to coat a metal spoon. Remove from heat and stir in vanilla extract and salt. Let cool to room temperature, then stir custard into strawberries. Chill for at least 1 hour, until mixture is fairly thick and quite cold.

Pour into the container of an ice cream maker and freeze according to manufacturer's directions. For the best flavor, serve ice cream immediately. (If that's not possible, transfer it to a freezer container, cover tightly, and keep for up to 2 days in the freezer. Soften at room temperature for 10 minutes before serving.)

166 calories, 4 g fat, 2 g saturated fat, 8.5 mg cholesterol, 4 g dietary fiber, 72 mg sodium

VARIATION: Peach Ice Cream. Instead of using strawberries, you can make this ice cream with very ripe peaches. Peel 6 to 7 medium peaches by dipping them in boiling water for 30 seconds, then slipping off the skins as soon as they're cool enough to handle. Cut in half and remove pits, then puree peaches in a food processor with 1 tablespoon lemon juice. You should have at least 3 cups puree.

Make the custard as directed and stir into 3 cups peach puree along with a pinch of salt, 2½ teaspoons vanilla extract, and ½ teaspoon almond extract. Chill and freeze as directed.

Appetizers, Salads, and Side Dishes

WHITE CORNMEAL AND GRITS SPOONBREAD

Spoonbread is really more a pudding than a bread. It makes a good side dish for all kinds of vegetable main courses. Try it with the Slow-roasted Vidalia Onions with Collard Greens on page 133.

Makes 8 servings

2½ cups water

1 cup white cornmeal

¼ cup old-fashioned grits

3 egg whites

1½ tablespoons unsalted butter or
    margarine, cut in ½-inch pieces

1 cup evaporated skim milk

½ teaspoon salt

¼ teaspoon white pepper

2 egg yolks

Bring the water to a boil in a large saucepan. Whisk in cornmeal and grits. Simmer until mixture is thick, whisking often to prevent lumps. This should take about 20 to 25 minutes.

While cornmeal and grits are cooking, beat the egg whites until they stand in soft, glossy peaks. Set aside.

When cornmeal is done, remove from stove. Mix in butter, milk, salt, pepper, and egg yolks. Fold in egg whites.

Preheat oven to 375°.

Pour batter into a lightly buttered 9-inch-round cake pan. Batter will fill pan. Bake in the center of the oven for 30 minutes, or until a tester inserted in the center comes out clean. Spoonbread will puff slightly. Serve immediately.

146 calories, 4 g fat, 2 g saturated fat, 60 mg cholesterol, 1.5 g dietary fiber, 193 mg sodium

"BARBECUED" BABY LIMAS

Like so many of us, lima beans are at their peak when they're young and fresh. Cooking them with a quick little barbecue-style sauce does something absolutely magical to these buttery textured beans. If you happen to have some good home-made or commercial barbecue sauce on hand, you can use a couple of tablespoons of it instead.

Makes 4 servings

*¾ pound small fresh lima beans (if
  unavailable, use frozen baby limas)*
*2 teaspoons unsalted butter or canola
  oil*
2 teaspoons ketchup
1 tablespoon vinegar

1 tablespoon sugar
*1 teaspoon Worcestershire sauce
  (see Note)*
Dash of Tabasco
¼ teaspoon salt
Pepper to taste

Cook lima beans in boiling water to cover until cooked through but still firm, about 10 to 20 minutes. (If using frozen limas, follow directions on package.) Drain.

Heat the pan used to cook the limas to dry it. Add oil, ketchup, vinegar, sugar, Worcestershire, Tabasco, and salt. Stir and cook for 2 minutes. Add beans and cook, stirring, until they've absorbed the liquid and are coated with the sauce. Season with pepper.

Serve warm.

Note: Traditional Worcestershire sauce contains anchovies. If you're a strict vegetarian, you can use a vegetarian Worcestershire-style sauce or soy sauce.

138 calories, 2 g fat, 1 g saturated fat, 5 mg cholesterol, 7 g dietary fiber, 196 mg sodium

SAVORY STUFFED MIRLITONS

The mirliton, a pear-shaped squash with a pale green skin, is popular in the Deep South. Mirlitons are available mostly in the South, but chayote squash, which is more widely available, is very similar and can be substituted. Almost the same texture as butternut squash and mildly flavored like summer squashes, mirlitons and chayotes cook fairly quickly. The skin is not eaten.

Makes 4 servings

2 mirlitons or chayote squash, washed
   and cut in half lengthwise
1 tablespoon whole allspice
1 tablespoon canola oil
2 cloves garlic, minced
¾ cup minced onion
½ cup diced celery

½ cup fine dry whole wheat bread
   crumbs
¼ teaspoon salt
½ teaspoon minced fresh marjoram or
   ¼ teaspoon dried
⅛ teaspoon red pepper flakes, or to
   taste

Using a spoon, scoop out seeds from squash.

Set squash on a steamer rack over hot, not boiling, water to which you've added the allspice. Cover. Steam until squash are fork tender.

Again, using a spoon, scoop out most of the pulp from squash. Place squash in a bowl, mash, and set aside. Reserve shells for stuffing.

Heat oil in a nonstick frying pan that has been sprayed with nonstick cooking spray. Sauté garlic, onion, and celery for 5 minutes over medium heat. Stir occasionally and cover pan if necessary to soften vegetables. Stir in bread crumbs, salt, marjoram, pepper flakes, and squash pulp. Mound filling into squash shells. Squash can be prepared to this point, refrigerated, and heated just before serving.

Preheat oven to 350°. Set stuffed squash shells on cookie sheet. Bake for 10 to 15 minutes, until heated through.

Remove from cookie sheet with a spatula and fork. Serve hot.

143 calories, 5 g fat, 0.5 g saturated fat, no cholesterol, 3 g dietary fiber, 313 mg sodium

SHIMMERING GAZPACHO

Florida has tomatoes and humidity that go on forever, which helps to explain why gazpacho, the chilled vegetable soup, is so popular there. We've turned the summer favorite into a pretty molded salad (or a congealed salad, to the southerners among you). If you'd rather not mess with molding it, you can enjoy the gazpacho in its standard form as a soup.

Agar, translucent white powder or flakes derived from seaweed, is used to gel the mold. It's available in health-food stores. If you are not strictly vegetarian, you can use two envelopes of gelatin (which is an animal product) instead.

The mold will slice better if the vegetables are cut in fine dice (about ¼ inch).

Makes 8 first-course servings

3½ cups (from about 2 pounds) finely diced, seeded tomatoes, preferably a combination of red, pink, and yellow
½ cup finely diced peeled cucumber
½ cup finely diced green or yellow bell pepper
⅓ cup finely chopped green onion
1 ripe avocado, peeled and finely diced
2 tablespoons finely chopped fresh parsley

¼ cup fresh lime juice, or to taste
4 teaspoons sugar (optional)
¼ teaspoon salt
Tabasco to taste
1 to 2 cups vegetable or tomato juice
1 cup water
3 tablespoons agar flakes or
    1 tablespoon powdered agar
    or 2 envelopes gelatin
Bibb lettuce leaves

Lightly oil a 6-cup ring mold.

Combine all the diced vegetables and parsley in a glass or ceramic bowl. Add lime juice, sugar, salt, and Tabasco. Stir gently and let stand for 10 to 15 minutes.

(If you want to serve gazpacho as a soup, add 2 cups vegetable or tomato juice at this point and omit water. Chill for up to 12 hours. Ladle into glass bowls to serve.)

Stir together vegetable or tomato juice, water, and agar in a small saucepan. Bring to a boil, then simmer over low heat, stirring frequently, until agar dissolves, 5 to 10 minutes. If using gelatin, sprinkle over juice and water and let stand for a minute to soften. Heat over low heat for a minute or two, just until gelatin dissolves.

Remove from heat and let cool for 5 minutes, then stir into vegetables. Pour into mold.

Chill for at least 3 hours, or until firmly set. To unmold, dip mold briefly in a bowl of hot water, hold a plate over top, and carefully turn over. If necessary, tap mold a couple of times to loosen gazpacho.

Line salad plates with lettuce leaves. Slice gazpacho mold and serve on lettuce.

90 calories, 4 g fat, 1 g saturated fat, no cholesterol, 3 g dietary fiber, 246 mg sodium

Soups

BISQUE OF FRESH PEAS

It's getting a little harder to find fresh shelling peas these days; nobody wants to do the work of separating all those peas from their pods. If you grow them or find them at the farmers' market, try them in this jade green soup.

This must be made with very fresh peas. If you use frozen (or older) peas, you'll have to push the soup through a strainer to remove the skins.

Makes 4 servings

1 tablespoon unsalted butter or olive oil
⅓ cup chopped green onion (with most of green tops)
3 cups (about 4 pounds in the pod) fresh or frozen peas
2 cups water
Dry sherry

1½ cups skim milk
½ teaspoon salt
¼ teaspoon white pepper
1 teaspoon finely chopped fresh tarragon or mint
1 teaspoon finely snipped fresh chives

Heat butter or oil in a large saucepan. Add green onion and sauté until slightly softened. Add peas, water, and a splash of sherry. Bring to a boil, then reduce heat to low and cook about 20 minutes, until peas are tender. Let cool slightly, then puree peas in a blender with milk, another splash of sherry, salt, and pepper until smooth. (If you can't get soup as smooth as you'd like, press it through a sieve.)

Return to pan and heat through; do not let it boil. Stir in tarragon or mint and chives.

Serve hot.

184 calories, 3 g fat, 2 g saturated fat, 8 mg cholesterol, 7 g dietary fiber, 371 mg sodium

SWEET POTATO–PEANUT SOUP

This African-inspired soup combines two basic southern foodstuffs in one savory blend of flavors. Sweet potatoes originated in Africa, where they're a major food source.

Makes 8 servings

3 medium-large (about 2 pounds total)
  sweet potatoes
1 tablespoon peanut oil
1½ cups chopped onions
3 cloves garlic, minced
1 tablespoon minced fresh gingerroot
1 to 2 teaspoons minced fresh chile
  peppers, to taste
4 cups coarsely chopped cauliflower or
  cabbage

3½ cups vegetable stock (page 17) or
  canned vegetable broth
2 cups water
⅔ cup (about 2½ ounces) roasted,
  unsalted peanuts, coarsely chopped
½ teaspoon salt (if using unsalted
  stock)
¼ teaspoon pepper

Peel sweet potatoes and cut into 1-inch cubes. Heat oil in a large pot and sauté onions, garlic, ginger, and chiles until onions are translucent. Add sweet potatoes, cauliflower or cabbage, vegetable stock or broth, and water. Bring to a boil, then reduce heat to low and simmer for 30 to 40 minutes, until vegetables are tender. Mash some of the sweet potatoes with the back of a spoon.

Stir in peanuts, salt, and pepper. Serve hot.

214 calories, 7 g fat, 1 g saturated fat, no cholesterol, 6 g dietary fiber, 475 mg sodium

A Genius at Agriculture

Sweet potatoes and peanuts rank as two of the South's most profitable food crops, thanks in large part to the efforts of George Washington Carver.

Carver, born in the 1860s to slaves in Missouri, enrolled in Simpson College in Iowa in 1889 and worked as a cook to earn his tuition. In 1896 he graduated with a master's degree in horticulture from Iowa State Agricultural College. That same year he was named head of the newly formed department of agriculture at Booker T. Washington's Tuskegee Institute, an industrial school for African-Americans in Tuskegee, Alabama.

Large-scale cultivation of cotton and tobacco had exhausted much of the South's good farming land. Carver experimented with ways to rebuild the soil and discovered that peanuts and sweet potatoes, both of which thrived in the South, improved the soil nicely. To make it worthwhile for farmers to grow large amounts of these crops, he developed more than three hundred by-products from peanuts and sweet potatoes, including cereals, oils, dyes, soaps, and assorted foodstuffs. He also began a "school on wheels," teaching Alabama farmers how to care for the soil.

By the time Carver died in 1943, he was one of America's most respected scientists and educators.

Entrées

BROCCOLI AND ROASTED PEPPER RISOTTO

Broccoli and red peppers are a classic southern combination. Here they get all gussied up in a risotto. Arborio rice is a short, plump, starchy rice that exudes a creamy gravy as it cooks. Rather than staying separate, the grains of rice cling and become pleasantly smooth and sticky. Arborio rice is available in Italian markets, specialty shops, and some supermarkets. You can substitute Valencia rice, which is the Spanish equivalent.

If you like, serve this with freshly grated Parmesan cheese on the side. Also, see Quicker Risotto (page 119) for faster versions.

Makes 4 servings

4½ to 5½ cups vegetable stock (page 17)
2 cups chopped fresh broccoli florets
1½ tablespoons olive oil
1 large clove garlic, minced
½ cup finely chopped shallots
1½ cups Italian Arborio rice
1 strip lemon or orange zest
1 teaspoon salt

1 medium red bell pepper, roasted, cored, and cut in half lengthwise (see page 14)
1 medium yellow bell pepper, roasted, cored, and cut in half lengthwise (see page 14)
¼ cup finely chopped fresh parsley
Pepper to taste

Bring stock to a boil in a saucepan. Add broccoli and cook over medium heat for 2 minutes, or until bright green and tender-crisp. Remove broccoli with a slotted spoon and set aside. Keep stock (and any broccoli bits floating in it) hot over a low flame.

Heat oil in another 4- to 6-quart heavy-bottomed saucepan. Add garlic and shallots, and sauté until softened. Add rice and lemon or orange zest, and stir to coat with oil. Stir in 1 cup hot stock and salt. Cook over low heat, stirring frequently, until stock is absorbed. Repeat with 3 more cups stock, 1 cup at a time, then add another ½ cup stock and stir until absorbed. If risotto is done, the rice will be cooked through but slightly chewy. If it is not done, stir in up to 1 more cup stock, ½ cup at a time.

Dice half of each pepper and cut the other half into thin strips. Stir diced peppers, parsley, and broccoli into risotto. Season with pepper.

Spoon risotto onto plates or into shallow soup bowls and top with strips of roasted peppers. Serve immediately.

352 calories, 7 g fat, 1 g saturated fat, no cholesterol, 2 g dietary fiber, 1,274 mg sodium

Quicker Risotto

Risotto is wonderful, but nobody would call it fast food. By the time you cut up the vegetables, heat the stock, and cook the rice, you've easily spent at least an hour. And it's not an hour you can spend playing catch with your kid while the risotto bubbles merrily. No, you have to stand there at the stove and stir the stuff for 30 minutes or more.

That's why we were intrigued when we learned from Lorna Sass, author of *Vegetarian Cooking Under Pressure* and *The Ecological Kitchen,* that one can make risotto in the pressure cooker in just minutes.

To pressure-cook risotto, heat the oil and sauté the garlic and shallots. Add 1½ cups Arborio rice and 3½ cups stock plus seasonings. Lock the lid and bring to pressure over high heat. Lower the heat just enough to maintain high pressure and cook for 5 minutes. Release the pressure quickly by letting steam escape through the nozzle or by holding the pan under cold running water. Let the rice stand for a minute. If it's not quite cooked through, add another ½ cup stock and cook over medium heat, stirring, until absorbed.

You can also microwave risotto, although it is not as creamy. To microwave the broccoli and pepper risotto: Use 3 to 3½ cups stock. Cook the broccoli in 3 cups stock on high (100 percent) until broccoli is tender-crisp, about 5 to 6 minutes. Remove the broccoli with a slotted spoon and set aside.

Stir oil, garlic, shallots, rice, and orange zest into stock. Microwave on medium high (80 percent power), stirring once or twice, until most of the stock has been absorbed and the rice is cooked through but still fairly chewy. This should take 10 to 20 minutes. Cover and let stand for 5 minutes. If rice is still too chewy, add another ½ cup stock and microwave another 1 to 3 minutes, then let stand for 5 minutes. If the liquid is completely absorbed after standing but rice is cooked through, stir in another ½ cup warm stock and let sit another minute before serving. Stir in salt.

Add broccoli, roasted peppers, and parsley as directed in recipe.

LOUISIANA RICE AND EGGPLANT

Wild Pecan rice, available in many supermarkets and specialty shops, is a special variety grown near New Iberia, Louisiana. It has a toasted pecan aroma that's memorable. You can substitute basmati or regular long-grain rice in this recipe.

Makes 4 servings

1 medium-large eggplant, peeled and
   diced
Salt
3 tablespoons canola oil
3 cloves garlic, minced
1 cup chopped onion
¾ cup chopped celery
1 green or red bell pepper, seeded and
   chopped
1 cup uncooked Wild Pecan, basmati,
   or regular long-grain rice

1 can (14½ ounces) whole tomatoes,
   chopped, including liquid
2 bay leaves
1 teaspoon fresh thyme leaves or
   ½ teaspoon dried
1 teaspoon fresh chopped marjoram or
   ½ teaspoon dried
¼ teaspoon pepper
¼ teaspoon Tabasco
¼ cup minced fresh parsley
½ cup hot water

Arrange eggplant in a large strainer or on a double thickness of paper towels. Sprinkle eggplant with salt and let stand for 30 minutes. Rinse and pat dry.

Heat 2 tablespoons oil in a large nonstick frying pan. Sauté eggplant and garlic over medium heat, stirring occasionally, until eggplant is tender and browned. Set aside.

Heat remaining 1 tablespoon oil. Sauté onion, celery, and bell pepper for 5 minutes. Stir in rice and cook for 4 to 5 minutes, stirring often. Add tomatoes and their liquid, bay leaves, thyme, marjoram, pepper, Tabasco, parsley, and hot water. Cover tightly and simmer for 20 minutes, or until rice is cooked.

Reheat eggplant separately.

To serve, discard bay leaves, spoon rice mixture onto dish, and sprinkle hot eggplant on top. Serve hot.

338 calories, 11 g fat, 1 g saturated fat, no cholesterol, 6 g dietary fiber, 198 mg sodium

RED BEANS AND RICE

Red Beans and Rice is an essential part of New Orleans's culture during Mardi Gras and all year long. World-famous jazz trumpeter and vocalist Louis Armstrong even used to sign letters "Red beans and ricely yours." Tradition has it that housewives served it on Mondays, washdays, because they could stick the beans in a pot and let them simmer while they did the laundry.

Makes 4 servings

1½ *cups dry red kidney beans*
1 *rib celery, including leaves, chopped*
1 *cup chopped onion*
2 *cloves garlic, minced*
3 *bay leaves*

½ *teaspoon Tabasco*
½ *teaspoon salt*
2 *cups cooked long-grain brown or*
   white rice

Pick beans over and rinse well. Place beans in a heavy pot and cover with 2 inches of water. Bring water to a boil and cook beans for 2 minutes. Reduce heat to medium-low. Stir in celery, onion, garlic, bay leaves, and Tabasco.

Continue cooking until beans are tender, 2 to 3 hours (depending on age of beans). Stir occasionally because they tend to stick to the bottom of pan. Keep beans covered with water, adding hot water as needed. When beans are cooked, season with salt.

Discard bay leaves.

To serve, spoon ½ cup rice in the center of each plate. Ladle beans and sauce over rice. Beans are even better a day or two after they're cooked; keep refrigerated and reheat over a low flame.

385 calories, 1 g fat, 0.5 saturated fat, no cholesterol, 16 g dietary fiber, 290 mg sodium

HOPPIN' JOHN BAKE
(BLACK-EYED PEAS AND RICE)

The black-eyed pea is named for the small black "eye" on its inside curve. Dining on Hoppin' John, a long-favored casserole of black-eyed peas and rice, on New Year's Day is said to invite prosperity, especially if you serve greens—the color of money—on the side.

Makes 4 servings

2 tablespoons canola oil

2 cloves garlic, minced

1 cup chopped onion

1 green bell pepper, chopped

1 cup sliced brown or white mushrooms

1 cup chopped fresh or canned tomatoes

½ teaspoon salt

½ teaspoon pepper, or to taste

¼ teaspoon Tabasco, or to taste

1 can (14½ ounces) crushed tomatoes

¾ cup cooked brown or white rice

2 cups cooked black-eyed peas (cooked with bay leaves and some parsley; if using canned peas, drain and rinse)

Preheat oven to 325°.

Heat oil in a nonstick skillet. Add garlic and onion, and sauté over medium heat until tender, stirring occasionally, about 5 minutes. Add green pepper, mushrooms, and chopped tomatoes. Continue cooking for 5 minutes, stirring occasionally. Season with salt, pepper, and Tabasco. Mix in crushed tomatoes, rice, and peas.

Pour mixture into a 1½-quart casserole dish. Bake for 1 hour, or until casserole is hot and flavors are blended.

Serve hot.

235 calories, 8 g fat, 1 g saturated fat, no cholesterol, 10 g dietary fiber, 458 mg sodium

SOUFFLÉD GRITS WITH RED PEPPERS

Grits can be down-home or they can be downright upscale, as they are in this soufflé served on a bed of scarlet peppers.

Makes 4 servings

2 teaspoons grated Parmesan cheese
¼ cup minced onion
¼ pound white or brown mushrooms, sliced
1 cup skim milk
¼ teaspoon salt
¼ cup old-fashioned grits
½ cup egg substitute
⅛ teaspoon ground nutmeg

⅛ teaspoon ground allspice
¼ cup grated reduced-fat Swiss cheese
1 tablespoon grated Parmesan cheese
4 egg whites
1 large red bell pepper
2 teaspoons canola oil
1 clove garlic, minced
1 vine-ripened tomato, peeled and chopped

Spray a 1½-quart soufflé dish with butter-flavored nonstick cooking spray. Sprinkle with 2 teaspoons Parmesan. Set aside.

Heat a nonstick frying pan that has been sprayed with butter-flavored nonstick cooking spray. Add onion and sauté over medium heat, stirring occasionally, until tender. Add mushrooms and cook until tender. If they start to become dry, cover them. Pour off any liquid from cooked mushrooms.

While onion and mushrooms are cooking, prepare grits. Bring milk and salt to a boil over medium heat. Whisk in grits and bring mixture to a boil. Reduce heat to low and cook until mixture thickens, about 5 to 8 minutes, whisking often to eliminate any lumps. Remove pan from heat. Whisk in egg substitute. Add nutmeg and allspice, Swiss cheese, 1 tablespoon Parmesan, and onion-mushroom mixture. Cool.

Preheat oven to 425°.

Beat egg whites until they stand in glossy peaks. Fold about ½ cup of egg whites into grits mixture to lighten it. Fold in remaining egg whites.

Pour mixture into prepared soufflé dish. Put dish in the middle of the oven. Reduce heat to 400°. Bake, without opening oven door, for 30 minutes, or until dry on the outside and slightly moist in the center when tested with a bamboo skewer or tester.

While soufflé bakes, core, seed, and chop red pepper. Heat oil in a nonstick frying pan. Add garlic and pepper, and cook just until pepper begins to soften and its skin darkens. Add tomato, and cook until heated through.

To serve, spoon vegetables onto a plate or dish. Use 2 large spoons to scoop out soufflé. Place on top of vegetables and serve at once.

181 calories, 6.5 g fat, 2 g saturated fat, 10 mg cholesterol, 2.5 g dietary fiber, 346 mg sodium

Grits Is (Are?) Good

You could write a book on whether grits, the corn cereal southerners love so much, is/are singular or plural. Southerners seem to disagree. Northerners, when they bother to think about grits at all, favor the plural.

There's little argument—at least in South Carolina—that South Carolinians put away more grits per capita than anybody else. They eat grits plain, fried, and gussied up in all sorts of chef's specials.

Grits, also known as hominy grits, are made from cooked, dried, coarsely ground corn that has had the skin and germ removed. The coarsest grits have a more satisfying "gritty" texture and rich hominy flavor, but they can take a half-hour or longer to cook into a creamy porridge. Regular grits, often labeled old-fashioned grits in the supermarket, take 15 to 25 minutes to cook. For the sake of convenience, many cooks use quick grits, which cook up in as little as 5 to 10 minutes.

Grits can be cooked in water, milk, vegetable stock, or just about any liquid you wish.

At their humblest and most traditional, grits are served as a breakfast dish, ideal for sopping up gravy. Southerners also love them cut into squares and fried. But like other mildly flavored cereals, grits can be used in everything from soufflés to puddings to casseroles.

FRIED GRITS AND CHEESE
FINGER SANDWICHES

Like their first cousin, cornmeal, grits can be turned into just about anything. In this variation on that old southern favorite, fried grits, we've turned them into flavorful little sandwiches. These are good with mango or peach chutney.

Makes 4 servings

¾ *cup old-fashioned grits*
¼ *teaspoon salt*
¼ *teaspoon white pepper*
4 *extra-thin slices reduced-fat Swiss*
   cheese

2 *teaspoons unsalted butter*
Sprigs of watercress or parsley

Bring 3½ cups water to a boil. Whisk grits into boiling water in a slow, steady stream. Reduce heat to a simmer. Cook for 20 to 25 minutes, whisking occasionally, or until grits have thickened. Add salt and pepper.

Pour grits into a lightly greased 8-by-4-inch loaf pan. Refrigerate for several hours or overnight, or until grits are firm. Unmold onto a plate. With a small, sharp knife, carefully cut grits crosswise into 16 slices.

Cut cheese into slices about the same size and shape as the grits rectangles. Place a slice of cheese between 2 slices of grits to make a sandwich. Repeat with remaining cheese and grits.

Heat butter in a nonstick frying pan sprayed with butter-flavored nonstick cooking spray. Fry sandwiches a few minutes on each side, until they're golden and cheese is melted. Place 2 sandwiches on each plate. Garnish with watercress or parsley. Serve hot.

193 calories, 6 g fat, 3.5 g saturated fat, 20 mg cholesterol, 3.5 g dietary fiber, 175 mg sodium

RATATOUILLE-FILLED CORN CREPES WITH DILL

Most of the eggplants in supermarkets are from the South, especially Florida. Eggplants come in many shapes and colors, ranging from white to deep purple and from round to pear-shaped. Salting and rinsing an eggplant before using it helps to counteract any bitter flavor in the juice. You can omit that step if you have a young, very fresh eggplant.

Both the ratatouille and the corn crepes can be prepared ahead of time and assembled when ready to serve.

Makes 4 servings

Ratatouille:

1 medium eggplant, peeled and cut into
   ½-inch pieces (about 2 cups)
Salt
1½ teaspoons olive oil
2 cloves garlic, minced
¾ cup chopped onion
1 heaping cup chopped zucchini
1 green bell pepper, seeded and finely
   chopped
1⅓ cups peeled and chopped fresh
   tomatoes

¼ cup chopped fresh parsley
2 tablespoons balsamic vinegar
2 tablespoons tomato paste
1 teaspoon minced fresh basil or
   ½ teaspoon dried
1 teaspoon minced fresh oregano or
   ½ teaspoon dried
¼ teaspoon pepper

Crepes:

½ cup egg substitute
1 egg white
1½ tablespoons olive or canola oil
6 tablespoons yellow or white cornmeal
6 tablespoons all-purpose flour

1½ cups skim milk
¼ teaspoon salt
2 rounded teaspoons dill seeds
Canola oil to brush crepe pan

To make ratatouille: Put eggplant in a large colander or on paper towels. Toss with 1 teaspoon salt, then let stand for 30 minutes. Rinse off salt and pat eggplant dry.

Heat oil in a nonstick frying pan that has been sprayed with nonstick cooking spray. Add garlic and onion, and cook, stirring occasionally, for about 5 minutes, or until onion is tender. Add eggplant and sauté until soft, stirring occasionally, about 8 to 10 minutes.

Add zucchini, green pepper, tomatoes, parsley, vinegar, and tomato paste. Stir in basil, oregano, and pepper.

Cook, covered, for 15 minutes. Uncover and cook, stirring occasionally, another 15 to 25 minutes, or until vegetables are soft and flavors are melded. Taste and adjust seasonings.

Let cool, then spoon into bowl, cover lightly, and refrigerate until needed.

To make crepes: Crepe batter can be made in a blender or in a bowl. If preparing crepes by hand, sift flour and use a whisk. Otherwise, place all ingredients except seeds in a blender. Mix only a few seconds or until batter is smooth. Mix in seeds. You can substitute 2 tablespoons fresh dillweed if desired.

Brush a heated 6-inch, preferably nonstick, crepe pan or frying pan with oil. It is not necessary to use much oil after the first few crepes. Pour 2½ to 3½ tablespoons batter in pan, tilting pan so batter covers bottom of pan. Pour off any excess batter.

Crepe is ready when it is set and firm around edges. Loosen edges with a knife. Turn crepe and cook only a few seconds. Stack crepes between pieces of aluminum foil or wax paper. Cover; if not using immediately, refrigerate.

To assemble crepes: Rewarm crepes if necessary in a 300° oven. Put 2 cups ratatouille in a bowl and microwave on high just until hot. Drain well.

Put about 3 tablespoons warm ratatouille in center of each crepe and roll it up. Allow 2 crepes per person. Serve individually, with remaining cold ratatouille on the side.

281 calories, 11 g fat, 2 g saturated fat, 2 mg cholesterol, 4 g dietary fiber, 329 mg sodium

Why Peel Tomatoes?

We recommend peeling fresh tomatoes if you're going to cook them for longer than 5 minutes. After they cook for a while, the skins on unpeeled tomatoes loosen from the flesh, resulting in little shards of tomato skin floating in your soup, sauce, or ratatouille. While these are hardly fatal, they do detract from the dish's appearance and texture.

To peel tomatoes, cut a slit in the skin near the stem end and drop them into boiling water for 30 seconds. Remove with tongs. When the tomatoes are cool enough to handle, peel off the skins. They should slip off easily if the tomato is ripe and the water was hot enough. (If you're going to use the tomatoes in a pasta sauce, put the tomatoes in the water you're boiling for pasta, remove with tongs, and peel.)

If you're peeling only one tomato and you have a gas stove, you may find it more convenient to roast the skin off. Hold the tomato in tongs over the flame, turning so that the tomato roasts evenly. When the skin begins to look blistered or loose, remove the tomato from the heat, let cool, and slip off the skin.

Unless the tomato skins would ruin a dish, our recipes call for peeling as an optional, not mandatory, step. We know that modern cooks, including us, don't always have the time or inclination to perform such little niceties.

TOFU SANDWICHES WITH BARBECUE SAUCE AND TANGY SLAW

Southern barbecue sauces vary greatly from region to region. Some are thick, red, and sweet. Some are tangy and mustard-based. Others are little more than vinegar and seasonings. This tofu sandwich, which is topped with slaw, Memphis style, has an all-purpose sauce that's similar to one you might find in Tennessee or the western Carolinas. It is simultaneously tangy, sweet, and hot.

This dish is best if started the day before serving since the tofu must marinate for several hours or overnight in the sauce.

Makes 4 servings

Barbecue sauce:

¾ cup ketchup
¼ cup molasses
2 tablespoons brown sugar
¼ cup cider vinegar
1 tablespoon Worcestershire sauce (see Note on page 112)
2 teaspoons chipotle chile sauce, or to taste (or 2 teaspoons hot red pepper sauce and a dash of Liquid Smoke)

1 tablespoon Tennessee whiskey or bourbon (optional)
Salt and pepper to taste

1 pound firm tofu

Slaw:

4 cups shredded green cabbage
½ cup shredded carrot
¼ cup red wine vinegar
1½ tablespoons sugar

½ teaspoon salt

Fluffy Buns (page 136) or whole wheat hamburger buns

To make sauce: Combine ketchup, molasses, brown sugar, vinegar, Worcestershire, and chipotle sauce in a nonaluminum saucepan. Simmer over low heat for 15 minutes, stirring frequently. Stir in whiskey if using and add salt and pepper. Remove from heat and let cool.

Use immediately or pour into a clean glass jar, cover tightly, and refrigerate.

To prepare tofu: Drain and rinse tofu. Cut crosswise into 8 thin slices. Wrap a thick paper towel around each slice and gently but firmly press tofu between the palms of your hands to squeeze out moisture. Place tofu slices in a glass baking dish or pie plate. Pour ½ cup barbecue sauce over tofu and turn tofu slices to coat evenly. Cover and refrigerate for several hours or overnight.

To make slaw: Place cabbage and carrot in a glass or ceramic bowl. Add vinegar, sugar, and salt, and toss well. Chill for at least 1 hour and up to 24 hours.

Heat coals. Grill tofu over medium-hot coals, turning once and basting once or twice with additional barbecue sauce, until nicely browned, 6 to 8 minutes. (Tofu also may be cooked under a broiler or in a nonstick pan that has been sprayed with nonstick cooking spray.)

Place buns, cut side down, on grill to lightly toast them. Place sliced tofu on bottom halves of buns. Spoon a scant ¼ cup slaw on top of tofu. Brush top halves of buns lightly with barbecue sauce, then place on top of tofu and slaw.

Serve sandwiches immediately, with remaining slaw on the side.

Leftover barbecue sauce can be refrigerated for up to three weeks.

350 calories, 8 g fat, 1 g saturated fat, 2 mg cholesterol, 6 g dietary fiber, 558 mg sodium

SPICE-CRUSTED TOFU WITH GREEN AND RED TOMATOES

"Blackening," which originated in Louisiana but has become a popular technique in every corner of the United States, involves cooking foods in spices in a superhot cast-iron frying pan, so the food chars and picks up a crust of spices. Tofu is too delicate to be "blackened" but will pick up a nice spice crust cooked over a somewhat lower flame.

Green tomatoes are widely used in the South, where the tomato-growing season goes on for ages. Both they and their red cousins make excellent partners for the spicy tofu.

Makes 4 servings

2 tablespoons minced dried onion
1 teaspoon garlic powder
½ teaspoon chili powder
½ teaspoon cayenne
¼ teaspoon salt
¼ teaspoon red pepper flakes

¼ teaspoon dried thyme
10½ ounces extra-firm tofu, preferably reduced-fat
2 teaspoons canola oil
2 large green tomatoes, sliced
2 firm but ripe red tomatoes, sliced

Mix all spices together in a small dish.

Drain tofu. Cut lengthwise into 4 slices and blot dry with paper towels.

Spray a nonstick frying pan with butter-flavored cooking spray. Add oil and heat over medium-high heat.

Sprinkle spices evenly over bottom of pan. Add tofu and fry for 1 to 2 minutes on each side, until it has a crispy-browned coating and is warmed through. To turn tofu, use a flexible spatula and a fork, being careful to keep tofu in one piece. Remove tofu to a plate and keep warm.

Add green and red tomatoes to pan and fry only until they pick up spice coloring and are warm.

Serve tofu hot with tomatoes.

110 calories, 6 g fat, 0.5 g saturated fat, no cholesterol, 2 g dietary fiber, 156 mg sodium

BOILED NEW POTATOES AND CUCUMBERS WITH SOUR ORANGE SAUCE

Think of this light entrée as a warm salad. We use a combination of orange juice and lime juice to produce a flavor similar to that of sour orange juice since sour oranges can be difficult to obtain.

You can substitute sliced hearts of palm—fresh or canned and rinsed—for the cucumbers.

Makes 4 servings

1 tablespoon unsalted butter or margarine
1½ teaspoons all-purpose flour
¼ cup orange juice
¼ cup lime juice
¼ teaspoon salt

⅛ teaspoon white pepper
8 small red boiling potatoes, boiled and halved or quartered
2 cucumbers, peeled, seeded, and sliced
¼ cup minced fresh parsley for garnish

Melt butter in saucepan over medium heat. Whisk in flour until absorbed. Stir in both juices. Continue whisking until sauce begins to boil. Simmer sauce for 2 minutes. Stir in salt and pepper.

Toss potatoes with cucumbers and pour hot sauce over them. Sprinkle with parsley. Serve warm.

204 calories, 6 g fat, 4 g saturated fat, 16 mg cholesterol, 4 g dietary fiber, 145 mg sodium

WILTED KALE AND BEET SALAD

If you like, you can leave the eggs out of this salad and serve it as a side dish. Or replace the eggs with 1 cup cubed smoked tofu (page 16).

Makes 3 to 4 servings as a main course

1 pound (2 bunches) kale
1 teaspoon chipotle chile sauce or
  1 teaspoon Tabasco and a dash
  of Liquid Smoke

Dressing:
3 tablespoons liquid from beets
2 teaspoons red wine vinegar
1 tablespoon soy sauce
2 teaspoons Dijon mustard
1 teaspoon dark sesame oil
1½ tablespoons olive or canola oil

1 cup sliced sweet-and-sour beets
  (page 26) or canned pickled beets,
  liquid reserved
1 hard-cooked egg, chopped

3 hard-cooked egg whites, chopped
  (discard yolks or reserve for another
  use)
¾ cup low-fat croutons

Strip kale leaves from stems and discard stems. Coarsely chop kale and rinse well.

Place kale in a large pot with chipotle sauce and ½ cup water. Bring to a simmer. Cover and cook over low heat, stirring once or twice, until kale is wilted and softened, about 10 to 15 minutes.

Meanwhile, make dressing: Whisk together beet liquid, vinegar, soy sauce, and mustard. Whisk in oils until incorporated.

Drain kale and toss with about ¾ of the dressing. Spread on a platter. Arrange sliced beets in a circle on top of kale. Place chopped egg and egg whites in middle of salad; drizzle remaining dressing over all. Scatter croutons on top.

4 servings: 266 calories, 11 g fat, 2 g saturated fat, 53 mg cholesterol, 14.5 g dietary fiber, 657 mg

SLOW-ROASTED VIDALIA ONIONS WITH COLLARD GREENS

Use only very fresh, tender greens here. Instead of collard greens, you can use kale or chard.

Makes 4 servings

2 medium-large Vidalia or other mild onions, outer skins removed

2 teaspoons cold unsalted butter or margarine, cut in ½-inch pieces

4 cloves garlic, minced

1 cup whole wheat bread crumbs

Salt and pepper to taste

Paprika to taste

1 bunch (about 1 pound) collard greens

2 teaspoons canola oil

4 cloves garlic, minced

Preheat oven to 350°. Cut onions into wedges and arrange on a sheet of aluminum foil large enough to wrap onions.

Toss together butter, garlic, crumbs, salt, pepper, and paprika. Sprinkle mixture over onions and seal in foil.

Bake in center of the oven for 45 minutes. About 10 minutes before onions are ready, rinse collard greens, trim stems, and cut in 2-inch pieces; you should have about 8 cups.

Heat oil in a nonstick frying pan. Cook garlic over medium heat about 2 minutes, stirring occasionally, until it browns lightly. Stir in greens and cook, stirring occasionally, until greens are limp, just a few minutes.

To serve, set onion wedges on a plate and set greens on the side.

161 calories, 7 g fat, 3 g saturated fat, 11 mg cholesterol, 4 g dietary fiber, 209 mg sodium

Glorious Greens

While much of the country thinks dark leafy greens are salad bar decorations, the South knows better. Of all Americans, southerners eat the most greens, according to the Leafy Greens Council (which, oddly, is based in Minnesota). People throughout the South eat all kinds of cooking greens: turnip and beet tops, collards, mustard greens, kale.

That puts them a step up, nutritionally speaking. Dark leafy greens are excellent sources of vitamin C and beta-carotene. They've long been an important source of calcium for African-Americans, Asians, and others who often are lactose-intolerant, which means they cannot easily digest the sugars in milk. Beet greens are rich in potassium. Mustard greens, turnip greens, and kale are good sources of folic acid.

Some of these nutrients leach into the cooking liquid, which is why drinking the "pot likker," or cooking liquid, is such a good idea.

Often, greens are cooked with salt pork or ham until they're meltingly soft. Any deeply flavored food or food flavoring can stand in for the pork: garlic, hot peppers, soy sauce, smoke flavoring, peanut butter, even miso (a fermented soybean paste with a unique winey-sweet-salty flavor).

Really fresh greens can be quick-cooked. Strip the leaves from the stems, tear the leaves into bite-size pieces, and "smother" them in a covered pan with a small amount of liquid until they soften.

GRATIN OF STRING BEANS AND YELLOW SQUASH

This summer medley has the velvety texture and dairy flavor of creamed vegetables, with a lot less fat. Accompanied by biscuits or French bread and maybe a tossed salad, this makes a good, light main course for a muggy summer day.

Despite the craze for serving vegetables half-raw, in dishes such as this one the vegetables taste better if they're allowed to get tender and sweet.

Makes 4 servings

1 pound string beans
1 pound yellow summer squash
¼ pound fresh mushrooms, trimmed and sliced
2 teaspoons canola or olive oil
2 tablespoons flour
1 cup evaporated skim milk

1 tablespoon chopped fresh marjoram or 1 teaspoon dried
Pinch of ground nutmeg
¼ teaspoon salt
¼ cup dry bread crumbs
1 teaspoon melted unsalted butter or olive oil

Preheat oven to 400°.

Cook beans in boiling water for 5 minutes, or until they just turn bright green. Drain well and set aside.

Trim squash and cut into ¼–inch slices. Heat oil in a large ovenproof nonstick frying pan that has been sprayed with nonstick cooking spray. Add squash and fry for a minute or two over medium heat, until squash begins to turn golden. Stir in mushrooms and cook for 1 minute, then stir in beans. Sprinkle vegetables with flour. Stir in milk, marjoram, nutmeg, and salt.

Cook, stirring, over medium–low heat until sauce thickens, about 2 to 3 minutes. Remove from heat.

Mix bread crumbs with melted butter. Sprinkle over vegetables. Bake until top is golden and sauce is bubbly, about 15 minutes.

179 calories, 4 g fat, 1 g saturated fat, 5 mg cholesterol, 6 g dietary fiber, 405 mg sodium

Breads and Desserts

FLUFFY BUNS

If New Englanders like their breads of the earth, southerners prefer them of the air. Southern breads are often ethereal, melt-in-the-mouth affairs. These fluffy buns can be eaten with a wide range of foods, but they really excel at soaking up barbecue sauce.

Makes 8 large buns

1 package (2¼ teaspoons) active dry yeast
1½ cups buttermilk, slightly warmed
Canola oil
2 tablespoons sugar

¾ teaspoon salt
1 cup whole wheat flour
2 cups plus 2 tablespoons bread flour, plus more if needed

In the large bowl of an electric mixer fitted with the dough hook, combine yeast, buttermilk, 1 tablespoon of oil, sugar, and salt. Stir in whole wheat flour and bread flour to make a soft, slightly sticky dough. Knead until smooth and elastic, working in small amounts of flour as needed to keep dough from sticking to the mixer bowl. Or knead by hand.

Place dough in an oiled bowl, turning to coat with oil. Cover and let rise in a warm place until doubled, about 1 to 1½ hours.

Punch dough down and divide into 8 equal pieces. Roll into balls and place on a greased cookie sheet. Press lightly to make disks of dough about ¾ inch thick. Cover loosely with a towel and let rise about 1 hour, until light.

Preheat oven to 400°.

Brush tops of buns lightly with oil. Bake about 15 minutes, or until golden but not hard. Let cool on racks. Store in plastic bags; these freeze well.

222 calories, 3 g fat, 0.5 g saturated fat, 2 mg cholesterol, 3 g dietary fiber, 250 mg sodium

FRENCH BREAD

Soft, tender French bread is a traditional accompaniment to meals in New Orleans. Day-old bread makes excellent garlic toast or bread pudding.

Makes 1 loaf; 8 servings

1¼ teaspoons active dry yeast   *½ teaspoon salt*
1 cup warm water (105° to 115°)   *2 tablespoons cornmeal*
2½ cups bread flour   *1 egg white, slightly beaten*
½ cup cake flour, or more if needed   *1 tablespoon sesame seeds*

Dissolve yeast in warm water.

Combine flours and salt in the large bowl of an electric mixer. Add dissolved yeast and mix until combined. Dough will be sticky. If it is too sticky to work with, add more cake flour, by the tablespoonful, until dough is manageable but still sticky.

Place dough in a bowl, cover lightly, and set aside in a warm place to rise until doubled in bulk, about 1½ hours.

Punch dough down. Roll dough on lightly floured cloth or board to make a long, thin loaf. Sprinkle cornmeal on a nonstick baking sheet or in a French bread pan. Make 3 diagonal slashes in top of dough with a razor blade or a very sharp knife. Cover lightly and let dough rise in a warm place until light.

Preheat oven to 400°.

Brush bread with egg white and sprinkle with sesame seeds.

Bake for 30 minutes, or until bread is golden brown and sounds hollow when tapped on the bottom.

180 calories, 2 g fat, 0.5 g saturated fat, no cholesterol, 1.5 g dietary fiber, 160 mg sodium

WHOLE WHEAT BISCUITS

Southerners pride themselves on biscuits that billow like clouds. Basically there are two secrets to making airy biscuits: Use a soft wheat flour and make the dough nice and wet. The steam created when the dough hits a superhot oven helps the biscuits to rise tall.

Whole wheat biscuits are not the impossibility they'd seem to be at first glance. Just be sure to use whole wheat *pastry* flour, which is much softer than regular whole wheat flour. For the white flour, use a low-protein flour designed for biscuits—no problem if you live in the South. If you don't live in the South, cake or pastry flour is your best bet.

Makes 12 biscuits

1 cup sifted soft white flour (cake or pastry flour), plus some for dusting
1 cup whole wheat pastry flour
2½ teaspoons baking powder
¼ teaspoon baking soda

¾ teaspoon salt
½ teaspoon sugar
2 tablespoons solid vegetable shortening
1¼ to 1⅓ cups buttermilk

Preheat oven to 450°. Spray a 10-inch-round cake pan or an 11-by-7-inch pan with nonstick cooking spray.

Mix flours, baking powder, baking soda, salt, and sugar in a bowl. With a pastry blender or 2 knives, work in shortening until mixture is crumbly. Stir in enough buttermilk to make a wet, very sticky dough.

Scrape dough out onto a heavily floured board. With floured hands, pat into a disk about ½ inch thick. Cut out rounds with a floured 2½-inch biscuit cutter. Gather up scraps, pat into a disk, and cut more biscuits. Don't cut scraps more than once, and try not to work too much flour into the dough.

Place biscuits in a cake pan, with sides touching. Bake for 10 to 12 minutes, until golden. Serve hot.

95 calories, 3 g fat, 1 g saturated fat, 1 mg cholesterol, 1.5 g dietary fiber, 278 mg sodium

SWEET POTATO–PECAN BREAD WITH SHERRIED FIG SPREAD

Sweet potato gives this bread a pretty orange color and a hint of sweetness. It's especially nice served with a sherried fig spread. We've made the spread with dried figs because they're more available. During the brief fresh fig season, you can make a breakfast of the bread with fresh figs that have been cut in half and sprinkled lightly with sherry.

Makes 1 loaf; 10 servings

1 package (2¼ teaspoons) active dry yeast
¼ cup warm water (105° to 115°)
2 tablespoons plus 1 teaspoon sugar
2 tablespoons unsalted butter or margarine, at room temperature, cut into ½–inch pieces
¾ cup cooked and mashed sweet potatoes, at room temperature

¾ teaspoon ground cinnamon
½ teaspoon salt
¼ teaspoon ground ginger
¼ teaspoon ground nutmeg
½ cup skim milk, warmed
3 cups bread flour
½ cup white cornmeal
⅓ cup chopped pecans
1 egg white, lightly beaten

Dissolve yeast in warm water with 1 teaspoon sugar.

In the large bowl of an electric mixer, cream 2 tablespoons sugar and butter. Mix in mashed sweet potatoes, cinnamon, salt, ginger, and nutmeg. Stir in yeast and milk. Stir in flour and cornmeal. Dough will be slightly sticky and soft.

Knead dough on a lightly floured board for a few minutes until smooth.

Place dough in a large bowl and cover with a damp towel. Let dough rise in a warm area until doubled in bulk, about 1½ hours.

Punch dough down, then knead for 2 to 3 minutes, mixing in the pecans.

Shape dough into a loaf. Set into a lightly greased nonstick 9-by-5-inch loaf pan. Let dough rise for 1 hour, or until light.

Preheat oven to 375°. Brush bread with egg white. Bake in the center of the oven for 35 minutes, or until it is golden brown on top and sounds hollow when tapped.

Cool for 5 minutes. Remove from pan and cool on a rack. This is very good the next day, toasted and spread with cream cheese or Sherried Fig Spread (recipe follows).

243 calories, 5.5 g fat, 2 g saturated fat, 6 mg cholesterol, 2 g dietary fiber, 130 mg sodium

SHERRIED FIG SPREAD

Makes 1¼ cups

1 cup dried figs   **⅓ cup sugar**
Boiling water   **1 tablespoon sherry, or to taste**

Using kitchen scissors, snip stems off figs. Cut figs into quarters. Place in a small, heavy saucepan and add boiling water to cover. Bring to a boil. Continue boiling for 15 minutes, stirring once or twice, until figs are very soft.

Cool, then puree in a food processor. Return to pan and stir in sugar. Cook over medium heat for 10 minutes, or until spread is desired thickness.

Remove pan from heat. Stir in sherry. Spoon into bowl and let cool. Cover and refrigerate.

Per tablespoon: 30 calories, no fat, no cholesterol, 1 g dietary fiber, 1 mg sodium

BENNE WAFERS

Benne is the southern name for sesame seeds. Sesame, which was brought from Africa, quickly caught on in the southeastern United States. This rich, crisp cookie is a classic way to use sesame seeds.

Makes 40 wafers

6 tablespoons unsalted butter, at room temperature, cut in ½-inch pieces
¾ cup packed light brown sugar
1 egg
¼ teaspoon baking powder
½ cup plus 2 teaspoons all-purpose flour
¼ cup toasted sesame seeds (benne)
½ teaspoon vanilla extract

Line 2 cookie sheets with aluminum foil. Preheat oven to 325°.

Using electric mixer, cream butter and sugar together. Mix in egg, baking powder, flour, sesame seeds, and vanilla extract.

Drop batter by teaspoonful onto baking sheets, spacing 2 inches apart.

Bake cookies on the center rack in the oven for 8 to 10 minutes, or until firm and beginning to brown around edges. The cookies brown quickly so keep a watch, making sure they don't brown too much. Let cookies stand for 2 minutes before removing with a spatula.

39 calories, 2.5 g fat, 1 g saturated fat, 10 mg cholesterol, negligible fiber, 6 mg sodium

PEACH CUSTARD RICE PUDDING

Georgia peaches are famous worldwide. This recipe is a good way to use up an overabundance of peaches, as well as leftover rice. It's very nice for breakfast as well as for dessert.

Check the pudding every half hour to make sure the water level in the outer pan remains constant. Add more hot water as necessary.

Makes 4 servings

3 cups skim milk

⅓ cup sugar

2 eggs

¼ teaspoon salt

1 teaspoon vanilla extract

½ teaspoon ground cinnamon

1¼ cups peeled, pitted, and chopped
   peaches

1¼ cups cooked long-grain rice, cooled

2 egg whites, beaten until soft, glossy
   peaks form

Lightly butter a 2-quart ovenproof bowl or soufflé dish. Preheat oven to 375°.

In a large bowl, beat 2 cups milk, sugar, eggs, salt, vanilla extract, and cinnamon until blended. Stir in remaining milk, peaches, and rice. Fold in egg whites.

Pour pudding into prepared dish. Set dish in a larger pan and add 1 inch of hot water to outer pan.

Bake pudding in the center of the oven for 1 hour, or until a tester inserted in the center comes out clean. Let cool in oven with door open. Serve warm or chilled.

289 calories, 3 g fat, 1 g saturated fat, 109 mg cholesterol, 1.5 g dietary fiber, 287 mg sodium

3

The Midwest and Heartland

Scandinavian-style Brunch

Chilled Yogurt Soup with Cucumbers, Tomatoes, and Dill

Swedish Pancakes with Cherry Sauce

Zucchini, Carrot, and Potato Pancakes

Plum Custard Bake

Midwest Family Reunion

Broccoli, Raisin, and Sunflower Seed Salad

Pea and Peanut Salad

Garden Pasta Salad with Basil Vinaigrette

Minty Fudge Snack Cake

A Stroll Down Devon Avenue

Cauliflower and Cashew Biryani

Fragrant Spinach

Eggplant with Cumin and Black Pepper

Honeyed Cheese Pudding with Fresh Fruit

Appetizers, Salads, and Side Dishes

Black Walnut and String Bean Spread with Pita Bread

Cherry Tomatoes Stuffed with Hummus

Green Salad with Dried Cranberries and Black Walnuts

Soups

Fresh Corn Chowder

Potato Soup with Pickle and Horseradish

White Bean and Yellow Pea Soup

Carrot Soup with Matzo Balls

Entrées

Whole Wheat Crepes Filled with Herbed Cheese

Large Pumpkin Ravioli with Asparagus and Tomato-Chive Sauce

Open-Face Cheddar and Farmstand Tomato Sandwiches

Barbecued Bean Sandwiches

Pepper and Egg Sandwiches

Bernice's Radish and Egg Sandwiches

Free-Form Country Pie

Root Vegetable Pasties with Saffron Crust

Warm Bean and Tomato Salad with Honey-Mustard Dressing

Risotto with Asparagus and Morels

Toasted Almond Tabbouleh

Pad Thai, Chicago Style

Slow-baked Sauerkraut with Carrots and Apples

Roasted Carrot and Potato Casserole

Savory Potato Pudding

Hot German-style Potato Salad

Whole Cabbage Stuffed with Spinach and Wild Rice

Four-Way Chili

"Unstuffing" with Carrot-Miso Gravy

Breads and Desserts

Milwaukee Potato Bread

Semolina Rolls with Parmesan and Pepper

Apple Bran Muffins

Whole Wheat Pita Bread

Cornflake-topped Noodle Pudding

Apple Currant Crisp

Berry and Cherry Compote with White Cheese Mousse

Maple-scented Tropical Fruits Délice

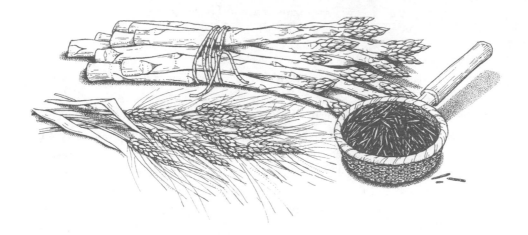

Carved by glaciers, tilled by native grasses, washed by the Great Lakes and the awesome Mississippi, the prairies at America's heart offered rich farming to the immigrants who poured in from the eastern United States and points abroad. The arable land went on farther than any eye could see. The newcomers broke the sod and quickly turned the Heartland into the nation's breadbasket. Mostly flat and fertile, the Midwest and Plains states support wheat, corn, soybeans, rye, barley, and oats.

The wheat raised in the central states feeds all of America and much of the rest of the world. The soft wheat of Ohio, Indiana, Illinois, and Missouri goes into flat breads, crackers, and pastries. The hard wheats of Kansas, Nebraska, and the Dakotas are turned into bread, pasta, and couscous.

How do midwesterners use wheat? Let us count the ways. They use it in spaetzle (German drop noodles), spaghetti, egg rolls, couscous, noodles, pizza crusts, tabbouleh, dumplings, wheat berry salads, kringles (a Scandinavian pastry), pancakes, bar cookies, strudels, sandwiches, and enough bread—pita, Jewish rye, lavash, potato, whole wheat—to fill in Lake Superior. Have we mentioned the turnovers yet? Try runzas (Czech turnovers made with bread dough), pasties (Cornish turnovers made with pastry dough), pierogi (Polish turnovers made with noodle dough), samosas (Indian turnovers made with pastry dough), spanakopitta (Greek turnovers made with phyllo dough), kolachky (Czech, Hungarian, or Polish turnovers made with cookie dough), won tons, and ravioli.

Attracted by the rich farmland and the industries gathered along the Great Lakes, the Germans, Dutch, Swiss, Swedes, Finns, Norwegians, Cornish, Belgians, Indians, Pakistanis, African-Americans, Mexicans, Poles, Hungarians, Czechs, Slovaks, Serbs, Ukrainians, Lithuanians, Croatians, Assyrians, Lebanese, Japanese, Thais, Koreans, Vietnamese, and Hmong have all made America's Heartland their home.

Commercial cereal makers and bakers also found the area attractive. The Midwest is home to Kellogg's, Post, General Mills and its ageless Betty Crocker, Quaker Oats, and Pillsbury.

It's not unusual for midwesterners to make an entire dinner of corn on the cob—or popcorn when the fresh stuff is out of season. And why shouldn't they? The world's best corn—no butter needed—comes from Indiana, Iowa, Illinois, and Ohio. America's most familiar popcorn king, Orville Redenbacher, hails from northwest Indiana, and the Amish and Mennonite farmers in eastern Indiana and western Ohio don't exaggerate when they paint WORLD'S BEST POPCORN on their roadside stands.

Corn and wheat are only part of the Midwest's agricultural bounty. From the lakes of Wisconsin and Minnesota come wild rice, some of it still hand-harvested by the Ojibway in canoes. Michigan produces asparagus, wild mushrooms, potatoes, peaches, plums, and blueberries, and is the U.S. capital for tart Montmorency cherries. Black walnuts are a Missouri specialty. Many of the beans we bake or put into soups come from Michigan or the Dakotas.

Wisconsin still reigns as king of the dairy states, and in addition to the traditional varieties favored by Germans and Swiss, it is home to makers of goat cheese, French cheeses, and the whole range of Italian cheeses from Parmesan to mascarpone.

Illinois and Iowa may feed most of their soybean crop to livestock, but an increasing percentage of it is making its way into tofu, the protein-rich soybean curd that has long found favor with vegetarians and has finally arrived in America's mainstream supermarkets.

Much of the central states' traditional fare is plain and hearty, meant to protect against winter cold or keep a farmer working from dawn to dusk. Although mid-westerners still like large portions, there are signs that the food is lightening up.

But it's still cooked from the heart.

• SCANDINAVIAN-STYLE BRUNCH •

The frigid northern Heartland felt like home to the hearty Nordic immigrants. The days shorten to almost nothing in the winter and lengthen to near infinity in the summer. Glacially chiseled bluffs rise above the Mississippi, and thousands of lakes dot the area. If you creep far enough north, you can even catch a glimpse of the Northern Lights.

Communities throughout the north-central states host dozens of festivals that transport the participants, if only briefly, to ancestral homes in Norway, Finland, or Sweden. Christmas brings forth a groaning board of cardamom-scented cookies, coffee cakes, and breads.

Although Chicago's thriving Swedish community has scattered by now throughout the city and suburbs, the Andersonville neighborhood on the city's north side still embraces the Swedish Museum; a bakery that makes wonderful coffee cakes, marzipan pastries, and seven-grain breads; and delicatessens where you can buy an endless assortment of flatbreads, a good bowl of yellow pea soup, and irons for making pancakes in the shape of butterflies.

Suggested Wines: Try a Chardonnay or white Burgundy with the yogurt soup and zucchini pancakes. It's harder to match a wine to the cherry pancakes; your safest bet is probably coffee.

Chilled Yogurt Soup with Cucumbers, Tomatoes, and Dill

For a prettier soup, use both yellow and red tomatoes.

There is no added liquid in this soup; the liquid comes from the vegetables.

Makes 8 servings

1 large cucumber, peeled
2 cups peeled, seeded, and chopped
*   yellow or red tomatoes*
4 cups plain nonfat yogurt, chilled

¼ cup minced fresh dillweed
2 cloves garlic, crushed
¼ cup chopped black walnuts or regular
*   walnuts*

Cut cucumber in half lengthwise. With a spoon scoop out seeds, starting at the top of the cucumber and pulling down with the spoon. Thinly slice seeded cucumber. Put in a deep bowl.

Mix tomatoes with cucumber. Stir in yogurt, dill, and garlic. Let stand for 10 to 15 minutes.

Ladle the soup into bowls. Sprinkle nuts on top just before serving.

108 calories, 3 g fat, 0.5 g saturated fat, 2 mg cholesterol, 1 g dietary fiber, 99 mg sodium

Swedish Pancakes with Cherry Sauce

Classically these delicate, small pancakes are made in a special pan that includes depressions to hold the batter. But we made ours in a nonstick frying pan.

Tart scarlet Montmorency cherries from Michigan and Wisconsin are in season for only a few short weeks in July.

Lingonberries, relatives of the cranberry, are often served with Swedish pancakes, and fresh or frozen cranberries can be substituted for the cherries in the sauce.

Makes 8 servings

Cherry sauce:

2 cups fresh tart cherries or 1 can (16 ounces) unsweetened red tart cherries, including liquid

¼ cup sugar

¼ teaspoon ground nutmeg

1½ tablespoons cornstarch

1 tablespoon cherry liqueur or brandy (optional)

Pancakes:

2 egg whites

1 cup all-purpose flour

1 teaspoon baking powder

2 egg yolks

1¼ cups skim milk

1 tablespoon unsalted butter or margarine, melted and cooled

To make sauce: If using fresh cherries, pit the cherries and let stand in a bowl for 20 minutes to collect juices.

Pour half of cherries and liquid into a small pan. Puree remaining half of cherries, in a food processor or blender, then pour in pan. Add sugar and nutmeg. Cook over medium heat until sauce begins to boil. If you're using fresh cherries, you may need to thin the sauce with a little water.

Remove ¼ cup of the liquid and whisk cornstarch into it. Return mixture to sauce, whisking occasionally until sauce thickens slightly. Remove from heat and stir in liqueur or brandy if using. Cool.

To make pancakes: Beat egg whites until they form firm, glossy peaks; set aside.

Sift flour and baking powder together. Set aside. In a separate bowl, beat egg yolks with milk and cooled butter. Stir in flour mixture.

Gently fold in beaten egg whites. Let batter stand for 20 minutes, then stir. Spray a nonstick frying pan with butter-flavored nonstick cooking spray. Make small, even pancakes, using about 2 tablespoons batter for each. Cook pancakes, turning once, until golden brown on each side.

Serve hot with Cherry Sauce.

150 calories, 3 g fat, 1.5 g saturated fat, 58 mg cholesterol, 2.5 g dietary fiber, 40 mg sodium

Zucchini, Carrot, and Potato Pancakes

Use a food processor, fitted with a grating disk with medium or large holes, to grate all the vegetables.

Makes 8 servings

2 cups grated zucchini

2 cups peeled and grated carrots

1 cup peeled and grated potato

½ cup chopped onion

½ cup egg substitute

2 teaspoons minced garlic

½ teaspoon salt

¼ teaspoon pepper

⅓ cup flour

About 1 tablespoon unsalted butter

Toss grated zucchini, carrots, potato, and onion in a bowl. Mix in egg substitute, garlic, salt, pepper, and flour. Let stand for 20 minutes.

Heat about 1 teaspoon butter over medium heat in a large nonstick frying pan that has been sprayed with butter-flavored nonstick cooking spray. Spoon pancake mixture into pan, using 2 to 3 tablespoons batter per pancake. Cook, turning once, until pancakes are firm and beginning to turn golden. Repeat until batter is used up, adding butter to pan as necessary.

Serve hot.

70 calories, 2 g fat, 1 g saturated fat, 4 mg cholesterol, 2 g dietary fiber, 173 mg sodium

Plum Custard Bake

When buying plums, choose those that are firm but not hard; they should give slightly under pressure. Unless plums are soft and fragrant when you buy them (meaning they're truly ripe), soften them at room temperature for two to three days before using. Once ripened, they can be refrigerated.

Makes 8 servings

4½ cups pitted and sliced small
  plums

½ cup sugar

½ cup all-purpose flour

⅛ teaspoon salt

1 egg, lightly beaten

2 egg whites, lightly beaten

1¼ cups skim milk

1 teaspoon vanilla extract

Confectioners' sugar (optional)

Preheat oven to 350°.

Spray a 9-inch pie pan with butter-flavored nonstick cooking spray. Arrange plum slices on bottom of dish and sprinkle with ¼ cup sugar.

Combine flour, remaining ¼ cup sugar, salt, egg, egg whites, milk, and vanilla extract in a deep mixing bowl or food processor bowl. Whisk or process until batter is smooth. Pour over plums.

Bake in the center of the oven for 1 hour, or until puffy and golden brown. Sprinkle lightly with confectioners' sugar if using and serve warm.

155 calories, 1.5 g fat, 0.5 g saturated fat, 27 mg cholesterol, 2 g dietary fiber, 75 mg sodium

· MIDWEST FAMILY REUNION ·

In the hazy days of August and early September, families gather in the Midwest for reunions, swatting yellow jackets away from the food, trying to guess which cousin is which, and exchanging gossip and news over cold beer.

The food, like all picnic food—and much of midwestern food in general—is the sort of basic stuff Grandma used to make. The spread always includes at least one pasta salad (what we used to call macaroni salad as kids), brownies or other bar cookies, breads, muffins, a fruit salad, chicken salad, a "newer" addition such as a broccoli salad with raisins and sunflower seeds, a wiggly gelatin concoction or two, and a random assortment of vegetable salads, usually heavy with mayonnaise.

In recent years the picnic dishes have changed oh so gradually, as some of the older family members get a scolding from their doctors and the younger generation trains for marathons. Suddenly there's a little less mayonnaise, a little less meat and chicken, and a few more vegetables, fruits, and grain salads.

But no matter what happens, there'll always be bar cookies. And wiggly gelatin things.

Suggested Wine: Family reunions almost always mean beer, usually in cans. Wine lovers can tote along a dry or medium-sweet Rhine-style wine. Several, in fact, are produced in Michigan.

Broccoli, Raisin, and Sunflower Seed Salad

Parents swear by this salad; the sunflower seeds and raisins encourage their kids to eat the broccoli. The dressing often is far too sweet; we've made an orange dressing with not too much sugar for a fresher flavor. Although we prefer the broccoli lightly blanched (it's prettier and easier to eat), you can leave it raw if you like.

Makes 8 servings

3 pounds (about 5 stalks) broccoli
2 medium carrots, peeled and grated
1 very small red onion, finely diced

½ cup raisins
⅓ cup roasted sunflower seed kernels

Dressing:

5 tablespoons orange juice
5 tablespoons reduced-fat mayonnaise
1 teaspoon raspberry vinegar (optional)

2 teaspoons sugar, or to taste
½ teaspoon salt

Trim bottom 2 inches from broccoli stalks. Cut off florets and separate into small pieces. Peel stems and dice. Blanch broccoli florets and diced stems in a large pot of boiling water for 1 minute, then drain, rinse under cold water, and drain again. Place broccoli in a large bowl with carrots, onion, raisins, and sunflower seed kernels.

Whisk together orange juice, mayonnaise, vinegar, sugar, and salt until smooth. Pour over broccoli salad and toss well. Keep cold until serving.

153 calories, 6.5 g fat, 1 g saturated fat, no cholesterol, 6 g dietary fiber, 248 mg sodium

Pea and Peanut Salad

Our friend Donna in Grand Rapids, Michigan, once engaged a group of fellow onliners on Prodigy in a lively discussion of the origins of pea and peanut salad. After tossing around ideas and wildly fantastical recipes for other regional oddities, they decided this salad is pretty much confined to western Michigan and environs. We've since found a pea and peanut salad recipe in a Pennsylvania Dutch cookbook, but the concoction is so popular in Michigan that we felt its home is truly there.

For a variation on the same theme, you can make Pea and Colby Salad, another midwestern picnic favorite.

Makes 8 servings

20 ounces frozen peas
2 tablespoons finely grated red onion
¼ cup reduced-fat mayonnaise
3 tablespoons nonfat sour cream or
  yogurt
¼ to ½ teaspoon sugar (optional)

1 tablespoon reduced-fat peanut butter
Pinch of cayenne
¼ teaspoon salt
Black pepper to taste
2 tablespoons dry-roasted peanuts,
  preferably unsalted

Cook peas according to package directions. Rinse under cold water until peas are cool and drain well. Place in a bowl with onion.

Whisk together mayonnaise, sour cream or yogurt, sugar if using, peanut butter, and cayenne. Add to vegetables and toss to coat. Season with salt and pepper. Refrigerate. Shortly before serving, toss peanuts with peas. Serve cold or slightly chilled.

112 calories, 4.5 g fat, 1 g saturated fat, no cholesterol, 4 g dietary fiber, 214 mg sodium

VARIATION: Pea and Colby Salad. Make the salad as directed except: Replace the peanuts with ½ cup reduced-fat Colby (or mild Cheddar) cheese cut into ¼-inch cubes, and replace the peanut butter and 1 tablespoon of sour cream or yogurt in the dressing with 2 tablespoons sweet pickle relish.

106 calories, 4 g fat, 1 g saturated fat, 2 mg cholesterol, 4 g dietary fiber, 236 mg sodium

Garden Pasta Salad with Basil Vinaigrette

Makes 8 large or 16 small servings

1 pound corkscrew pasta or elbow macaroni, preferably whole wheat
1 cup fresh or frozen corn kernels
½ cup finely diced red onion
1 (5 to 6 ounces) zucchini squash, finely diced
6 medium radishes, trimmed and diced
2 large ripe tomatoes, cored, seeded, and finely diced

1 green bell pepper, cored, seeded, and finely diced
1 red bell pepper, cored, seeded, and finely diced
¼ cup finely chopped fresh parsley

Vinaigrette:
5 tablespoons white wine vinegar
3 tablespoons honey
½ teaspoon salt

6 tablespoons olive oil
½ cup fresh basil leaves
Freshly ground black pepper

Cook pasta in boiling water until al dente, about 10 to 12 minutes depending on size. After 8 to 10 minutes of cooking time, add corn to pasta. When pasta is done, drain pasta and corn and rinse thoroughly under cold running water.

While pasta is cooking, prepare onion, zucchini, radishes, tomatoes, bell peppers, and parsley; place vegetables in a very large bowl.

Make vinaigrette by placing vinegar, honey, salt, oil, basil leaves, and pepper in a blender or food processor. Process on high until basil is very finely minced.

Add drained pasta and corn to vegetables in bowl. Add vinaigrette and stir well. Season with pepper. Refrigerate at least 1 hour before serving.

8 servings: 352 calories, 11.5 g fat, 1.5 g saturated fat, no cholesterol, 3 g dietary fiber (6.5 g with whole wheat pasta), 146 mg sodium

Minty Fudge Snack Cake

Nobody who tastes this moist, intensely chocolate cake, which falls somewhere between a devil's food cake and a brownie, will believe a serving has only 4 grams of fat. This recipe can be cut in half and baked in an 8-inch-square pan.

Indiana is one of the country's leading growers of peppermint and spearmint, which are used in everything from cooking extracts to medicinal rubs.

Makes 32 bars

6 tablespoons canola oil
1 cup plain low-fat yogurt
1 cup granulated sugar
1 cup packed light brown sugar
2 tablespoons light corn syrup
1 tablespoon vanilla extract
1 teaspoon peppermint extract

4 egg whites, lightly beaten or ½ cup
    egg substitute
1 cup all-purpose flour
1 cup unsweetened cocoa powder
½ teaspoon salt
¼ teaspoon ground cinnamon
¼ teaspoon baking soda

Icing:

1 ounce unsweetened chocolate

1 tablespoon unsalted butter

1 cup confectioners' sugar

½ teaspoon peppermint extract

⅛ teaspoon vanilla extract

1 to 2 tablespoons water

Preheat oven to 350°. Spray a 13-by-9-inch baking pan with nonstick cooking spray.

In a medium mixing bowl, beat oil, yogurt, sugars, corn syrup, vanilla and mint extracts, and egg whites just until smooth. In another bowl, stir together flour, cocoa, salt, cinnamon, and baking soda. Add to oil-sugar mixture and stir just until mixed.

Pour batter into pan. Bake for 25 to 30 minutes, or until center no longer looks wet. Let cool.

While cake cools, make icing: Place chocolate and butter in a small microwave-proof glass container and microwave on 80 percent power for 1 minute 15 seconds, or until chocolate is mostly melted. Stir until smooth. (Or melt butter with chocolate in the top of a double boiler.) Let cool.

In a small bowl, beat chocolate mixture with confectioners' sugar, mint and vanilla extracts, and water to make a smooth, spreadable icing.

Spread icing evenly over cooled cake. Refrigerate cake for at least 15 minutes to firm it and set the icing. Before serving, cut across 8 times and lengthwise 4 times to make 32 bars (it's easier if you dip the knife in hot water between cuts). Store bars in a single layer in a loosely covered container.

117 calories, 4 g fat, 1 g saturated fat, 2 mg cholesterol, 1 g dietary fiber, 56 mg sodium

• A STROLL DOWN DEVON AVENUE •

Like all large cities, Chicago has many fascinating ethnic neighborhoods. Our favorite, hands down, is Devon Avenue on the city's far north side.

The eastern part of the avenue, toward the lake, is Hispanic and includes one of our favorite Cuban groceries, which carries at least three different kinds of masa for tamales (Mexican, Cuban, and Guatemalan) at Christmastime. (Masa is a corn dough made from ground corn that has been treated with lime.)

The liveliest part of the strip kicks in west of Western Avenue. Here Devon is dominated by Indians and Pakistanis, and the sidewalks are filled with women wearing bangles and brilliantly hued saris. On Friday evenings many of the men are dressed in flowing white shirts and trousers as they return from prayer.

Devon Avenue bears a ceremonial street sign proclaiming it "Gandhi Street" after the renowned founder of modern India. The next block is known as "Mohammed Ali Jinnah Way," after the founder of Pakistan. Only in America. . . .

The spices here come in half-pound bags, and the aromas of cumin, coriander, and garlic waft on the breeze. The rice comes in 10- to 20-pound bags and includes imported basmati, a slender-grained, fragrant variety that can make anyone fall head over heels for rice.

It's no problem finding ingredients here for vegetarian specialties, from elaborate pilafs to chickpea fritters. Indians have a long tradition of vegetarian cooking, and many remain vegetarian even after moving to the meat-happy United States.

There's a Mediterranean presence on Devon as well. The Assyrian Cultural Center is here, as is a Middle Eastern grocery store that sells lavosh and pomegranate molasses, and a Greek-run produce market that carries sesame bread, kalamata olives, and four different kinds of feta cheese along with Indian ingredients such as fresh fenugreek.

Farther west, the bright saris give way to black coats and hats and side whiskers. The signs in the delis turn Ukrainian or Russian, the breads are braided, and the chief spice is horseradish. Historically, the Russian Jews were the most prominent of the neighborhood's residents, and a new wave of immigrants from the former Soviet Union has joined the ocean of newcomers who stroll Devon.

We've created a menu that celebrates Devon Avenue's chief ethnic group, Indian, and offers a hint of the Middle East as well.

Suggested Wines: Because of the hot spices, Indian food is often served with beer, and an Indian beer would be appropriate. But the biryani is more fragrance than heat. A fairly fruity Sauvignon Blanc or a lighter red, such as Pinot Noir, can carry you through the courses.

Cauliflower and Cashew Biryani

Biryani is an elegant pilaf made by folding korma (a meat or vegetable stew made with yogurt) into basmati rice. In the United States many Indian restaurants carry this fragrantly spiced Moghul dish on their menus.

Basmati rice, which grows in Texas as well as in India and Pakistan, is a marvelously aromatic rice that smells like buttered popcorn as it cooks.

This biryani tastes best when the korma is made the day before and refrigerated, allowing all the flavors to meld. There is not much liquid in this dish because the rice should be dry and fluffy, and have separate grains.

A true biryani, like many Indian dishes, is made with whole spices so as not to "muddy" the rice. We use ground spices, however, because many people do not like biting into a whole clove or cardamom pod. Whether you use whole or ground spices, make sure the spices are fresh.

This complex recipe requires some time and patience, but the results are worth it. It is not difficult if you take it in steps.

Makes 8 servings

Vegetable stew:

1¼ cups plain nonfat yogurt

⅓ cup (about 1½ ounces) plain or dry-roasted cashews

1½ tablespoons canola oil

2 medium onions, quartered and very thinly sliced

1 tablespoon minced garlic

2 tablespoons grated or finely minced fresh gingerroot

2 to 3 chile peppers, seeded and finely minced

1½ teaspoons ground cumin

¾ teaspoon ground coriander

¾ teaspoon ground cardamom

2 sticks cinnamon, broken in half

¼ teaspoon ground cloves

1 teaspoon salt

3 medium (1½ to 1¾ pounds) boiling potatoes, peeled and diced

2 small to medium (¼ pound) carrots, peeled and sliced

2 cups cauliflower florets

2 cups ¾-inch pieces green beans or an additional 2 cups cauliflower florets

1½ cups water

¼ cup frozen peas

Biryani:

2 cups basmati rice

Fresh cilantro leaves, coarsely chopped

1 tablespoon finely chopped cashews

To make the stew: Puree yogurt and cashews in a blender or food processor until cashews are finely ground. Set aside.

Heat oil in a large, heavy saucepan or wok that has been sprayed with nonstick cooking spray. Add onions and fry over medium-high heat, stirring frequently, until they are a deep golden brown. Watch carefully and reduce heat if necessary so onions don't burn. Remove ¼ cup of fried onions to paper towels; blot and refrigerate until needed for garnish.

To remaining onions in pan, add garlic, gingerroot, and chiles; fry for 1 minute over medium heat. Add cumin, coriander, cardamom, cinnamon, and cloves; fry for 1 minute. Stir in about half of the yogurt-cashew mixture and cook over medium heat for 5 minutes, stirring frequently. Stir in remaining yogurt mixture and salt.

Stir in potatoes, carrots, cauliflower, and green beans if using. Add water; the liquid will not cover vegetables. Bring to a simmer, loosely cover pot, and simmer over medium-low heat, stirring 3 or 4 times, until vegetables are barely tender, about 25 minutes. Add more water if vegetables start to stick. Uncover and cook another 5 to 10 minutes, or until vegetables are tender and the liquid is thick and silky. Stir in peas.

At this point the stew can be covered and refrigerated several hours or overnight; reheat to warm before mixing with rice.

To prepare rice and assemble biryani: Place rice in a bowl and rinse 3 times by covering with cold water, swishing the rice around, then carefully draining off most of the water. (This removes some of the starch from the rice so that the grains will cook up dry and separate.)

To make biryani: Place rice in a pot with enough water to cover by 2 inches. Bring to a boil, reduce heat to low, and cook for 5 minutes. Drain rice and rinse well under cold water. (Again, this helps to remove some of the starch.)

Preheat oven to 350°.

Place rice in a large bowl and add vegetable stew. Stir thoroughly to mix. Turn rice out into a buttered or oiled 13-by-9-inch baking dish, cover with foil, and bake for 30 minutes, or until rice is tender and fluffy.

Sprinkle cilantro, reserved fried onions, and chopped cashews over top of biryani. Serve warm.

342 calories, 6 g fat, 1 g saturated fat, 1 mg cholesterol, 5 g dietary fiber, 325 mg sodium

Fragrant Spinach

Spinach braised with spices and yogurt is a dish found in almost every Indian restaurant on Devon Avenue (and probably in the United States). The dish often includes meat or handmade cheese, but we like the spinach alone, as a side dish. You can add a few cubes of cheese (such as feta, dry ricotta, or farmer cheese) and serve this with whole wheat pita as a light main course for four.

Makes 8 small side-dish servings

2 pounds fresh spinach
2 teaspoons canola oil
½ cup finely chopped onion
2 teaspoons minced fresh gingerroot
½ cup seeded and chopped tomatoes
   (fresh or canned)
¼ cup plain nonfat yogurt or
   3 tablespoons vegetable stock
   (page 17)

¼ teaspoon ground turmeric
¼ teaspoon freshly ground black
   pepper
¼ teaspoon ground cinnamon
½ teaspoon ground cumin
¼ teaspoon salt
⅛ to ¼ teaspoon hot red pepper, or
   to taste

Trim large stems from spinach and rinse leaves thoroughly. Place in a large pot with just the water clinging to the leaves and cook, uncovered, over medium heat, stirring frequently, until spinach darkens and wilts. Drain and set aside.

Heat oil in a heavy-bottomed saucepan. Add onion and sauté over medium-high heat, stirring frequently, until onion is golden. Watch carefully and lower heat if onion begins to brown too rapidly. Stir in gingerroot, tomatoes, yogurt, and spices. Cook over medium heat for 5 minutes, stirring frequently; add a little water if mixture starts to stick to bottom of pan.

Chop spinach. Add to spice mixture in pan and stir over low heat until spinach is heated through and coated with sauce.

This can be served immediately but tastes even better several hours or a day later. Rewarm gently over low heat.

43 calories, 1.5 g fat, no saturated fat, no cholesterol, 3 g dietary fiber, 151 mg sodium

●━━━◆━━━●

Eggplant with Cumin and Black Pepper

Eggplant is popular among those who shop on Devon Avenue: the Russians, the Indians, and the Middle Easterners. The younger and smaller the eggplant, the less likely it is to be bitter.

Makes 8 servings

*2 pounds small eggplants (baby or
 Japanese eggplants are ideal)*
8 teaspoons olive oil
3 cloves garlic, finely minced
½ teaspoon salt
½ teaspoon ground cumin

*½ teaspoon freshly ground black
 pepper*
1 lemon, cut in half
*2 tablespoons finely chopped fresh
 mint, cilantro, or parsley*

Preheat oven to 500°.

  Trim eggplants and peel. Cut lengthwise into slices about ⅛ inch thick. Brush 4 teaspoons oil evenly over 1 very large or 2 smaller cookie sheets. Lay eggplant slices on cookie sheets, overlapping slightly if necessary. Brush remaining 4 teaspoons oil very lightly over eggplant.

  Bake eggplant, turning once, for 15 to 25 minutes, or until soft and beginning to turn golden. If eggplant is on 2 cookie sheets, transfer it all to 1 cookie sheet at this point. Mix garlic with salt, cumin, and black pepper. Sprinkle over eggplant, then sprinkle with juice of lemon half. Toss well. Return to oven for another 5 minutes, until eggplant is very soft.

Place eggplant on a plate or in a shallow glass bowl and season with juice of remaining lemon half. Scatter herbs over eggplant and toss. This tastes best if refrigerated for several hours and then brought to room temperature before serving.

70 calories, 4.5 g fat, 0.5 g saturated fat, no cholesterol, 2.5 g dietary fiber, 137 mg sodium

●━━●━━●

Honeyed Cheese Pudding with Fresh Fruit

Many Indian and Middle Eastern desserts start with homemade cheese or milk that is boiled for hours to make a thick (and high-fat) fudgy confection. Others are dumplings in syrup. Nearly all of them are very rich and very sweet.

This dessert is an Americanized variation on those rich, syrupy desserts. It's easy to make and just sweet enough to satisfy a dessert craving.

This pudding is also good for breakfast, with fresh berries and a bit of honey or maple syrup.

Rosewater is available in Indian and Middle Eastern groceries and some specialty shops.

Makes 8 servings

1 cup light ricotta cheese
1½ cups low-fat (1-percent) cottage cheese

3 tablespoons honey
¼ cup whole wheat flour

Syrup:

*1 cup unsweetened or naturally
    sweetened peach, mango, apricot, or
    papaya juice*

1 tablespoon honey

¼ teaspoon almond or vanilla extract

1 to 2 drops rosewater (optional)

*2 cups peeled and thinly sliced fresh
    peaches, mangos, apricots, or
    papaya*

To make pudding: Preheat oven to 350°.

Place ricotta, cottage cheese, and honey in a food processor or blender and blend until smooth. Add flour and pulse just to mix. Pour into an 8-inch-square baking pan (preferably nonstick) that has been sprayed with nonstick cooking spray. Bake for 30 to 40 minutes, until pudding is puffy, golden, and firm. Let cool, then refrigerate for at least 2 hours.

To make syrup: Place fruit juice and honey in a stainless steel saucepan. Cook over high heat until liquid is reduced to ½ cup. Add extract and rosewater if using. Chill until serving time.

Peel and slice fresh fruit just before serving. Cut pudding into 16 squares and lay 2 squares in each dessert bowl. Top with fruit and drizzle about 1 tablespoon syrup over each serving.

145 calories, 3 g fat, 2 g saturated fat, 11 mg cholesterol, 1 g dietary fiber, 212 mg sodium

Appetizers, Salads, and Side Dishes

BLACK WALNUT AND STRING BEAN SPREAD WITH PITA BREAD

Tired of the same old party themes? Throw a "Jerry Party" or a "Joe Party" or a "Susan Party"—and invite people you know who have those names or are married to someone who does.

Barbara first encountered this appetizer at a "Jerry Party," a wonderful, creative, warm party designed by her friends Judy and Sam Weiss. Barbara made the guest list because her husband is a Jerome. The Jerrys and their spouses greatly enjoyed this pâté-type spread of green beans and black walnuts.

Makes 4 servings

1 tablespoon canola oil
1¼ cups chopped onions
1 clove garlic, minced
2 cups cooked and drained string beans
    (fresh or frozen)
4 hard-cooked egg whites, chopped

½ cup black walnuts or pecans,
    chopped
Salt and pepper to taste
4 rounds Whole Wheat Pita Bread
    (page 204), or store-bought pitas

Heat oil in a nonstick frying pan that has been sprayed with nonstick cooking spray. Sauté onions and garlic over medium heat, stirring occasionally, until soft. Stir in beans, egg whites, nuts, salt, and pepper, and toss together.

Using a food processor, finely chop all ingredients. Taste and adjust seasonings. Spoon into a serving bowl and serve with pita bread that has been cut into triangles and warmed in the oven.

302 calories, 13 g fat, 1 g saturated fat, no cholesterol, 8 g dietary fiber, 364 mg sodium

CHERRY TOMATOES STUFFED WITH HUMMUS

Hummus, or *hummus bi tahini,* may have originated in the Middle East, but this puree of chickpeas seasoned with sesame sauce, garlic, and lemon has become an American staple as well. We've even ordered hummus and pita in a Chicago hotdog shop.

In a pinch you can use canned chickpeas in this, but the dip will take on a slightly tinny flavor. It's best to cook dried chickpeas or use the quick-cooking packaged chickpeas found in some produce departments.

Makes 6 appetizer servings

*18 to 24 medium-to-large cherry
   tomatoes*
1 cup cooked chickpeas (garbanzos)
2 teaspoons tahini (sesame butter)
1 small clove garlic, minced
1 teaspoon fresh lemon juice

1 teaspoon extra-virgin olive oil
Pinch of cayenne
2 to 3 tablespoons cold water
Salt and pepper to taste
*Chopped fresh parsley, plus parsley
   sprigs for garnish*

With a small, sharp paring knife, shave a little off the bottom of each cherry tomato so it will stand upright when filled with hummus. From the stem side, carefully cut out and discard seeds from each tomato. Drain tomato shells and stand upright on a plate, leaving the center of the plate free.

In a food processor or blender, puree chickpeas with tahini, garlic, lemon juice, oil, cayenne, and enough water to make a smooth puree. Season with salt and pepper.

Spoon hummus into the hollow of each cherry tomato. Sprinkle chopped parsley over hummus-stuffed tomatoes and garnish with parsley sprigs. Serve with crackers or triangles of toasted Whole Wheat Pita Bread (page 204). Spoon any leftover hummus onto center of plate.

76 calories, 2.5 g fat, 0.5 g saturated fat, no cholesterol, 3 g dietary fiber, 97 mg sodium

GREEN SALAD WITH DRIED CRANBERRIES AND BLACK WALNUTS

Black walnuts, used mostly in midwestern and southern cooking, taste sweeter and muskier than regular English walnuts. They're available in some supermarkets or specialty shops and through the mail (See Sources and Resources, page 329). If you cannot get them, make this salad with regular walnuts.

Dried cranberries are available in many supermarkets or by mail.

Makes 4 servings

4 cups salad greens, such as romaine,
   red leaf lettuce, and radicchio,
   washed, dried, and torn into bite-
   size pieces

¼ cup dried cranberries
⅓ cup chopped black walnuts
2 cups sliced white mushrooms
1 red onion, cut into rings

Cranberry vinaigrette:

3 tablespoons Cranberry Vinegar
   (recipe follows) or raspberry vinegar
¼ cup canned whole-berry cranberry
   sauce
¼ cup extra-virgin olive oil

2 cloves garlic, minced
2 teaspoons fresh oregano or
   1 teaspoon dried
½ teaspoon salt
¼ teaspoon freshly ground black pepper

In a salad bowl, toss torn greens with dried cranberries, walnuts, mushrooms, and onion rings.

To make vinaigrette: Combine vinegar and cranberry sauce in a small bowl. Whisk in the oil, a little at a time. Add the garlic, oregano, salt, and pepper. If you want to make the dressing ahead of time, cover and refrigerate for up to 5 days.

Drizzle dressing over greens, toss, and serve.

245 calories, 20 g fat, 2.5 g saturated fat, no cholesterol, 3 g dietary fiber, 278 mg sodium

CRANBERRY VINEGAR

Makes 1¼ cups

1¼ cups red wine vinegar
½ cup dried cranberries

1 tablespoon sugar
½ teaspoon whole allspice

Pour vinegar into a saucepan, stir in cranberries, and add remaining ingredients. Bring mixture to a boil over medium heat. Reduce heat to a simmer and cook for 3 minutes.

Cool vinegar to room temperature. Pour vinegar and cranberries into a sterilized bottle. Cover, seal, and store in a cool, dark place or refrigerate. Wait at least 1 week before using.

Soups

FRESH CORN CHOWDER

Anybody who lives in corn country knows you shouldn't mess much with one of nature's tastiest foods. If you buy too many ears or just need a change, try this chunky soup, which tastes like liquid corn on the cob.

Makes 4 servings

5 to 7 ears fresh sweet corn
2 cups skim milk
2 teaspoons unsalted butter or
  margarine
1 cup finely chopped onion

½ teaspoon paprika
Pinch of ground cumin
¼ teaspoon salt, or to taste
Freshly ground black pepper to taste

Cut corn kernels from the cob, then scrape the dull side of the knife over each cob to release more juice. You should have 6 cups kernels and juice.

Place 4 cups of corn kernels in a blender or food processor with milk. Blend on high speed until mixture has the consistency of a milkshake. Set aside.

Heat butter in a large saucepan. Add onion, paprika, and cumin, and sauté until onion softens. Add corn-milk mixture and whole corn kernels. Bring to a boil, reduce heat to medium, and cook, stirring frequently, until corn is tender, about 20 to 25 minutes. Season with salt and pepper.

275 calories, 5 g fat, 2 g saturated fat, 7 mg cholesterol, 11 g dietary fiber, 231 mg sodium

POTATO SOUP WITH PICKLE
AND HORSERADISH

Unless you have a Polish mom who made similar soups, this combination of ingredients may strike you as odd. Be assured that this slightly spicy, slightly tart white borscht (*barszcz,* in Polish) is delicious hot or cold. Serve it with a good rye bread.

Makes 4 to 5 servings as a main course

2 slices light rye bread, crusts removed
4 cups vegetable stock (page 17) or
    2 cups canned broth diluted with
    2 cups water
1 large (about ¾ pound) baking potato,
    peeled and cut into ½-inch dice
2 cups water
1 cup light sour cream
½ cup skim milk
1 tablespoon flour

⅓ cup (about 2 spears) finely chopped
    dill pickle
2 tablespoons dill pickle juice
3 to 5 teaspoons grated horseradish, to
    taste
1 tablespoon snipped fresh dill
¼ teaspoon salt (omit if using canned
    stock)
Freshly ground black pepper to taste
Dill sprigs for garnish

Tear the bread into small pieces and place in a large saucepan. Pour stock over bread and let stand for 5 minutes.

Cook potato in 2 cups water until very tender, about 15 to 20 minutes.

Meanwhile, whisk together sour cream, milk, and flour until smooth. Stir into bread and stock. Bring to a simmer, stirring occasionally. Mixture may curdle slightly. Add pickle and pickle juice, and simmer over low heat for 10 minutes.

When potato chunks are tender, mash them with their liquid until smooth. Stir into soup, along with horseradish. Cook on low heat for 1 to 2 minutes, just until soup is heated through. If desired, puree soup in a blender or food processor for a smoother texture. Stir in dill, salt, and pepper. Serve immediately or chill and serve cold.

Garnish with dill sprigs.

208 calories, 5 g fat, 2 g saturated fat, 21 mg cholesterol, 2 g dietary fiber, 810 mg sodium

WHITE BEAN AND YELLOW PEA SOUP

Split yellow peas and white beans go into the thick, hearty soups that are winter favorites in the Midwest and Plains states. We've combined the two in this zesty soup that takes the chill off, whether you're slogging through the snow in Duluth, Minnesota, or hunkering down against the January breezes in Topeka, Kansas.

Makes 8 servings

2 tablespoons olive oil
1½ cups chopped onions
4 cloves garlic, minced
1 cup sliced celery
6 cups vegetable stock (page 17) or
    4 cups canned broth diluted with
    2 cups water
1 can (14½ ounces) tomatoes, chopped
    and liquid reserved
2 cups dry navy or Great Northern
    beans

1½ cups dry yellow split peas
1 green or red bell pepper, seeded and
    chopped
⅓ cup minced fresh parsley
1 teaspoon dried tarragon
1 teaspoon dried oregano
½ teaspoon pepper
¼ teaspoon ground coriander
½ teaspoon salt (omit if using canned
    broth)

Heat oil in a large pot. Add onions, garlic, and celery, and cook over medium heat, stirring occasionally and covering pot if necessary, until vegetables are tender, about 5 minutes. Add stock, tomatoes and their liquid, beans, split peas, bell pepper, parsley, tarragon, oregano, pepper, and coriander.

Bring soup to a boil and boil for 2 minutes. Reduce heat to a simmer. Cover and simmer for 3 to 3½ hours, stirring occasionally and adding water if soup becomes too thick. Add salt. Taste and adjust seasonings.

377 calories, 5 g fat, 0.5 g saturated fat, no cholesterol, 17 g dietary fiber, 651 mg sodium

CARROT SOUP WITH MATZO BALLS

Matzo balls—dumplings made of matzo meal, finely ground unleavened crackers—turn a savory carrot soup into substantial comfort food.

Makes 4 generous servings

2 tablespoons canola oil
1 cup chopped onion
1 pound (about 6 large) carrots, peeled
  and sliced
1 cup peeled and cubed potato
5 cups vegetable stock (page 17), or
  3 cups canned broth diluted with
  2 cups water

½ teaspoon salt (omit if using canned
  broth)
½ teaspoon white pepper
1 teaspoon crushed fresh sage or
  ½ teaspoon dried and crumbled
Matzo Balls (recipe follows)

Heat oil in a nonstick pot that has been sprayed with nonstick cooking spray. Sauté the onion over medium heat until tender, about 5 minutes. Add carrots and potato cubes; sauté for 5 minutes, stirring often.

Stir in stock, salt, pepper, and sage, and bring to a boil. Partially cover pot, reduce heat to simmer, and cook for 40 minutes, or until carrots and potato cubes are very tender. Cool. Puree vegetables in 2 or 3 batches in a food processor or blender. Pour back into pan. Taste and adjust seasonings.

Heat soup before serving. Ladle into bowls and set 1 or 2 matzo balls in the center.

MATZO BALLS

Makes 8 small matzo balls

½ cup egg substitute
¼ cup vegetable stock (page 17) or
  water
½ cup matzo meal

2 teaspoons canola oil
¼ teaspoon salt
¼ teaspoon white pepper
½ teaspoon dill seeds

Put egg substitute in a bowl. Stir in stock, matzo meal, oil, salt, pepper, and dill seeds. Cover and refrigerate for 20 minutes.

Bring a large pot of lightly salted water to a boil.

With wet hands, shape matzo dough into 4 to 6 large balls or 8 smaller ones.

Slide matzo balls into boiling water. Reduce heat to simmer and cover pot. Continue cooking for 20 minutes, or until matzo balls are cooked through and tender. Do not uncover pot until the 20 minutes are up.

Use matzo balls immediately in soup, or cover and refrigerate for up to 2 days. Heat in soup before serving.

231 calories, 11 g fat, 1 g saturated fat, no cholesterol, 5 g dietary fiber, 1,187 mg sodium

Entrées

WHOLE WHEAT CREPES FILLED WITH HERBED CHEESE

When it comes to dairy products, the Midwest is still the Big Cheese. Wisconsin produces about a third of the nation's cheese and ranks second, just behind California, in butter production.

Makes 4 servings

Batter:

2 eggs

2 egg whites

1 tablespoon melted unsalted butter, cooled

1 tablespoon canola oil

½ cup whole wheat flour

½ cup all-purpose flour

2¼ cups skim milk

½ teaspoon salt

1 tablespoon finely chopped fresh oregano, or 1½ teaspoons dried

Filling:

1¼ cups fat-free cottage cheese or pot cheese

¼ cup plain nonfat yogurt

1 teaspoon finely chopped fresh basil

1 teaspoon finely chopped fresh oregano, or ½ teaspoon dried

Topping:

1 cup peeled and chopped tomatoes, for topping

1 teaspoon finely chopped fresh basil

1 tablespoon melted unsalted butter, for cooking crepes

Crepe batter can be made in a blender, food processor, or by hand. If preparing crepes by hand, sift flour and use a whisk. Otherwise, place all ingredients in a food processor or blender. Blend only a few seconds until batter is smooth. Let batter stand for 20 minutes.

Heat a 6–inch nonstick crepe pan or frying pan that has been sprayed with butter-flavored nonstick cooking spray. Pour 2½ to 3 tablespoons batter into pan, tilting pan so batter evenly covers bottom. Pour off any excess batter. If batter seems too thick, add a small amount of water to batter in bowl.

Crepe is ready when it is set and firm around edges. Loosen edges with a knife and turn it using a spatula or fingers. Let cook only a few seconds on the other side. Stack crepes between pieces of aluminum foil or wax paper. Cover and refrigerate crepes if not using immediately. You'll have some leftover crepes; freeze for later use.

Blend filling ingredients together in a bowl.

Toss tomatoes and basil for topping. Set aside.

Put 2 to 3 tablespoons of filling in center of each of 8 crepes, and roll each crepe around filling. Tuck in ends, envelope style.

Heat 1 tablespoon butter in a large nonstick skillet that has been sprayed with butter-flavored nonstick cooking spray. Cook crepes in 2 batches, turning once, until warmed through.

Remove crepes with a spatula and set 2 crepes on each plate. Spoon basil-flavored tomatoes over crepes. Serve immediately.

305 calories, 9 g fat, 4.5 g saturated fat, 127 mg cholesterol, 2.5 g dietary fiber, 673 mg sodium

LARGE PUMPKIN RAVIOLI WITH
ASPARAGUS AND TOMATO-CHIVE SAUCE

Illinois produces plenty of pumpkins, and most of the crop is canned for year-round use. Morton, Illinois, celebrates each year with a pumpkin fest.

If you prefer, ravioli can be cut smaller. Use the ravioli attachment on the pasta machine or cut each piece of dough into 16 rectangles about 2½ × 3 inches. Use 2 to 3 teaspoons of filling for each.

This can be served as a first course for eight; double the number of asparagus spears or scallions.

Makes 4 servings as a main course

Sauce:
2 teaspoons canola oil

2 cloves garlic, minced

½ cup minced onion

2 cups peeled and chopped fresh
   tomatoes

1½ teaspoons chopped fresh basil or
   oregano or ¼ teaspoon dried

¼ cup snipped chives

Dough:
1¾ cups all-purpose flour, plus some
   for kneading

2 eggs

1 egg white

Filling:
1½ cups cooked and pureed pumpkin
   (canned is fine)

1 egg white

2 cloves garlic, minced

Salt and white pepper to taste

¼ teaspoon ground nutmeg

¼ teaspoon dried marjoram

1 egg white, slightly beaten, to seal
   ravioli

12 spears trimmed asparagus or green
   onions, for garnish

To make sauce: Heat oil in a nonstick frying pan. Sauté garlic and onion over medium heat until tender, about 5 minutes. Stir in tomatoes, basil or oregano, and chives. Cook just until tomatoes are heated through.

To prepare dough: Place flour, eggs, and egg white in the bowl of a food processor fitted with the steel blade. Process only 10 to 12 seconds, or until dough forms a ball. Dough should be pliable but dry. If it is sticky, knead in a little more flour by hand. Cover dough and allow to rest for 20 minutes.

While dough is resting, combine pumpkin, egg white, garlic, salt, pepper, nutmeg, and marjoram in a bowl. Cover filling and refrigerate until needed.

Divide dough into 4 portions. Knead each piece on a lightly floured board or pastry cloth until smooth, keeping unused portions of dough covered with a damp cloth until needed.

At this point you can roll dough by hand or in a pasta machine according to manufacturer's directions. We rolled the pasta by machine.

Roll 1 piece of dough at a time, as thinly as possible. Brush off excess flour. Gather dough scraps and reroll.

Use a sharp knife or pizza or ravioli cutter to cut dough into 4 large rectangles, about 5 inches by 6 inches. Repeat with remaining dough to make 16 large rectangles in all.

Place about 2½ to 3 tablespoons filling in the center of half the pieces of dough. Moisten edges with egg white. Set second piece of dough on top. Press edges firmly with fingers or the tines of a fork to seal. At this point, ravioli can be cooked immediately or dried slightly for later cooking. To dry them, arrange in a single layer on a rack that has been lightly sprayed with nonstick cooking spray. Let dry for 1 hour, then refrigerate, still on rack. Ravioli should be cooked the same day they are made.

Bring 8 quarts of lightly salted water to a rolling boil. Add asparagus spears or green onions. Blanch asparagus for 1 minute or green onions for 30 seconds. Remove with a slotted spoon and set aside. Arrange asparagus spears or green onions in a fan shape in the center of 4 plates.

When the water in the pot returns to a boil, add ravioli. Cook for 3 to 5 minutes, or until tender. Drain.

Place 2 ravioli on each plate, overlapping slightly in center and making sure asparagus tips or ends of green onions peek out from under ravioli. Spoon sauce over ravioli.

Serve immediately.

343 calories, 6 g fat, 1 g saturated fat, 106 mg cholesterol, 5.5 g dietary fiber, 216 mg sodium

OPEN-FACE CHEDDAR AND
FARMSTAND TOMATO SANDWICHES

This is *the* sandwich to have when the first giant, juicy beefsteak tomatoes hit the roadside stands and farmers' markets.

Makes 4 servings

4 teaspoons sharp brown mustard
4 slices Milwaukee Potato Bread
(page 199) or bread of your choice
4 slices (1 ounce each) reduced-fat
Wisconsin Cheddar cheese
4 slices ripe beefsteak tomato, or
8 slices from smaller tomatoes

2 teaspoons unsalted butter or
margarine
1 red onion, sliced thin and separated
into circles
¼ cup chopped fresh parsley

Spread 1 teaspoon mustard on each slice of bread. Top with a slice of cheese, then a slice or two of tomato.

Heat butter in a large nonstick frying pan that has been sprayed with butter-flavored nonstick cooking spray. Add sandwiches and fry until golden brown on the bottom and cheese is soft and warm. Remove from frying pan with a spatula.

Place sandwiches on plates. Sprinkle with onion slices and parsley. Serve immediately.

351 calories, 11.5 g fat, 4.5 g saturated fat, 25 mg cholesterol, 3 g dietary fiber, 355 mg sodium

Paint It Orange

Let Vermonters eat those pale white Cheddars. In Wisconsin, Cheddar is orange. The practice of coloring the cheese probably began because milk tends to be paler in the summer, and cheese makers and their customers wanted consistency. Natural vegetable dyes are used to dye Cheddar orange.

Midwesterners also like their Cheddars mellow. Wisconsin Cheddars can age for three or four years and still lack the mouth-puckering sharpness of their eastern kin.

"Cheddar," by the way, refers to a process, not a cheese culture. After they're cut, the slabs of curd are cheddared, or stacked on top of one another, and turned regularly to drain off the whey.

Colby, a mildly flavored orange cheese that originated in Wisconsin, is made with the same cultures as Cheddar but is not cheddared.

A Seedy Lot

Imagine Virginia's surprise when she learned that the brown, fine-grained, zesty mustard she'd known as Belgian mustard while growing up (there are Flemish branches on her dad's side of the family tree) is actually German mustard. Or is it French? No doubt the Austrians, Dutch, and Lux-embourgers claim it as well.

By whatever name you call it, the European-style brown mustard, which can be bought smooth or coarse with whole seeds, is found in refrigerators all over the Midwest. Its hot sharpness makes it the ideal partner for sturdy bread, robust cheeses such as Cheddar, and pungent vegetables such as brussels sprouts and sauerkraut. It's also nice in a vinaigrette for potato salad.

BARBECUED BEAN SANDWICHES

Carbondale, Illinois, is home to Southern Illinois University and its medical school, where Barbara's daughter, Dorothy, is a student. It is also the capital of Downstate Illinois "bar-bee-cue," including a hefty sandwich served with a side of barbecued beans—flavored like chili—and coleslaw.

We like those beans so much we've decided to make a sandwich out of them.

Makes 4 servings

2 cups cooked red kidney beans (if
    canned, drain and rinse)
3 cloves garlic, minced
½ cup minced green onion
½ cup old-fashioned uncooked oats
2 teaspoons chili powder
1½ teaspoons cumin
¼ teaspoon salt
⅛ teaspoon pepper

3 tablespoons tomato paste
1 tablespoon canola oil
4 Fluffy Buns (page 136) or whole
    wheat hamburger buns
Barbecue Sauce with Beer (recipe
    follows)
1 cup radish sprouts or sprouts of your
    choice

Mash beans in a deep bowl. Mix in garlic, onion, oats, chili powder, cumin, salt, pepper, and tomato paste. Let stand for 20 minutes so oats soften and flavors blend. Shape into 4 patties.

Heat oil over medium heat in a nonstick frying pan that has been sprayed with nonstick cooking spray. Cook patties, turning once, until crusty on both sides and heated through.

Slather cut sides of buns generously with barbecue sauce. Place patties on bottoms of buns. Top with sprouts. Replace top half of each bun. Serve in buns, with or without a side of coleslaw.

With sauce: 529 calories, 8 g fat, 1 g saturated fat, 2 mg cholesterol, 13 g dietary fiber, 917 mg sodium

BARBECUE SAUCE WITH BEER

Makes 4 servings

½ cup ketchup
½ cup flat beer
2 teaspoons stone-ground mustard
¼ cup molasses

1 teaspoon Worcestershire sauce (see
    Note on page 112)
½ teaspoon ground cumin
⅛ teaspoon ground cinnamon

In a small saucepan, stir together ketchup, beer, mustard, molasses, Worcestershire sauce, cumin, and cinnamon. Bring sauce to a boil over medium heat. Reduce to a simmer and continue cooking for 5 minutes, stirring occasionally. Taste and adjust seasonings.

Cool. Cover and refrigerate until serving time.

102 calories, no fat, no cholesterol, no dietary fiber, 418 mg sodium

PEPPER AND EGG SANDWICHES

This recipe is inspired by a specialty that many of Chicago's Italian sandwich shops serve on Fridays during Lent. It's so popular that some eateries serve it all the time, to plenty of folks who are not the slightest bit Italian.

Makes 4 servings

4 French-bread or Italian-bread rolls
1 tablespoon olive oil
3 to 4 cloves garlic, finely minced
1 cup thinly sliced onion
2 green bell peppers, cored, seeded, and
    thinly sliced
2 tablespoons water
2 eggs

4 egg whites, or ½ cup egg substitute
½ teaspoon dried oregano
½ teaspoon seasoned salt, or
    ¼ teaspoon regular salt
¼ teaspoon black pepper
1 tablespoon freshly grated Parmesan
    cheese

Split rolls and open like a book. Toast in a preheated 375° oven until crusty and beginning to turn golden, 5 to 8 minutes.

Heat oil in a nonstick skillet that has been sprayed with nonstick cooking spray. Add garlic, onion, and green pepper. Sauté for 4 to 5 minutes over medium heat, until onion begins to turn golden. Add water and cover pan until onion and peppers soften, 2 to 3 minutes. Beat together eggs, egg whites, oregano, salt, and pepper. Add to green peppers and onion, and cook, stirring, until eggs set. Stir in Parmesan.

Spoon egg mixture into rolls. Serve immediately.

351 calories, 10 g fat, 2.5 g saturated fat, 107 mg cholesterol, 1 g dietary fiber, 769 mg sodium

BERNICE'S RADISH AND EGG SANDWICHES

Virginia's maternal grandmother used to make her own version of egg sandwiches in the summer when she was too hot or busy to cook an elaborate lunch for her ten children. She would cook the eggs with radishes from her garden.

To make radish and egg sandwiches for 2: Chop up 3 or 4 radishes, the fresher the better, and a green onion. Film a nonstick skillet with oil and add the vegetables plus 1 egg and 2 egg whites (or replace both with ½ cup egg substitute). Scramble the eggs until softly set, then season with a bit of salt and pepper.

Take a couple of slices of bread—whole wheat or pumpernickel is nice—smear them thinly with unsalted butter if you like, then top with the egg-radish mixture.

These messy sandwiches should be eaten right away.

FREE-FORM COUNTRY PIE

As its name implies, this recipe allows plenty of creativity. We've flavored the crust with dill and combined three mushrooms in the filling, but you can use your favorite filling and flavor the crust accordingly.

You can make it like a pizza, flavoring the crust with dried oregano and smearing it lightly with pizza sauce; omit the bread crumbs. Fill with blanched, seasoned broccoli or lightly cooked spinach and sautéed mushrooms. Dust the top with a little grated low-fat mozzarella.

Makes 4 servings

Crust:

1¼ teaspoons active dry yeast	*2 teaspoons dill seeds or dried herbs of your choice*
½ teaspoon honey	
⅓ cup warm water (105° to 115°)	*2 egg whites*
1 cup bread flour, plus more as needed	*2 tablespoons canola oil*
½ cup whole wheat flour	*1 tablespoon warm skim milk*
¼ teaspoon salt	

Three-mushroom filling:

1 tablespoon unsalted butter or margarine	*6 ounces oyster mushrooms, cleaned*
4 large shallots, minced	*1 cup chopped red bell pepper*
1 pound white mushrooms, cleaned and sliced	*¼ teaspoon salt*
	¼ teaspoon pepper
6 ounces brown mushrooms, cleaned and sliced	*1 tablespoon crumbled dried sage leaves*
	1 cup whole wheat bread crumbs
	1 egg white, slightly beaten

Dissolve yeast with honey in warm water. Combine flours, salt, and dill seeds in the large bowl of a heavy-duty electric mixer. Add yeast mixture, egg whites, oil, and milk. Dough will be soft. If dough is sticky, add flour, by the tablespoonful, until dough is manageable but still soft. Knead dough only a few minutes until smooth and even.

Place dough in a bowl, cover lightly, and set aside in a warm place to rise until doubled in bulk, about 1 hour.

Punch dough down. Let rest for 10 minutes before rolling.

To make filling and assemble pie: Melt butter in a nonstick frying pan that has been sprayed with butter-flavored nonstick cooking spray. Add shallots and sauté for 3 minutes over medium heat, stirring occasionally. Add white and brown mushrooms. Cook over medium-low heat, covering pan if necessary, until mushrooms are cooked through; drain off liquid. Remove from heat and add oyster mushrooms, red pepper, salt, pepper, and sage.

Preheat oven to 400°.

Roll out dough to a 12- to 14-inch circle directly on a nonstick or greased and floured cookie sheet. (If you do not have a cookie sheet without sides, roll out the dough on a sheet of wax paper, then gently flip onto a baking sheet.)

Drain mushroom mixture. Sprinkle crumbs over crust. Arrange mushroom filling evenly over crust. Pull up 2 inches of dough around edges, pleating every 1 or 2 inches, to make a free-form "dish" for the filling. Brush rim of crust with slightly beaten egg white.

Bake for 15 minutes, or until crust is golden. Cut into wedges and serve hot.

384 calories, 12 g fat, 3 g saturated fat, 8 mg cholesterol, 7 g dietary fiber, 437 mg sodium

ROOT VEGETABLE PASTIES WITH SAFFRON CRUST

Pasties are hearty individual pies or turnovers, originally brought to Michigan's Upper Peninsula by the Cornish miners in the late 1800s.

You can also make these in miniature for appetizers. Wrap well, freeze, and reheat in the microwave or oven.

Serve any extra filling as a warm side dish.

Makes 8 servings

Crust:

3 cups all-purpose flour	*½ cup plain nonfat yogurt*
1 teaspoon baking powder	*⅛ teaspoon saffron*
¼ teaspoon salt	*4 to 6 tablespoons hot water*
¼ cup vegetable shortening	

Filling:

*1½ cups peeled and diced rutabaga or
  potato*
1 cup peeled and diced carrots
1 cup peeled and diced parsnips
1 tablespoon canola oil
1 cup coarsely chopped onion
2 cloves garlic, minced

⅓ cup egg substitute
*1 teaspoon minced fresh basil, or
  ½ teaspoon dried*
Salt and pepper to taste

1 egg white, lightly beaten

Use a food processor to prepare crust. Put flour, baking powder, salt, shortening, and yogurt in machine. Turn machine on and off until ingredients are mixed well. Soften saffron in 4 tablespoons hot water. With machine running, add hot saffron water to dough and continue processing, adding more hot water as necessary, until dough forms a ball, only a few seconds. Gather dough into a ball, cover, and chill for 20 minutes.

To prepare filling: Cook rutabaga, carrots, and parsnips together in lightly salted boiling water for 20 to 25 minutes, until tender. Drain and let cool.

Heat oil in a nonstick frying pan that has been sprayed with nonstick cooking spray. Add onion and garlic, and sauté for 5 minutes over medium heat until softened, covering pan if necessary to sweat them. Put cooked vegetables and sautéed onion and garlic in a bowl together. Chop vegetables in a food processor for just a few seconds. Mix in egg substitute, basil, salt, and pepper.

Divide dough in half. Roll one half out on a lightly floured board or pastry cloth. Cut 4 circles, each about 5 inches in diameter. Repeat with remaining dough.

Preheat oven to 400°.

Roll each piece of dough to a 6- to 6½-inch circle. Spoon ¼ cup filling onto bottom half of each circle. Use water to moisten edges of dough. Fold dough over and crimp edges, pleating as necessary and pressing them together to seal. Set pastries on a nonstick cookie sheet. Brush with egg white. Bake for 40 minutes, or until crust is a light golden brown. Serve hot.

300 calories, 9 g fat, 2 g saturated fat, 0.5 mg cholesterol, 4 g dietary fiber, 175 mg sodium

WARM BEAN AND TOMATO SALAD WITH HONEY-MUSTARD DRESSING

According to one story, the navy bean got its name during the War of 1812 when Captain Oliver H. Perry was pursuing the British in the Great Lakes and fed his sailors plenty of white beans, which kept well at sea.

Michigan and the northern Plains states such as North Dakota are the leading producers of the navy bean and its close cousin, the Great Northern bean. Both are pearly white and mildly flavored, but the Great Northern is slightly larger.

Use the best, juiciest tomatoes you can find in this salad—either warm from your garden or from the farmers' market. If you must buy them in a store, try to get organically grown tomatoes, which generally are higher quality.

Makes 4 servings

Bean and Tomato Salad:

2 teaspoons olive or canola oil

4 cloves garlic, minced

⅓ cup chopped shallots

1 cup cooked and drained navy or Great Northern beans (rinse well if canned)

½ cup minced fresh parsley

1½ cups seeded and chopped ripe tomatoes

⅛ teaspoon red pepper flakes

¼ teaspoon salt

¼ teaspoon freshly ground pepper

Dressing:

3 tablespoons balsamic vinegar or red wine vinegar

2 teaspoons honey mustard

3 tablespoons olive oil or canola oil

1½ teaspoons chopped fresh basil, or ¾ teaspoon dried

Salt and pepper to taste

4 cups bite-size pieces washed, dried romaine lettuce

To make the salad: Heat oil in a nonstick frying pan that has been sprayed with nonstick cooking spray. Sauté garlic and shallots about 3 minutes over medium heat.

Stir in beans and parsley. Add tomatoes and pepper flakes. Season with salt and pepper. Remove from heat.

To make the dressing: Whisk vinegar and mustard together in a small bowl. Slowly whisk in the oil, basil, salt, and pepper. Taste and adjust seasonings.

Toss beans with dressing and lettuce. Divide salad among individual plates. Serve warm with a crusty whole wheat bread.

214 calories, 13 g fat, 2 g saturated fat, no cholesterol, 6 g dietary fiber, 315 mg sodium

RISOTTO WITH ASPARAGUS AND MORELS

Nothing says spring in Michigan better than asparagus and morels. Wild rice, another midwestern delicacy, is not traditional to risotto but adds a wonderful nutty flavor and chewy texture.

To make risotto in the pressure cooker or microwave, see page 119; use 3 to 3½ cups stock. We made this risotto with dried morels, which are available year-round in specialty shops and some supermarkets.

Makes 4 servings

6 medium morels, fresh or dried
½ cup wild rice
Vegetable stock (page 17) or equal parts canned vegetable broth and water
1 bunch asparagus, cut into 1-inch pieces (about 2 cups)
2 teaspoons unsalted butter or margarine

2 teaspoons olive oil
1 cup finely chopped red onion
1 cup Italian Arborio rice
1 tablespoon minced fresh marjoram or 1 teaspoon dried
1 teaspoon salt
2 tablespoons nonfat sour cream (optional)
Pepper to taste

If using fresh morels, trim stems and soak caps for 10 minutes in salted water. (This helps rid them of bugs.) Rinse under cold water and pat dry.

Cut each cap into several pieces.

If using dried morels, soak in warm water to cover for 20 to 30 minutes, until softened. Strain soaking liquid into a measuring cup. Cut caps into several pieces.

Place wild rice and ½ cup vegetable stock or water in a microwave-proof bowl. Microwave on high (100 percent) for 5 minutes. Set aside.

Blanch asparagus in a pot of boiling water for 1 minute; drain and rinse under cold water. Set aside.

In a saucepan, bring 4½ cups vegetable stock—or the morel soaking liquid and enough stock to equal 4½ cups—to a boil. Keep hot over a low flame.

Heat butter and oil in another 4- to 6-quart heavy-bottomed saucepan. Add onion and morels, and sauté until onion softens. Stir in Arborio rice, wild rice, and marjoram. Stir in 1 cup of hot stock and salt. Cook over low heat, stirring frequently, until stock is absorbed. Repeat with 3 more cups stock, 1 cup at a time. When risotto is done, the rice will be cooked through but slightly chewy, and suspended in a creamy sauce. If necessary, stir in up to ½ cup more stock to achieve this consistency.

Stir in asparagus and sour cream. Season with pepper.

Spoon risotto onto plates or into shallow soup bowls. Serve immediately.

337 calories, 5.5 g fat, 1.5 g saturated fat, 5 mg cholesterol, 2.5 g dietary fiber, 765 mg sodium

Mad About Morels

When May rolls around, you'll see a number of people roaming the woods in Michigan and thereabouts. They trip over tree roots as they attempt to walk while peering at the ground. They creep out of the house shortly after dawn, carrying wicker baskets and brown paper bags. They brandish pocket knives.

The object of this intense activity is *Morchella esculenta*—the morel, for short. This wild fungus, which is distributed throughout North America and, yes, much of the temperate world, pops up in the northern Midwest in May. It's the state mushroom of Minnesota, and the object of the annual World Mushroom Hunting Championship in Boyne City, Michigan, which draws people from all over the country.

The morel has a whimsically conical, pitted cap that looks like a hat for a gnome. But it's the fungus's flavor that woos people. Morels are rich and nutty, with traces of earthiness and green pepper.

Virginia still remembers, with great wistfulness, the two years when morels popped up, like magic, in her backyard. The next year they were gone—just like that. Morels are capricious, and hunters never count on their coming up in exactly the same place year after year.

Maybe that's why they inspire fanatical devotion: They play hard to get.

TOASTED ALMOND TABBOULEH

Tabbouleh, a Middle Eastern summer salad of finely cracked wheat and parsley, has grown popular in the United States, especially in the Midwest, which has a sizable Arab population. You can buy tabbouleh mixes, complete with cracked wheat and dried herbs, in many supermarkets. However, tabbouleh is supposed to be a *fresh* salad, with plenty of parsley. If you can't find plain bulgur (try the health-food store), buy boxed tabbouleh and save the dried spice packet for something else.

Be sure to use the finely cracked bulgur suitable for salads. The coarser grind is for cooking.

Makes 4 servings

1 scant cup fine bulgur (cracked wheat)
1 cup cold water
½ cup finely chopped Italian (flat-leaf) parsley or more if desired
2 tablespoons finely chopped fresh mint (optional)
2 green onions, including green tops, finely diced
2 tablespoons lemon juice

2 tablespoons extra-virgin olive oil
½ teaspoon salt
Pinch of red pepper
2 tablespoons toasted, finely chopped blanched almonds
1 small tomato, seeded and chopped
Shredded romaine lettuce
1 cucumber, preferably seedless
Lemon wedges for garnish

Place bulgur in a bowl and stir in cold water. Let stand for 30 minutes, or until bulgur has completely absorbed liquid. Fluff with a fork. Stir in parsley, mint if using, green onions, lemon juice, oil, salt, and red pepper. At this point, tabbouleh may be refrigerated for up to 4 hours.

Just before serving, stir almonds and tomato into tabbouleh. Line a platter with lettuce. Remove alternating strips of peel from cucumber to give it a striped look, then thinly slice. Arrange cucumber slices toward the outside of platter. Mound tabbouleh in center of platter and garnish with lemon wedges.

221 calories, 9.5 g fat, 1 g saturated fat, no cholesterol, 8 g dietary fiber, 282 mg sodium

PAD THAI, CHICAGO STYLE

We all need our little rituals. Virginia's is to have pad Thai—spicy rice noodles redolent of garlic, with peanuts, bean sprouts, and cilantro—for lunch every Tuesday. The pad Thai she likes best is what she calls Chicago style—orange, brawny, and bold, with enough garlic to turn heads when she walks into a room with it.

To our mind the best pad Thai is made with nam pla, Thai fermented fish sauce. It smells about as awful as you think it would but adds deliciously salty-pungent flavor overtones. It is, of course, not vegetarian. If you're a strict vegetarian or you can't get Thai fish sauce (a facsimile can be made by steeping a couple of anchovy fillets in soy sauce), substitute soy sauce.

Makes 4 to 5 servings

1 pound ¼–inch–wide rice noodles

4 ounces firm tofu or 2 egg whites plus
   ½ egg yolk

2½ tablespoons fish sauce or soy sauce

3 tablespoons sugar

¼ cup ketchup

7 tablespoons rice vinegar

1 to 2 teaspoons red chile paste (or
   omit in the recipe and serve on the
   side)

2 tablespoons canola oil

1 packed tablespoon crushed garlic
   or 2 tablespoons minced garlic
   (8 to 10 cloves)

1 cup fresh bean sprouts, rinsed

4 green onions, thinly sliced

3 tablespoons finely chopped unsalted
   peanuts

3 tablespoons finely chopped fresh
   cilantro

Place noodles in a large bowl. Add hot water to cover and let soak for 30 minutes, or until softened.

If using tofu, cut into slices about ¼ inch thick. Squeeze tofu slices between paper towels to press out some of the liquid. Generously coat a small nonstick skillet with nonstick cooking spray. Add tofu and cook over medium heat, turning once, until lightly browned, about 7 to 8 minutes. Remove to a plate and cut into narrow strips. Set aside.

If using egg, beat whites and half egg yolk together, then pour into a small nonstick skillet coated with nonstick cooking spray. Cook until egg is set. Let cool, then cut into narrow strips. Set aside.

Mix fish sauce, sugar, ketchup, vinegar, and chile paste. Set sauce aside.

Heat a wok or deep, heavy skillet until nearly smoking. Add oil and heat until nearly smoking. Add garlic and stir-fry about 10 seconds, until fragrant. Add sauce and cook, stirring once or twice, about 2 minutes, until syrupy.

Add noodles and cook over high heat, tossing, for 3 to 4 minutes, until soft and thoroughly coated with sauce. Remove from heat and stir in bean sprouts, onions, tofu or egg, and peanuts. Sprinkle with cilantro.

Serve immediately with additional chile paste on the side.

Note: For a more authentic pad Thai, substitute 3 tablespoons chopped Thai pickled turnip (available in Asian groceries) for the ketchup.

For 5 servings: 507 calories, 12 g fat, 1 g saturated fat, no cholesterol, 2 g dietary fiber, 664 mg sodium

SLOW-BAKED SAUERKRAUT WITH CARROTS AND APPLES

This dish would be appropriate for a celebration of Oktoberfest, a German-inspired harvest festival that's a staple on the autumn calendars of many a midwestern city and town.

Makes 4 servings

1½ cups diced red potatoes

1 tablespoon unsalted butter or margarine

1 cup sliced onion

1 cup sliced cooking apples

2 cups grated carrots

1 pound sauerkraut, drained and rinsed

4 bay leaves

1 tablespoon juniper berries

½ teaspoon salt

½ teaspoon pepper

10 to 12 ounces smoked tofu (page 16) or plain tofu, firm or extra-firm, cut into ½-inch slices

1 cup dry white wine

Cook unpeeled potatoes in water to cover until tender but firm, about 10 minutes, then drain.

Melt butter or margarine in a nonstick frying pan that has been sprayed with nonstick cooking spray. Sauté onion for 3 to 4 minutes over medium heat, stirring occasionally. Stir in apple slices and cook for 2 minutes. Put apples and onion in a 9-by-13-inch ovenproof casserole.

Preheat oven to 325°.

Toss onion and apples with carrots and sauerkraut. Add bay leaves, juniper berries, salt, and pepper. If using unsmoked tofu, wrap a thick paper towel around each slice and gently but firmly press tofu between palms of hands to squeeze out moisture. Add tofu and wine to sauerkraut and vegetables.

Bake, covered, for 30 minutes. Uncover and continue baking for 2 hours. Stir casserole 2 or 3 times during cooking. If it starts to dry out, add a little more wine or some water.

Discard bay leaves. Serve hot.

236 calories, 7.5 g fat, 2.5 g saturated fat, 8 mg cholesterol, 7 g dietary fiber, 700 mg sodium

ROASTED CARROT AND POTATO CASSEROLE

Thanks to all the carrots, this casserole is sweet—even before you add the honey—and extremely rich in beta-carotene.

To make this dish even better, spoon Savory Potato Pudding (page 193) over the top about 35 to 40 minutes before end of baking time. Continue baking, uncovered, until crust is golden.

Makes 4 servings

1 cup chopped onion
¼ pound dried pitted prunes or
  apricots
2 large white potatoes, washed, peeled,
  and cut in 1-inch pieces
¼ cup golden raisins
1 pound carrots, sliced
2 large sweet potatoes, washed, peeled,
  and cut in 1-inch pieces

3 tablespoons honey
½ cup sweet red wine
3 tablespoons lemon juice
1 cup vegetable stock (page 17) or
  canned broth

Preheat oven to 350°.

Spray a bowl-shaped, 2-quart lidded casserole with nonstick cooking spray. Mix all ingredients in casserole. Tightly cover casserole and bake in center of oven for 1½ hours.

Uncover. Stir ingredients, taste and adjust seasonings, and continue cooking for 1 more hour. Vegetables will be very soft and some will be crushed.

380 calories, 1 g fat, no saturated fat, no cholesterol, 10.5 g dietary fiber, 312 mg sodium

SAVORY POTATO PUDDING

Barbara's mother taught her to make tzimmes, the Jewish holiday stew on which the carrot casserole on page 192 is based, with a savory crust of potato pudding. Spoon it over the casserole 35 to 40 minutes before end of baking time.

Makes 4 servings

1½ pounds baking potatoes,
   peeled
½ cup grated onion
1 clove garlic, minced
½ cup egg substitute

2 egg whites
½ cup unsalted matzo meal or all-
   purpose flour
¼ teaspoon salt
¼ teaspoon pepper

Grate potatoes and mix with onion. Stir in garlic, egg substitute, egg whites, matzo meal or flour, salt, and pepper.

    Spoon it into an 8-inch-square baking pan that has been sprayed with nonstick cooking spray and bake at 400° for 45 minutes, or until golden.

240 calories, 2 g fat, 0.5 g saturated fat, no cholesterol, 2.5 g dietary fiber, 224 mg sodium

HOT GERMAN-STYLE POTATO SALAD

This popular Midwest sweet and sour salad is best served right away so the potatoes stay firm.

Makes 4 servings as a main course

24 new red potatoes
2 tablespoons olive or canola oil
¼ cup finely diced smoked tofu
   (optional, page 16)
1 red onion, minced
1 cup vegetable stock (page 17)

1 tablespoon cornstarch
2 tablespoons red wine or cider vinegar
2 teaspoons sugar
¼ teaspoon dried thyme
1 bay leaf
Salt and pepper to taste

Cook potatoes in lightly salted boiling water until they can be pierced easily with a knife but are still firm. Remove from heat and rinse under cold water. Cut in halves or quarters, depending on size, and place in a serving bowl.

While potatoes are cooking, prepare dressing. Heat oil in a nonstick frying pan that has been sprayed with nonstick cooking spray. Add tofu if using and cook until golden. Add onion and sauté over medium heat, stirring occasionally, until soft. Add all but 2 tablespoons of stock and bring to a simmer. Whisk cornstarch into remaining stock. Stir into mixture in skillet, then stir in vinegar, sugar, thyme, bay leaf, salt, and pepper. Simmer, covered, for 2 to 4 minutes, until thickened. Discard bay leaf. Toss potatoes with hot dressing. Serve at once.

286 calories, 8 g fat, 1 g saturated fat, no cholesterol, 3 g dietary fiber, 146 mg sodium

WHOLE CABBAGE STUFFED WITH SPINACH AND WILD RICE

When you slice into this cabbage, you see a gorgeous tweed filling flecked with green.

To give the rice a deeper, nuttier flavor, toast it before cooking. Heat the rice in a dry skillet over medium heat until it turns golden and begins to smell toasted. Then cook as usual.

For a more traditional stuffed cabbage, see Sweet-and-Sour Stuffed Cabbage Rolls, page 195.

Makes 6 servings

1 head (about 3 pounds) cabbage

Filling:

1¾ cups cooked brown rice

¾ cup cooked wild rice

¼ cup chopped fresh parsley

½ cup egg substitute, or 1 egg and
1 egg white

1 package (10 ounces) frozen chopped
spinach, thawed and squeezed dry
with paper towels

½ teaspoon salt

3 cloves garlic, very finely minced

¼ teaspoon pepper

¾ cup water

Tomato sauce:

1 tablespoon olive oil

½ cup chopped onion

1 can (14½ ounces) crushed tomatoes

2 tablespoons lemon juice

2 teaspoons chopped fresh basil, or
1 teaspoon dried

¼ teaspoon salt and pepper

Remove any bruised outer leaves of cabbage. Place whole cabbage in lightly salted boiling water to cover. Cover pan, reduce heat to medium, and cook for 5 minutes. Drain and cool. Core cabbage and remove inside of cabbage, leaving a ½- to 1-inch-thick shell. Reserve insides of cabbage for another use, such as soup.

Mix together brown and wild rice, parsley, egg substitute, spinach, salt, garlic, and pepper. Stuff cabbage with rice mixture.

Preheat oven to 350°. Carefully place cabbage in a deep ovenproof casserole. Add water. Cover casserole and bake for 25 minutes, or until cabbage is tender.

While cabbage is cooking, prepare sauce. Heat oil in a nonstick pan that has been sprayed with nonstick cooking spray. Sauté onion until soft, about 5 minutes. Stir in remaining ingredients. Simmer for 5 minutes, stirring occasionally.

Remove cabbage to cutting board. Using a sharp knife or cleaver, cut cabbage into 6 wedges. Set a wedge on each dinner plate and spoon hot sauce over. Serve hot. This is good with potatoes.

193 calories, 4 g fat, 0.5 g saturated fat, negligible cholesterol, 7 g dietary fiber, 490 mg sodium

VARIATION: Sweet-and-Sour Stuffed Cabbage Rolls. The brown and wild rice filling is also nice in a more standard stuffed cabbage. Blanch the cabbage as directed, then peel off 8 of the larger leaves. Reserve the rest of the cabbage for another use.

Spoon the rice mixture onto leaves, then roll them up, tucking in ends to make bundles. Place, seam side down, in a 9-by-13-inch baking dish that has been sprayed with nonstick cooking spray.

Pour ¼ cup lemon juice over the cabbage rolls, then sprinkle with ¼ cup dark brown sugar and ½ cup gingersnap crumbs. Pour 1 can (28 ounces) crushed tomatoes and 1 cup tomato juice over cabbage rolls. Cover with aluminum foil and bake at 375° for 1 hour, then remove foil and bake another 30 minutes.

332 calories, 4 g fat, 0.5 g saturated fat, no cholesterol, 8 g dietary fiber, 819 mg sodium

FOUR-WAY CHILI

This Cincinnati favorite is a baroque variation on chili mac (chili with macaroni). A heap of pasta is topped with chili, cheese, and a sprinkling of chopped onion. Hints of chocolate and cinnamon are the secret ingredients in the bean chili.

Makes 4 servings

1 tablespoon olive oil
½ cup chopped onion
2 cloves garlic, minced
2½ cups cooked kidney beans, canned
   or cooked from dry, with
   ½ cup liquid
1 cup canned crushed tomatoes
1 teaspoon ground cinnamon
¼ teaspoon ground allspice

½ teaspoon salt
¼ teaspoon cayenne
¼ teaspoon dried thyme
½ teaspoon chocolate chips
8 ounces pasta (preferably whole
   wheat)
1 cup (4 ounces) grated part-skim
   mozzarella cheese
2 cups minced red onions

To make chili: Heat oil in a large heavy-bottomed saucepan that has been sprayed with nonstick cooking spray. Sauté onion and garlic, loosely covering pan if necessary, until softened. Stir occasionally. Add beans and liquid, tomatoes, spices, and chocolate chips. Continue cooking over medium heat, stirring occasionally, for 3 to 4 minutes. Crush some of the beans with the back of a spoon as chili cooks.

While chili is cooking, cook pasta in a large pot of lightly salted water just until tender. Drain. Divide pasta among plates or shallow soup bowls. Ladle chili over pasta, sprinkle with cheese, and top with red onions.

483 calories, 10 g fat, 4 g saturated fat, 15 mg cholesterol, 17 g dietary fiber, 586 mg sodium

"UNSTUFFING" WITH CARROT-MISO GRAVY

A vegetarian we know once said she encountered no problems hosting Thanksgiving; even when she used to serve turkey, people filled up on the side dishes. So she just started serving the side dishes and forgot the turkey.

We feel much the same way about stuffing: Why stuff it into anything? This "unstuffing" has the bread, the sage, the onions—all the stuff that makes it such a popular comfort food for any time of year.

Although the miso is optional—you can replace it with 1 tablespoon soy sauce—its "winey" saltiness and sweetness give the gravy a greater depth of flavor. See Miso Magic (page 199).

Makes 8 servings

10 slices stale whole wheat bread or a mixture of white and whole wheat, torn into small pieces (about 8 cups)
3 to 4 teaspoons poultry seasoning, to taste
1 teaspoon dried savory
¼ cup finely chopped fresh parsley
2 tablespoons canola oil
1 cup finely diced fresh mushrooms (preferably shiitake)

1 cup finely diced celery
1½ cups finely diced onions
½ cup egg substitute
1½ to 1¾ cups vegetable stock (page 17) or water
¼ teaspoon salt
Pepper to taste

Gravy:

2 teaspoons canola oil

1½ cups diced onions

3 cups vegetable stock (page 17), or
   2 cups canned broth diluted with
   1 cup water

1 small clove garlic (optional)

2 medium (5 to 6 ounces total) carrots,
   peeled and diced

Pinch of ground nutmeg

1½ tablespoons white miso

Preheat oven to 350°. Spray a 9-by-5-inch loaf pan, preferably nonstick, with nonstick cooking spray.

Place bread in a large bowl and toss with poultry seasoning, savory, and parsley. Set aside.

Heat oil in a medium frying pan. Add mushrooms, celery, and onions, and sauté until onions begin to soften. Add to bread mixture along with egg substitute and toss well.

Add enough stock to make a very moist mixture. Season with salt and pepper. Spoon mixture into loaf pan, then smooth top with the back of a spoon. Cover tightly with foil and bake for 30 minutes, then uncover and bake another 25 to 35 minutes, until top is browned and crusty.

While stuffing bakes, make the gravy: Heat oil in a nonstick frying pan or saucepan that has been sprayed with nonstick cooking spray. Add onions and cook over medium heat, stirring frequently, until golden. Stir in vegetable stock and bring to a boil. Add garlic, carrots, and nutmeg. Cook over low heat until carrots are very tender, about 30 minutes. Let cool slightly, then blend in a blender or food processor with miso until smooth.

When stuffing is done, remove from oven and let stand for 10 minutes. Cut into slices and spoon some of the carrot-miso gravy over each slice. (If necessary, reheat gravy briefly over a low flame or in the microwave on 70 percent power.)

214 calories, 8 g fat, 1 g saturated fat, no cholesterol, 5 g dietary fiber, 844 mg sodium

Miso Magic

Given the acreage devoted to soybeans in the Midwest, it's ironic that so much of it goes to livestock instead of people. However, soy products such as tofu and miso are winning a lot of respect for their healthful properties. For one thing, they're the only foods that contain significant amounts of genistein, a possible cancer fighter. Soybean oil—which food processors use in everything from salad dressings to cakes—does not contain many of soy's healthful elements, which are found in the protein.

If you've eaten Japanese food, you've undoubtedly had miso, a fermented flavoring paste made from rice, soybeans, and other grains as well. Miso soup is commonly served as a first course in Japanese restaurants.

Miso's winey-sweet-salty flavor is not to everyone's taste. If you haven't yet met miso, start with light or white miso, also labeled *shiro miso,* which is the sweetest and most delicate. Use dark misos, often made with barley, to flavor robust soups and gravies.

Like yogurt, miso contains beneficial live cultures. It should not be boiled. Add it to foods just before serving. It's easier to dissolve miso if you mix it with a little of the hot soup, sauce, or gravy before adding it to the pot.

Breads and Desserts

MILWAUKEE POTATO BREAD

The potato is a very important vegetable in Milwaukee, Wisconsin, a city steeped in German ancestry. You can use leftover mashed potatoes in this moist, fairly sweet bread.

Makes 2 loaves; 24 servings

1 package (2¼ teaspoons) active dry
   yeast
1 teaspoon honey
1¼ cups warm water (105° to 115°)
5½ to 6 cups bread flour
¼ cup canola oil
⅓ cup sugar

¼ cup egg substitute, or 2 egg whites
1¼ cups plain mashed potatoes,
   slightly warm or at room
   temperature
½ teaspoon salt
⅓ cup sunflower seed kernels

Mix yeast and honey in ½ cup of the warm water and let stand until foamy. Mix in ⅔ cup flour. Place bowl in a warm place for 10 minutes, or until mixture becomes spongy and bubbly.

With an electric mixer, fitted with a dough hook, blend oil, sugar, yeast-honey mixture, egg substitute, potatoes, and salt. Blend in about 5 cups flour alternately with remaining water to make a soft dough. Knead until smooth and elastic, working in a little additional flour if necessary. Turn out onto a floured board and knead in sunflower kernels by hand, reserving 1 tablespoon sunflower kernels for top of loaf.

Place dough in an oiled bowl, cover with a damp towel, and set aside in a warm place to rise until doubled in bulk, about 2 hours.

Punch dough down, divide in half, and place in 2 nonstick 9-by-5-inch loaf pans that have been sprayed with nonstick cooking spray. Sprinkle loaves with remaining 1 tablespoon of sunflower kernels.

Let dough rise until light, about 45 minutes to 1 hour.

Preheat oven to 350°. Set loaf pans in center of oven. Bake breads about 45 minutes, until they are golden and sound hollow when tapped. Cool for 5 minutes, then turn out of pans and finish cooling on a wire rack.

232 calories, 4 g fat, 0.5 g saturated fat, no cholesterol, 1.5 g dietary fiber, 66 mg sodium

SEMOLINA ROLLS WITH PARMESAN AND PEPPER

Semolina flour, used to make couscous and macaroni, is ground from the durum wheat that blankets much of North Dakota. Sometimes labeled pasta flour, it's sold in health-food stores, Middle Eastern or Indian stores, and specialty shops.

These rolls are inspired by two breads we've enjoyed in Chicago: a pepper-cheese loaf and a velvety semolina bread.

Makes 10 rolls

2⅔ cups fine semolina (pasta flour)
1 teaspoon active dry yeast
⅓ cup warm water (105° to 115°)
1 cup skim milk
Olive oil
1¼ teaspoons salt

1 to 1⅓ cups bread flour, plus more
  as needed
1 teaspoon cracked black pepper
Grated fresh Parmesan cheese
Cornmeal

Combine 1 cup semolina, yeast, and water in a small bowl to make a soft, sticky dough. Cover and let rise for 1 hour, or until light and spongy.

To make the dough: In the large bowl of an electric mixer fitted with the dough hook, mix the semolina-yeast mixture, milk, 1 tablespoon oil, and salt. Stir in remaining 1⅔ cups semolina, then enough bread flour to make a soft, slightly sticky dough. Knead by machine for 5 minutes, adding small amounts of bread flour as necessary to keep dough from sticking to bowl, until dough is smooth and elastic. Or mix and knead by hand.

Place dough in an oiled bowl, cover lightly, and set aside in a warm place to rise until doubled in bulk, about 1 to 3 hours. Punch dough down, sprinkle with pepper, and knead, incorporating as evenly as possible.

Divide dough into 10 pieces. Pat each piece into a rectangle. Sprinkle 2 teaspoons Parmesan evenly over each rectangle. Roll up tightly, starting with a long end, and tuck and smooth ends to make cigar-shaped rolls.

Sprinkle a baking sheet generously with cornmeal. Place rolls on baking sheet, cover loosely with plastic wrap, and let rise until light, 30 to 60 minutes.

Preheat oven to 400°. Lightly brush tops of rolls with oil. Bake for 15 minutes, then remove from baking sheet and place directly on oven rack. Bake another 5 minutes, or until crisp and golden. Remove to a rack to cool.

270 calories, 4 g fat, 1.5 g saturated fat, 4.5 mg cholesterol, 1.5 g dietary fiber, 373 mg sodium

APPLE BRAN MUFFINS

For a change of pace, serve these as a supper accompaniment. To rewarm the muffins, heat them in a 450–degree oven for 5 minutes.

Makes 12 muffins

2 cups All–Bran or 100% Bran
   breakfast cereal
1½ cups flour
½ cup sugar
1 teaspoon baking soda
1½ teaspoons baking powder
¼ teaspoon salt

¼ cup canola oil
¼ cup dark molasses
2 egg whites
1½ cups buttermilk
¾ cup golden raisins
2 cups peeled, chopped apples

In a deep bowl, combine cereal, flour, sugar, baking soda, baking powder, and salt. Stir in remaining ingredients; do not overmix. Let stand for 1 hour. (This allows cereal and flour to fully absorb the liquid, making for a more tender muffin.)

Preheat oven to 375°. Fit a muffin tin with paper liners. Ladle batter into muffin cups, filling almost to the top.

Bake for 20 to 25 minutes, until a tester or bamboo skewer inserted in the center comes out clean. Cool for 5 minutes, then remove muffins from tin and complete cooling on rack. Store in an airtight container.

239 calories, 5.5 g fat, 0.5 g saturated fat, 1 mg cholesterol, 6.5 g dietary fiber, 377 mg sodium

Snap and Crackle

In the late nineteenth century, an energetic twenty-something health reformer named Dr. John Harvey Kellogg took over a sanitarium in Battle Creek, Michigan, and promptly made it famous. Before long, Kellogg had begun marketing granola and cornflakes to the "hygiene" movement, which considered cereals an especially healthful breakfast.

Kellogg's success put Battle Creek on the map, won a cult of followers for "muscular vegetarianism," and inspired the birth of more than forty manufacturers of cereals and health foods. (One of the survivors was C. W. Post, makers of the popular Grape Nuts.)

Around the turn of the century, a Yale researcher conducting research on protein needs pitted hale, meat-eating Yale athletes against the sedentary, vegetarian staff of Kellogg's Battle Creek sanitarium in endurance tests. The vegetarians clearly emerged as the more fit of the two. Mainstream scientists and nutritionists, utterly convinced of the superiority of diets rich in animal protein, ignored the vegetarians' victory.

In 1984, Kellogg's decided to charge into the fray again by putting a message about fiber's possible links to cancer prevention on its boxes of All-Bran. At the time, government rules banned all health claims on food labels. Rather than telling the cereal company to cease and desist, however, the U.S. Food and Drug Administration decided to study the matter.

Eventually, the FDA's study led to new labeling regulations that do allow certain carefully worded health claims. Among them are fiber's possible links to cancer prevention.

Incidentally, the "Kellogg" that still graces billions of cereal boxes is based on the signature of John Harvey's younger brother Will. It was he who first realized the enormous potential of turning a small amount of cheap grain into a box of high-priced allure.

WHOLE WHEAT PITA BREAD

Thanks to the large Middle Eastern and Indian populations, a lot of the bread sold in Chicago is flat. As nice as bakery pita is, this popular flat bread is even better fresh from your oven.

Makes 12 pita breads

1 package (2¼ teaspoons) active dry
  yeast
1 teaspoon sugar
1 cup warm water (110°)

2 cups all-purpose flour
1 cup whole wheat flour
½ teaspoon salt
2 tablespoons olive oil

Dissolve yeast and sugar in warm water in a small bowl.

Mix all-purpose flour, whole wheat flour, salt, and oil in a large bowl. Make a well in the center of the flour mixture, pour the yeast mixture into the well, and stir until blended, making a soft dough. Or use an electric mixer with the dough hook attached.

Knead on a lightly floured surface until smooth, about 3 to 5 minutes.

Place the dough in a large bowl, cover with a damp towel, and let rise in a warm place until doubled in bulk, 1 to 1½ hours.

Punch dough down and knead again for 2 to 3 minutes. Divide dough into 12 equal parts, shape each part into a smooth ball, and set on a nonstick baking sheet. Cover the dough balls lightly with a clean towel and let stand for 20 minutes.

Preheat oven to 475°. Place a large ungreased nonstick baking sheet in the oven and heat for 10 minutes.

Use a rolling pin to pat or roll each ball of dough into a 5- or 6-inch round.

Arrange pita breads 2 inches apart on the preheated baking sheet. Bake on the lowest oven rack for 5 minutes, or until they are puffed and light brown.

Wrap the pita breads in a towel as they cool, about 5 minutes. Serve warm.

130 calories, 2.5 g fat, 0.5 g saturated fat, no cholesterol, 2 g dietary fiber, 90 mg sodium

CORNFLAKE-TOPPED NOODLE PUDDING

Noodle puddings are served all around the country, but it is only proper to use the recipe in the Midwest chapter because both the yolk-free noodles we use and the cornflakes are manufactured in the Midwest.

The pudding can be served as dessert or as a breakfast or brunch dish.

Makes 8 servings

3 ounces light cream cheese, at room
  temperature
1 cup egg substitute
¼ cup sugar
3 tablespoons melted unsalted butter or
  margarine, cooled

8 ounces yolk-free egg noodles
1 cup warm skim milk
¼ cup golden raisins

Topping:
2 tablespoons sugar
¾ teaspoon ground cinnamon
¼ teaspoon ground nutmeg

1 cup crushed cornflakes or other plain
  cereal

Grease an 8-inch-square nonstick baking pan.

Beat together cream cheese, egg substitute, sugar, and butter in a bowl.

Cook noodles just until tender, according to package directions. Drain. Stir cheese mixture into warm noodles. Mix in milk and raisins. Pour pudding into prepared pan.

Preheat oven to 350°.

To make topping: Toss sugar, cinnamon, nutmeg, and cornflakes together. Sprinkle over top of the pudding.

Bake for 30 minutes. Remove pudding from oven and cut into 8 pieces but do not remove from pan. Return it to the oven and bake another 30 minutes, or until firm. Serve warm or at room temperature.

Noodle pudding freezes well. Defrost before reheating.

272 calories, 8.5 g fat, 4.5 g saturated fat, 22 mg cholesterol, 1 g dietary fiber, 150 mg sodium

APPLE CURRANT CRISP

Oats give the topping for this crisp a good crunch and toasted-grain flavor. Use a good pie apple in this, such as Pippin, Wealthy, Greening, Northern Spy, Jonathan, or Ida Red.

Makes 8 servings

1 cup dry bread crumbs
⅓ cup old-fashioned oats
3 tablespoons all-purpose flour
¼ cup packed light brown sugar
2 tablespoons unsalted butter or
  margarine, cut into small pieces

4 cups peeled and diced apples
¾ cup fresh red currants or raspberries
½ cup granulated sugar
2 tablespoons cornstarch

Preheat oven to 350°. Spray an 8-inch nonstick baking pan with butter-flavored nonstick cooking spray. Sprinkle bread crumbs evenly over bottom of pan.

In a mixing bowl or the bowl of a food processor, combine oats, flour, and brown sugar. Cut in butter until mixture is crumbly.

Toss apples and currants with granulated sugar and cornstarch until well mixed. Spoon fruit into prepared baking pan. Sprinkle oat mixture evenly over fruit.

Bake, uncovered, in the center of the oven for 30 minutes, or until topping begins to turn golden and filling is bubbling hot.

Serve warm, with nonfat frozen vanilla yogurt or light ice cream.

216 calories, 4 g fat, 2 g saturated fat, 8 mg cholesterol, 3 g dietary fiber, 111 mg sodium

The Apple Man

One of America's most endearing eccentrics was Johnny Appleseed. Born John Chapman around 1774, he migrated westward from Massachusetts, planting apple seeds and pruning trees along the Ohio River and giving and selling apple seeds to travelers heading farther west.

Compassionate to the core, Johnny Appleseed was also a vegetarian. He strongly believed it was wrong to harm any of God's creatures and allegedly expressed deep sorrow after killing a rattlesnake that had bitten him.

Johnny made it as far west as Indiana. He died in Allen County in 1845. A statue commemorating him stands in Fort Wayne, Indiana, the county seat.

In his own way, the odd wanderer guaranteed his immortality. Orchardists estimated that by 1838 the seeds from his stock had grown into trees covering more than one hundred thousand square miles.

BERRY AND CHERRY COMPOTE WITH WHITE CHEESE MOUSSE

This easy, luscious summer dessert is from Carl Jerome at the Cooking and Hospitality Institute of Chicago, one of the oldest professional cooking, restaurant, and hotel management schools in America.

Dried tart cherries can be found in specialty shops, some supermarkets, or by mail; see Sources and Resources (page 329). The fresh berries can vary according to what's available.

Makes 6 servings

1 tablespoon finely chopped dried tart
   cherries
¼ cup Grand Marnier
1 pint fresh raspberries
1 pint fresh blackberries

1 pint fresh blueberries
4 to 5 tablespoons sugar, preferably
   superfine
½ cup light ricotta cheese
¼ cup light cream cheese

In a small glass or ceramic bowl, combine cherries and Grand Marnier and let stand until cherries soften, about 30 minutes.

Meanwhile, place raspberries, blackberries, and blueberries in a large bowl. Sprinkle with just enough sugar to lightly sweeten, about 1 to 2 tablespoons. Add cherries and gently toss. Cover and refrigerate until needed, 2 hours to overnight.

Combine ricotta, cream cheese, and 3 tablespoons sugar in a food processor or mixer bowl and blend thoroughly until mixture is very smooth and has the consistency of thick mayonnaise. Transfer to a covered bowl and refrigerate until needed.

To serve, toss the fruits, then arrange in 6 soup plates. Top each with a dollop of the cheese mousse. Set the soup plates on dinner plates and serve.

187 calories, 3 g fat, 1 g saturated fat, 6 mg cholesterol, 5.5 g dietary fiber, 34 mg sodium

MAPLE-SCENTED TROPICAL FRUITS DÉLICE

Traces of the tropics—a murmur of ginger here, a stroke of Gauguin color there—enliven the menu at Froggy's, a French cafe north of Chicago. That's no surprise: Chef Thiérry LeFeuvre once was chef to the governor of Tahiti. This dessert that he shared is gorgeous, easy to make, and virtually fat free.

The maple syrup is a midwestern touch; as far as we know, sugar maples don't grow in Tahiti.

Makes 4 servings

2 medium papayas
2 mangos
¼ to ½ cup skim milk
2 tablespoons maple syrup or honey

Pinch of ground cinnamon
Strips of lemon zest, fresh raspberries,
   and mint leaves for garnish

Cut the papayas in half lengthwise. Scoop out the seeds and discard. Carefully scoop out the flesh, leaving the shells intact.

Peel the mangos. Slice through each mango as close to the large pit as possible. Slice off each mango until it is free of the pit.

Cut half of the mango and papaya flesh into cubes. Place the remaining half in a food processor with ¼ cup skim milk, maple syrup, and cinnamon. Puree until smooth. You should have a thick, silky, smooth puree; add more milk if necessary. Mix puree with cubed fruits.

Place papaya shells on dessert plates and press to flatten slightly so they stand without tilting. Spoon fruits and puree into papaya shells. Garnish with lemon zest, raspberries, and mint leaves.

174 calories, 0.5 g fat, no saturated fat, 1 mg cholesterol, 6 g dietary fiber, 39 mg sodium

4

The West

Southwestern Breakfast for Four

Quesadillas with Tomato-Mango Salsa

Denver-style Egg White Omelet

Spicy Hashed Brown Potatoes

Pinto Quick Bread with Dates

Dinner in the Desert

Warm Fig Salad with Pine Nuts

Minted Garlic Tortilla Soup

Black Bean Crepes with Salsa Cruda

Coffee Flan

Après-Ski Party

Winter Vegetable Soup with Blue Cheese Croutons

Fettucine with Creamy Porcini-Sage Sauce

Dried Fruit Compote

Chocolate Cinnamon Meringue Peaks

Appetizers, Salads, and Side Dishes

Basic Southwest Beans

Baked Potato Wedges with Mustard and Rosemary

Warm Winter Lettuce with Sesame and Pickled Ginger Dressing

Soups

Quinoa, Barley, and Brown Mushroom Soup

Pozole (Mexican-style Hominy Soup)

Two-Chile Lentil and Shiitake Chili

Entrées

Salad of Orange Lentils and Brown Rice

Gingered Pinto Bean Salad

Bean Burritos with Tomatillo Sauce

Enchiladas with Roasted Peppers and Onions

Pan-fried Tofu with Pico de Gallo and Green Peppers

Layered Buckwheat-Ricotta Crepes with Tomato-Chive Salsa

Fire-roasted Sweet and White Potatoes and
Quinoa, Couscous, and Chickpea Packets

Grilled Peppers with Whiskey Black Beans and Radish–Jicama Salsa

Pan-fried Chiles Rellenos with Melon Salsa

Mashed Potato Cakes with Basque-style Tomato and Pepper Sauce

Texas Caviar Salsa on a Baked Potato

Scrambled Huevos Rancheros with Refried Beans

Vegetable Chili with an Herbed Cornbread "Hat"

Breads and Desserts

Flour Tortillas

Whole Wheat Tortillas

Corn Tortillas

Layered Canyon Cornbread with Dried Tomato Butter

Whole Wheat Sourdough Bread

Cinnamon Rolls

Trail Mix Truffles

Huckleberry Yogurt Pie

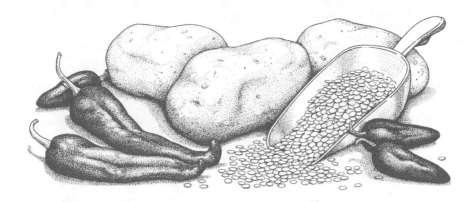

The West offers proof of just how restless a people we are. In the late nineteenth and early twentieth centuries, settlers pointed their covered wagons toward the setting sun in search of cheap land, gold, or just a change of landscape. Even today people from both coasts and the country's middle are heading West again, in search of mountain beauty, peace of mind, and high-tech jobs.

This has always been a land for folks who like the outdoors. The Native American peoples who weren't farming corn followed the buffalo from pasture to pasture. The settlers from the East tended toward outdoorsy occupations as well: panning gold, herding sheep, raising cattle.

Today, people may have jobs that keep them indoors, but on the weekends westerners golf, climb rocks and peaks, ski, or mountain-bike with a vengeance. Who can blame anyone for wanting to be outdoors where "purple mountain majesties" rise above the fruited plains?

It's no surprise that slow-simmering chili has reached the status of an art form in the West, that quick-cooking tortillas and long-rising sourdough—a bread you can leave until you get around to it—are staple breads, and that energy bars and trail mix never go out of fashion here.

The southern part is a beautiful desert of cliffs, bluffs, canyons, and mountains. Once owned by Mexico, the Southwest still favors the earthy and bold flavors of Mexican cooking, which in turn bears heavy influences of the native peoples: hominy, garlic, cumin, cinnamon, chocolate, beans, pumpkin, pine nuts, quinoa, amaranth, corn, and plenty of chiles.

The north's rugged mountains traditionally have seen plainer cooking. Except for that of the Basques, which is heavily accented with garlic, the cooking of the Rockies is the cooking of the Scandinavians, Germans, and Scots who settled there.

The volcanic soils of central Idaho proved to be the perfect home for the starchy potato that Luther Burbank developed. The giant russet Idaho baking potatoes are famous for their thick, crisp skin and fluffy flesh that was born to be baked, mashed, and turned into mountains of fast-food french fries.

The Palouse, an area straddling west-central Idaho and eastern Washington, grows just about all our lentils, plus beans and wheat.

Berries, cherries, and mushrooms thrive in the woods of Idaho and Montana. Colorado is experimenting with growing quinoa, a high-protein grain that thrives at high altitudes. Teff, a grain native to Ethiopia, and wild rice grow in northern Idaho.

The West also serves up evidence of humankind's amazing ability to transform landscapes for better or worse. Who could have dreamed that arid Arizona would become one of the country's biggest growers of lettuce?

With yet another influx of newcomers, western cooking continues to evolve. Fresh spring rolls have popped up alongside fajitas, and bagels are almost as common in some parts as rattlesnakes.

Southwestern chefs are adding Italian and Asian touches to foods that have been native American staples for centuries. Californians seeking a new paradise are bringing in espresso bars. New Yorkers and Chicagoans have brought a love of bagels and pizza with them to their new high-altitude nests.

New Age farmers are experimenting with organically grown heirloom seed crops. And yes, even here, smack in the middle of cattle country, vegetarianism has begun to make inroads. But with all those vibrant flavors, who'll miss the meat?

• SOUTHWESTERN BREAKFAST FOR FOUR •

The Southwest is America's Provence, complete with rugged landscape, brilliant sun, and flavors that linger long in the memory. The colors associated with southwestern decor are desert pastels, but the ingredients and flavors of southwestern cuisine—chiles, garlic, cinnamon, cumin, cilantro, corn, dried tomatoes, beans, dates—are as simultaneously bold and lyrical as a Georgia O'Keeffe painting.

This breakfast, suitable for those times when you have a couple of house guests, is a good candidate for alfresco dining on the patio or deck.

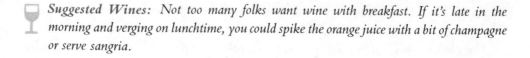 *Suggested Wines: Not too many folks want wine with breakfast. If it's late in the morning and verging on lunchtime, you could spike the orange juice with a bit of champagne or serve sangria.*

Quesadillas with Tomato-Mango Salsa

Quesadillas, or cheese-filled tortilla turnovers, are satisfying any time of day as a snack or appetizer. With a slightly sweet mango salsa, they're perfect for breakfast. Please note that the salsa needs to stand at least one hour before serving to let the flavors blend.

Makes 4 servings

Salsa:

1 cup chopped ripe tomatoes
¼ cup chopped green onion
2 tablespoons minced fresh cilantro
¾ cup chopped ripe mango

2 tablespoons lime juice
1 jalapeño pepper, seeded and minced
2 cloves garlic, minced

Quesadillas:

1¼ cups 1-percent cottage cheese or fat-free ricotta cheese
½ cup shredded reduced-fat Monterey Jack cheese
3 tablespoons diced mild or spicy chiles, such as finger peppers

½ teaspoon cumin seeds
4 corn or whole wheat flour tortillas about 7 inches wide

To make salsa: Combine all ingredients in a bowl. Stir, cover, and refrigerate. Let salsa stand for 1 hour or refrigerate up to 12 hours. Stir before serving.

To make quesadillas: In a small bowl, combine cottage cheese and Monterey Jack cheese with diced chiles and cumin seeds.

Spread each tortilla with the cheese mixture. Fold in half.

Heat a nonstick frying pan that has been sprayed with nonstick cooking spray.

Add quesadillas and cook on each side over medium heat until warm and beginning to brown. Serve warm with salsa on the side.

With salsa: 237 calories, 6 g fat, 3 g saturated fat, 16 mg cholesterol, 4 g dietary fiber, 541 mg sodium

Without: 177 calories, 5.5 g fat, 3 g saturated fat, 16 mg cholesterol, 2 g dietary fiber, 534 mg sodium

Denver-style
Egg White Omelet

For greater volume, always have egg whites at room temperature before beating.

Makes 4 servings

4 egg whites, at room temperature
1 cup egg substitute
1 tablespoon canola oil
½ cup minced onion
¾ cup cooked, diced, and cooled
    potato

½ cup diced green bell pepper
¾ cup diced firm tofu, preferably
    smoked (page 16)
½ teaspoon salt
¼ teaspoon white pepper

Beat egg whites until they stand in stiff, glossy peaks. Fold in egg substitute. Set aside.

Heat oil in a nonstick frying pan that has been sprayed with nonstick cooking spray. Cook onion over medium heat until soft, stirring occasionally and covering pan if necessary to soften onion. Stir in potato and bell pepper. Cook another 3 to 4 minutes. Gently stir in tofu and sprinkle with salt and pepper. Fold in egg mixture. As eggs set, fold over with a spatula. Eggs will have a somewhat "scrambled" look.

Cut omelet into slices and put on individual plates. Serve with Spicy Hashed Brown Potatoes (below).

156 calories, 6.5 g fat, 0.5 g saturated fat, 0.5 mg cholesterol, 1 g dietary fiber, 437 mg sodium

Spicy Hashed Brown
Potatoes

Makes 4 servings

2 large (¾ pound each) Idaho baking
    potatoes, baked or microwaved until
    nearly tender
½ teaspoon salt
½ teaspoon freshly ground black
    pepper

¼ to ½ teaspoon hot red pepper, to
    taste
¼ teaspoon ground coriander
1½ tablespoons olive or canola oil

Grate potatoes on the large holes of a hand grater or a food processor disk. Toss with salt, black pepper, red pepper, and coriander. Heat 1 tablespoon oil in a 10- to 12-inch nonstick frying pan that has been sprayed with nonstick cooking spray. Add potatoes in a single layer, flattening them into a cake. Cook over medium-high heat, uncovered, for 7 to 8 minutes. Do not stir.

When potatoes are nicely browned on the bottom, drizzle remaining oil over top. Flip potatoes—you'll have to break them up a bit to do this—and cook on the other side for 2 to 3 minutes, until golden. Serve warm.

235 calories, 5 g fat, 0.5 g saturated fat, no cholesterol, 4 g dietary fiber, 280 mg sodium

Pinto Quick Bread
with Dates

The beans are the "secret ingredient" in this dessert bread. Without imposing much of their own flavor, they make this spicy loaf moist and full-bodied.

Makes 1 loaf; about 12 servings

½ cup granulated sugar

¼ cup light brown sugar

¼ cup canola oil

1 cup cooked, drained, and pureed
   pinto beans (if using canned beans,
   drain and rinse well)

½ teaspoon salt

¾ cup buttermilk

¼ cup egg substitute

1¾ cups all-purpose flour

1 teaspoon baking powder

1 teaspoon baking soda

1 teaspoon ground cinnamon

¼ teaspoon freshly ground nutmeg

¼ teaspoon ground cloves

½ cup chopped dates

Preheat oven to 350°. Spray or grease a 9-by-5-inch loaf pan.

In the large bowl of an electric mixer, beat sugars with oil. Blend in beans, salt, buttermilk, and egg substitute. Mix in flour, baking powder, baking soda, spices, and dates. Spoon into pan.

Bake in the center of the oven for 50 minutes, or until a tester inserted in the center comes out dry. Cool for 5 minutes, then unmold onto a rack to finish cooling. Slice and serve cool.

201 calories, 5 g fat, 0.5 g saturated fat, 0.5 mg cholesterol, 3 g dietary fiber, 223 mg sodium

• DINNER IN THE DESERT •

One of our favorite things about the desert—just about any desert—is its intensity. It's a vast, unforgiving, humbling place that's home to cacti taller than a man, snakes that rattle, and flowers that stun the senses.

During the day, the baking heat rises off the parched earth in shimmering waves. The sky is very blue and very close. As the evening shadows lengthen, the heat lets go, and by nightfall the temperature plummets by twenty, thirty, or even forty degrees. If you're lucky enough to be well away from city lights, the stars burn in the pitch-black sky with a diamond-edged brilliance.

This intensely flavored, robust dinner warms body and soul on a crisp desert evening.

 Suggested Wines: The fig salad should be served alone. A buttery Chardonnay or a lighter red, such as a Merlot or Pinot Noir, would pair well with both the garlic soup and the crepes.

Fruits of the Desert

Not surprisingly, desert peoples long have harvested cacti, those superb water-storers, for food and liquid. Two parts of the Opuntia cactus family are still widely used as food: nopales (no-PAH-les), or nopalitos, also called cactus pads, and cactus pears, also called prickly pears and Indian pears.

Slippery like okra, with a tart, green-peppery flavor, nopales can be boiled, steamed, sautéed, fried, or used in soups. They go nicely with tomatoes and onions. The nopales available in supermarkets have had the stickers removed and generally need just a light peeling before cooking. They're available off and on from early spring through late fall.

Oval and 3 to 4 inches long, cactus pears—which are actually large berries—are available off and on in supermarkets from summer through early spring. The skin color ranges from a dull green to purplish. The watery, sweet flesh is a stunning deep rose and is filled with hard black seeds.

Cactus pear juice makes a gorgeous rosy-hued cocktail that can play as the opening act for this desert menu. For four cocktails: Cut two large cactus pears in half and spoon the pulp into a blender container. Add ¼ cup lime juice, 1 tablespoon orange liqueur, and 1 teaspoon sugar. Puree on high speed until liquefied. Push through a strainer to get rid of the seeds. Fill four small cocktail glasses with chipped or crushed ice. Pour ½ ounce (1 tablespoon) of tequila into each glass and then the cactus pear mixture.

Warm Fig Salad
with Pine Nuts

Makes 8 servings

8 cups washed and dried bite-size
   pieces of greens, such as oak leaf, red
   leaf, or Bibb lettuce
10 large fresh figs

2 cups 1% cottage cheese
3 tablespoons nonfat vanilla yogurt
¼ cup pine nuts, preferably toasted

Arrange lettuce on 8 salad plates.

Wipe figs using a damp paper towel. Warm figs in a 350° oven for 1 to 2 minutes.

Quarter 8 of the figs. Set 1 quartered fig on each lettuce-lined plate in the shape of an **X**.

Coarsely chop remaining 2 figs. In a food processor, puree cottage cheese, yogurt, and figs until smooth. Spoon mixture in the center of the plate. Sprinkle with pine nuts and serve immediately.

122 calories, 3 g fat, 1 g saturated fat, 2.5 mg cholesterol, 3 g dietary fiber, 237 mg sodium

Minted Garlic Tortilla Soup

Makes 8 servings

2 teaspoons olive oil

5 cloves garlic, crushed

¼ to ½ teaspoon salt

¾ cup fresh mint leaves

½ cup chopped fresh cilantro or parsley

4 cups cooked chickpeas (garbanzos)

1 quart vegetable stock (page 17) or
    3 cups canned broth and 1 cup
    water

1 tablespoon canola oil

4 flour tortillas

Heat olive oil in a nonstick frying pan that has been sprayed with nonstick cooking spray. Sauté garlic with salt for 2 minutes, stirring occasionally. Place sautéed garlic, mint, cilantro, and 3 cups of chickpeas in a food processor and puree until smooth. Place chick-pea puree in a soup pot. Stir in vegetable stock.

Bring soup to a boil, then reduce heat to a simmer. Add remaining 1 cup of chickpeas and cook to heat through.

While soup is heating, cook tortillas: Heat canola oil over medium heat in a nonstick frying pan that has been sprayed with nonstick cooking spray. Cook tortillas on each side until warm and beginning to brown. With kitchen shears or a pizza cutter, cut tortillas into strips.

Pour soup into bowls and sprinkle with tortilla strips. Serve hot.

227 calories, 6.5 g fat, 0.5 g saturated fat, no cholesterol, 6 g dietary fiber, 537 mg sodium

Black Bean Crepes
with Salsa Cruda

The salsa adds a splash of scarlet to the deep purplish-black crepes in this beautiful entrée. The next time you cook black beans, reserve some liquid for this recipe (it can be stored in an airtight container in the freezer). Do not use the liquid from canned beans, which is much too salty.

   You can eliminate the salsa and serve the crepes with a dollop of nonfat sour cream and some chopped fresh tomato.

Makes 8 servings (2 crepes per serving)

Salsa:

1½ cups peeled and chopped vine-
   ripened tomatoes
½ cup roasted, peeled, seeded, and
   chopped poblano pepper (page 14) or
   drained canned chiles

⅓ cup minced red onion
1 to 2 jalapeño peppers, seeded and
   chopped
¼ teaspoon salt

Crepes:

1¼ cups skim milk
1¼ cups liquid from cooked (not
   canned) black beans
2 egg whites
1¼ cups egg substitute
¾ cup cornstarch

¾ cup all-purpose flour
2 teaspoons minced fresh oregano, or
   1 teaspoon dried
¼ teaspoon salt (omit if using liquid
   from canned beans)
1 tablespoon canola oil

Filling:
3 cups Refried Beans (page 257)

To make salsa: Mix together all ingredients in a bowl. Cover and refrigerate until serving time. Toss salsa before serving. Taste and adjust seasonings.

To make crepes: Place all ingredients in a blender or food processor and blend a few seconds, just until smooth. Or sift flour with cornstarch and place in a bowl. Whisk in remaining ingredients until smooth.

Let batter stand for 20 minutes.

Heat a nonstick crepe pan that has been sprayed with nonstick cooking spray. Pour about 3 tablespoons of batter into pan (enough to cover bottom of pan). Tilt pan from side to side so that pan is covered with batter. If batter becomes too thick, add water, 1 tablespoonful at a time, until desired consistency.

Cook only until crepe is firm. Turn crepe over and cook until done. Stack crepes between sheets of aluminum foil or wax paper. (Crepes may be refrigerated or frozen at this point; reheat in a 300° oven.)

Heat refried beans either over low heat or in a microwave.

To serve, spoon about 3 tablespoons of hot refried beans in the center of each crepe and roll the crepe around the filling. Put 2 crepes on each plate (you may have some crepes left over). Spoon salsa on the crepes and serve.

291 calories, 7 g fat, 1 g saturated fat, 1 mg cholesterol, 8.5 g dietary fiber, 379 mg sodium

Coffee Flan

Historically, this baked custard made its way from Spain to Mexico and then the southwestern states. But the garnish—chocolate-covered coffee beans—is a modern touch.

Makes 8 servings

1 cup sugar

3 tablespoons water

1 cup egg substitute

1 can (12 ounces) evaporated skim milk

2 cups fresh skim milk

1½ tablespoons instant French roast
  or espresso coffee

1½ teaspoons vanilla extract

Chocolate-covered coffee beans for
  garnish

Melt ½ cup of sugar and water in a small, heavy saucepan until the syrup is golden brown. Stir often and make sure the sugar syrup does not burn. Pour syrup into the bottom of a 4-cup metal ring mold, turning and tipping the mold to coat the bottom. Put mold in the refrigerator so that the syrup will harden.

Preheat oven to 350°. Fill a shallow pan that is large enough to hold the mold with 1 inch of hot water.

In a deep bowl, mix egg substitute with remaining ½ cup of sugar, evaporated skim milk, and 1½ cups of fresh skim milk.

Heat remaining ½ cup of skim milk in the microwave or in a small saucepan until scalding hot. Dissolve coffee in the hot milk. Let cool slightly, then stir back into the remaining flan mixture. Stir in vanilla extract.

Pour flan into the mold and set it gently in the water-filled pan.

Bake in the center of the oven for 1 hour and 15 minutes, or until a knife inserted in the custard comes out clean. Cool the flan in the oven with oven door ajar for 1 hour, then refrigerate.

Loosen the edges of the mold with a sharp knife. Unmold flan onto a serving dish. Refrigerate. Serve cold, sprinkled with chocolate-covered coffee beans.

178 calories, 1 g fat, 0.5 g saturated fat, 3 mg cholesterol, no dietary fiber, 136 mg sodium

• APRÈS-SKI PARTY •

Come December the lodge operators in Colorado, Idaho, Utah, New Mexico, and other western parts walk around with big smiles. So do the skiers, who have been making do with machines and roller skates for months, just waiting for the first real snow.

Skiing—downhill, cross-country, or even by machine—is one of the best all-around exercises for burning calories, which is why skiers can really pack it away after a day on the slopes. A ski party by its nature is casual. Seeing your sunburned slopemates in magenta Lycra does not evolve naturally into white tablecloths and crystal.

Like all athletes, skiers need an abundance of carbohydrates, which help replenish the stores of glycogen that the muscles in turn convert to glucose for energy. This menu is rich in carbohydrates and in the dusky-spicy flavors of the West.

 Suggested Wines: A red Burgundy makes a good partner for the soup if you're serving it with the blue cheese croutons. If you're omitting the croutons, a Riesling would pick up the sweetness of the squash. The garlicky, creamy tofu sauce for the pasta suggests a Chardonnay or champagne.

Or drink a rich full-bodied beer such as stout with the soup and a creamy ale with the pasta.

Winter Vegetable Soup
with Blue Cheese Croutons

The pungent brininess of blue cheese complements both sweet vegetables, such as acorn squash, and members of the cabbage family, such as kale.

Teff, a grain used extensively in Ethiopian cooking but still little known in the United States, is grown in Idaho. Look for it in North African groceries or health-food stores. Its tiny seeds have a wheaty-yeasty flavor and can be used in baked goods or to thicken soups.

To peel a hard-shell squash, cut it into large chunks, stand it skin side down on a cutting board, and run a sharp paring knife between the squash and its peel.

Makes 8 servings

2 tablespoons olive oil

2 medium onions, cut in half
lengthwise and thinly sliced
(4 cups)

4 cups peeled and diced butternut or
acorn squash

1 large (½ to ¾ pound) boiling
potato, peeled and diced

1 teaspoon dried marjoram

8 cups vegetable stock (page 17), or
5 cups canned broth diluted with
3 cups water

½ teaspoon salt (omit if using canned
broth)

⅓ cup teff (optional)

4 cups finely chopped kale

2 tablespoons Cognac or brandy
(optional)

Croutons:

8 thin slices cut from a baguette
(preferably whole wheat)

2 ounces (about ½ cup) crumbled blue
cheese

Cracked black pepper

Heat oil in a large pot. Add onions and cook over medium heat, stirring frequently, until they are a deep golden color. This may take 20 to 25 minutes or longer; watch the onions as they begin to brown so they don't burn.

Stir in squash, potato, and marjoram. Stir in vegetable stock and salt if using. Bring to a boil, then reduce heat to low and simmer for 20 minutes, or until the vegetables are tender. Stir in teff and kale, and cook about 5 minutes, until softened. Stir in Cognac or brandy and remove from heat. Let soup cool slightly, then puree about half of it in a blender or food processor until the kale is finely minced. Add puree back to the soup in the pot.

Serve soup immediately or refrigerate overnight and reheat the next day.

Just before serving, make the croutons: Preheat oven to 400°. Place bread slices on a baking sheet. Toast in the oven for 7 to 8 minutes, until crisp. Sprinkle crumbled blue cheese evenly over the bread, then sprinkle generously with pepper. Return to the oven for 2 to 3 minutes to soften the cheese.

Ladle hot soup into bowls. Top each serving with a blue cheese crouton.

217 calories, 7 g fat, 2 g saturated fat, 4 mg cholesterol, 7 g dietary fiber, 752 mg sodium

Fettucine with Creamy Porcini-Sage Sauce

Porcini, also called by their French name of cepes or their American moniker, the King Bolete, are highly prized members of a wild mushroom family that thrives in the West. Packaged dry porcini, sold in pieces or slices, have an outstanding smoky, almost bacony, flavor. They can be found in specialty shops, Italian groceries and some supermarkets, or ordered by mail (see Sources and Resources, page 329).

We really like garlic-parsley–flavored fettucine with this dairy-free sauce. If possible, use eggless, fresh fettucine.

Makes 8 servings

2½ tablespoons olive oil

7 to 9 medium cloves garlic, finely minced

1¾ cups vegetable stock (page 17), or 1 cup canned broth diluted with ¼ cup water

3 tablespoons chopped fresh sage, or 1 tablespoon dried and crumbled

3 tablespoons tomato paste

¼ cup dried porcini mushroom pieces

½ to 1 teaspoon salt (use lesser amount with canned broth)

1 package (10 to 11 ounces) soft silken tofu

2 pounds fresh fettucine, or 1½ pounds dried

2 tablespoons pine nuts, toasted and chopped

Freshly ground black pepper

1 to 2 roasted red peppers, cut into strips (see page 14)

Sprigs of fresh sage for garnish (optional)

Bring a very large pot of water to a boil.

Heat 1 tablespoon oil in a small saucepan. Add garlic and cook for a few seconds, just until fragrant, then add vegetable stock, sage, tomato paste, porcini, and salt.

Bring to a simmer and cook for 15 minutes. Let cool slightly, then place in a food processor or blender with tofu. Blend until smooth. Set aside.

Cook pasta in boiling water for 2 to 3 minutes if fresh, or about 10 minutes if dried, until al dente. Drain well.

Toss hot pasta with tofu–garlic sauce, remaining 1½ tablespoons oil, pine nuts, and a generous amount of black pepper. Garnish with roasted pepper and sage sprigs. Serve immediately.

412 calories, 10 g fat, 1.5 g saturated fat, 79 mg cholesterol (with egg noodles), 6.5 g dietary fiber, 328 mg sodium

Dried Fruit Compote

Serve this naturally sweet compote as a side dish or dessert.

Makes 8 servings

16 dried apricot halves
16 dried apple rings
8 pitted prunes
**½ cup dried tart or sweet cherries, or
    dried cranberries**

2 sticks cinnamon
1 teaspoon vanilla extract
1½ cups apple or cherry cider
1 tablespoon lemon juice

Place all fruits in a large stainless steel, nonstick, or enameled pan. Stir in cinnamon sticks, vanilla extract, cider, and lemon juice. Bring to a boil. Reduce heat to a simmer and cook, stirring occasionally, until fruit is tender and most of the liquid has been absorbed, about 20 to 25 minutes.

Remove and discard cinnamon. Serve warm or at room temperature.

114 calories, no fat, no cholesterol, 2.5 g dietary fiber, 15 mg sodium

Chocolate Cinnamon Meringue Peaks

Bitter chocolate nicely cuts the sweetness in these baby mountains of meringue. Outside, they're so crisp they'll shatter if you don't handle them carefully, but inside they're chocolaty and chewy. For more information about meringues, see Perfect Meringue (page 232)

Makes 2 dozen

3 egg whites, at room temperature
Pinch of salt
⅔ cup sugar

½ teaspoon vanilla extract
1 ounce unsweetened chocolate, grated
¾ teaspoon ground cinnamon

Preheat oven to 250°. Line a large baking sheet with wax paper, then lightly spray the paper with nonstick cooking spray.

Beat egg whites with salt until foamy. Gradually beat in sugar and continue beating on high speed until the meringue stands in firm, glossy peaks. Beat in vanilla extract, then stir in chocolate and cinnamon.

Using a pastry bag fitted with a large star tip, pipe rosettes of meringue onto the prepared baking pan, pulling up the tip to create twirly peaks. Or drop meringue from a tablespoon and swirl the spoon to make peaks.

Bake for at least 1 hour, until the meringues are very dry and crisp to the touch. Let cool, then carefully peel off the paper. Store in an airtight container.

Per meringue: 30 calories, 0.5 g fat, 0.5 g saturated fat, no cholesterol, no dietary fiber, 18 mg sodium

Perfect Meringue

When beating meringue, it's best to have the egg whites at room temperature. Be sure there's absolutely no trace of yolk in the whites; any fat at all keeps them from beating properly. A little acid—cream of tartar, lemon juice, or vinegar—or a bit of salt helps break down the proteins in the egg whites, making it easier to whip them to greater volume.

Beat the egg whites and sugar just until the egg whites stand in stiff peaks when you lift up the beaters. A good meringue has a brilliant gloss; an overbeaten one looks dry and spongy.

Do not try to make meringue on a humid day; it will absorb moisture and turn into gum. For the same reason, store baked, cooled meringue in an airtight container.

Meringue can be spread into just about any shape you like. Try piping or spreading the chocolate cinnamon meringue into eight disks, building up the sides a bit to make shallow "dishes." Bake for 1½ to 2 hours or longer. Meringue for shells should be crisp inside as well as out; check that the inside is dry by prying up a small piece with a knife.

Use the meringue shells as containers for low-fat vanilla, chocolate, or strawberry ice cream. Drizzle the ice cream and meringue with a little fat-free chocolate or strawberry sauce.

Appetizers, Salads, and Side Dishes

BASIC SOUTHWEST BEANS

Over the years, beans have made the move from the great open range to the indoor range. Pinto beans, with their mealy texture, are *the* bean to use in refried beans.

If you plan to make the Black Bean Crepes on page 224, cook black beans rather than pintos and reserve some of the cooking liquid. These beans are best made the day before serving.

Makes 8 to 10 servings

1 pound dried pinto beans   **4 cloves garlic, crushed**
2 medium onions, cut in half

Wash and drain beans. Remove and discard any stones or shriveled beans. Cover beans in a large pot with 2 to 3 inches of water. Mix in onion and garlic.

Bring mixture to a boil, cook for 2 minutes, then reduce heat to a simmer and continue cooking until beans are tender, which will take anywhere from 2 to 3½ hours depending on the age of the beans. After about 1½ hours, stir beans once or twice if needed. If they become dry, add more water, except during the last hour. Let cool, then refrigerate overnight.

Remove onions and reheat beans before serving.

154 calories, 0.5 g fat, no saturated fat, no cholesterol, 13 g dietary fiber, 3 mg sodium

BAKED POTATO WEDGES
WITH MUSTARD AND ROSEMARY

Makes 4 servings

4 medium-large Idaho baking potatoes,   **½ teaspoon salt**
  scrubbed   **¼ teaspoon cayenne**
1 tablespoon olive or canola oil   **1 tablespoon minced fresh rosemary, or**
1 tablespoon stone-ground mustard   **½ tablespoon dried and crumbled**

Preheat oven to 375°.

Cut potatoes in half lengthwise and then cut each half into 3 wedges. Put potatoes on a cookie sheet that has been sprayed with nonstick cooking spray.

Mix oil, mustard, salt, and cayenne in a small bowl. Brush potatoes with mustard mixture, then sprinkle with rosemary. Bake in the center of the oven until fork-tender and crisp on the outside, about 1 hour. Turn potatoes every 20 minutes, so that all sides brown.

Serve hot. Squeeze roasted garlic (page 316) over potatoes if desired. Allow 1 head of garlic per person.

254 calories, 4 g fat, 0.5 g saturated fat, no cholesterol, 4.5 g dietary fiber, 332 mg sodium

WARM WINTER LETTUCE WITH SESAME AND PICKLED GINGER DRESSING

It seems amazing that Arizona, a desert state, is a major grower of cool-weather, water-loving romaine, leaf, and iceberg lettuce, broccoli, and cauliflower. Yuma, in the far southwest corner of the state, is the winter lettuce capital of the United States.

Few Americans cook lettuce. Yet, like spinach, it can be delicious lightly cooked. Here it takes on an Asian accent. Pickled ginger, which really makes this dish, is available in Asian groceries, health-food stores, and some supermarkets.

Makes 4 servings

1½ teaspoons canola oil
4 green onions, cut into long shreds
4 cups shredded iceberg lettuce

4 cups shredded romaine lettuce
1 cup thinly julienned carrots

Dressing:
2 teaspoons soy sauce
1 teaspoon dark sesame oil
1 tablespoon cider vinegar
2 teaspoons sugar

1 teaspoon sesame seeds, preferably toasted
1 tablespoon shredded pickled ginger

Heat oil in a nonstick skillet or saucepan that has been sprayed with nonstick cooking spray. Add green onions and cook a few seconds. Add iceberg and romaine lettuce and carrots, and cook over medium heat, stirring, until they just begin to wilt. Remove from heat.

Whisk the dressing ingredients together. Pour over the lettuce and stir to coat. Serve immediately.

70 calories, 3.5 g fat, 0.5 g saturated fat, no cholesterol, 2 g dietary fiber, 191 mg sodium

Soups

QUINOA, BARLEY, AND BROWN MUSHROOM SOUP

The Incas called quinoa (KEEN-wah), a high-protein, mildly flavored seed, "the mother grain." Most of the quinoa sold in health-food stores here is imported from Bolivia or Peru, but it grows in Colorado and California as well.

Quinoa looks like plump sesame seeds. In its natural state it contains a soapy, bitter coating and must be rinsed several times. However, the packaged quinoa sold in health-food stores has been scrubbed; we usually give it just a quick rinse before cooking.

When you cook this soup, you'll notice the little white quinoa sprouts floating in the broth. We think these "curlicues" are just part of the charm of this nutritious, fluffy grain.

This hearty soup tastes better a day or two after you make it.

Makes 8 servings

2 tablespoons canola oil

1 cup chopped onion

2 cloves garlic, minced

1 cup sliced carrots

½ cup pearl barley (not quick-
cooking)

7 cups water or vegetable stock (see
page 17)

1 can (16 ounces) stewed and sliced
tomatoes

2 bay leaves

1 teaspoon honey

¾ teaspoon salt

¼ teaspoon pepper

2 tablespoons chopped fresh basil, or
1 tablespoon dried

1 cup sliced brown or white mushrooms

½ cup quinoa, rinsed

Heat oil in a Dutch oven or soup pot. Add onion and garlic, and sauté for 5 minutes, stirring occasionally. Add remaining ingredients. Bring soup to a boil, reduce heat to simmer, and cook, partially covered, about 1 hour, or until all ingredients are tender.

Stir occasionally as the soup cooks. Discard bay leaves before serving. Serve hot.

142 calories, 4.5 g fat, 0.5 g saturated fat, no cholesterol, 4.5 g dietary fiber, 364 mg sodium

POZOLE (MEXICAN-STYLE HOMINY SOUP)

Pozole is a green corn that is steamed and dried on the cob, then stripped from the cob. Canned hominy makes a good substitute.

This soup, which originated in the Jalisco region on Mexico's western coast, is a popular Christmas season favorite among Mexican-Americans. It usually is made with pork, but the meatless version has a good, well-rounded flavor—and doesn't have to cook as long.

Makes 4 servings

1 tablespoon canola oil

4 cloves garlic, minced

1 cup chopped onion

2 teaspoons chili powder

2 teaspoons minced fresh oregano, or
½ teaspoon dried

½ teaspoon honey

½ teaspoon salt

3 cups vegetable stock (page 17), or
2 cups canned broth and 1 cup
water

2 tablespoons freshly squeezed lime
juice

1 fresh jalapeño pepper, seeded and
chopped

1 can (4 ounces) mild green chile
pepper, chopped

1 can (29 ounces) white hominy,
drained

1 cup peeled and chopped tomatoes
(fresh or canned)

⅓ cup chopped fresh cilantro

1 tablespoon sliced black olives

2 limes, cut in wedges

Heat oil in a large nonstick saucepan that has been sprayed with nonstick cooking spray. Add garlic and onion, and sauté over medium heat until tender, stirring occasionally. Add remaining ingredients except cilantro, olives, and limes.

Bring to a boil, reduce heat, and simmer, covered, for 15 minutes.

Taste and adjust seasonings.

Ladle pozole into bowls and sprinkle with cilantro and olives. Serve hot. Pass lime wedges at the table.

256 calories, 7 g fat, 1 g saturated fat, no cholesterol, 6 g dietary fiber, 1,000 mg sodium

TWO-CHILE LENTIL AND SHIITAKE CHILI

This is unadorned Tex-Mex-style chili with no tomatoes or other "frivolous" ingredients—just plenty of heat from two widely used chiles. A combination of shiitakes and lentils gives the stew body and a meaty chewiness.

Like any chili, this tastes best served a day or two after it's made.

Makes 6 servings

1½ cups lentils
5 cups vegetable stock (page 17) or
3 cups canned broth diluted with
2 cups water
6 dried ancho chiles
4 dried guajillo chiles
4 cups warm water
2 tablespoons olive oil
2 tablespoons chopped garlic

3½ ounces fresh shiitake mushrooms
1 tablespoon ground cumin
1 tablespoon paprika
1 teaspoon dried oregano
¼ teaspoon ground cinnamon
1 tablespoon brown sugar
1 teaspoon salt (use less with canned broth)

Rinse lentils. Place in a saucepan with vegetable stock. Bring to a boil, then reduce heat and cook for 10 minutes. Remove from heat and set aside.

Place chiles in a large bowl with warm water. Let soak for 30 minutes, or until chiles are softened. Remove chiles, reserving soaking liquid. Cut out stems, cores, and seeds, and discard. Cut chiles into pieces. Strain soaking liquid. Place chiles and soaking liquid in a blender or food processor. Process on high speed until smooth.

Heat oil in a Dutch oven or soup pot. Add garlic and shiitakes, and sauté until shiitakes begin to soften, about 3 minutes. Add chile mixture and cook over medium heat for 5 minutes, stirring often.

Stir in cumin, paprika, oregano, cinnamon, sugar, and salt. Reduce heat to low and cook, partially covered, for 30 minutes. Add lentils and stock, and cook another 30 minutes, or until lentils are cooked through but not mushy.

Although chili can be served immediately, it tastes better if you let it cool, refrigerate it overnight, and reheat the next day.

243 calories, 8 g fat, 1.5 g saturated fat, no cholesterol, 8 g dietary fiber, 369 mg sodium

Packing Heat

America likes it hot these days, and chiles show up in abundance everywhere from Hispanic groceries to farmers' markets to supermarkets to fancy food stores. Here's a handful of chiles commonly used in southwestern cooking.

Jalapeño, the most commonly found in supermarkets, is a short, fairly squat green chile that's medium hot. It's often canned. It's a good all-purpose chile for dips, soups, guacamole, pepper jelly—wherever you want a good jolt of heat without being overpowered.

Smoked, the jalapeño becomes the trendy chipotle, sold canned or dried. Chipotles are very smoky; use them sparingly in soups, sauces, and grilled foods.

Serranos are medium to dark green or scarlet, and average about 2 inches long. These thin peppers are widely used in salsas and guacamole. They pack a real punch; use them sparingly. Like jalapeños, they are often canned.

The Anaheim, also known as the New Mexico chile or chile Colorado, is long, narrow, and slightly bumpy. It has light to medium green, tough skin and benefits from roasting. It's mildly hot and is often stuffed. It is widely used in sauces and in egg and cheese dishes.

Poblano is a large heart-shaped fresh chile with very glossy skin that ranges from greenish purple to almost black. It tastes like a mildly hot, more intense green pepper. The skin is tough, and poblanos are usually roasted and peeled. They can be stuffed, or cut into strips and added to a variety of dishes; try them with zucchini and corn.

The chile ancho is a dried red poblano. It is reddish black and leathery. If it were a wine, its flavor would be described as tobacco and leather, with some sharp fruit. Anchos are one of the most widely used chiles and are good in all kinds of sauces. The chile mulato is a relative, but it has a smoother skin and a soft, chocolaty flavor.

The chile guajillo is a long, slender dried chile with a tough maroon skin. It's semi-hot to hot and has a fruity-herbal flavor. It's used most often in cooked sauces.

The pasilla is a long, thin dried chile with a wrinkled reddish black skin. It ranges from hot to very hot and has a fairly sharp flavor.

It's a good idea to wear rubber gloves when handling chiles. Remove the seeds and ribs—especially the ribs—to reduce the chile's heat. If you think gloves are for wimps, just be sure you don't rub your eyes for the next day or so.

Entrées

SALAD OF ORANGE LENTILS AND BROWN RICE

Almost all the lentils grown in the United States hail from the dusty-colored hills of the Palouse, a region embracing part of west-central Idaho and east-central Washington.

Orange lentils—or call them red or pink, if you prefer—aren't grown as widely in the United States as the brown variety. They're husked, and thus cook much more quickly than the standard brown lentils. A pretty coral, they turn golden when cooked.

This can be used as a salad, as a filling for crepes, or as a main dish.

Makes 4 servings as a main course

½ cup brown rice	*3 tablespoons canola or olive oil*
1 cup orange lentils	*3 tablespoons freshly squeezed lime*
2 whole cloves garlic	*juice*
1 onion, cut into quarters	*2 tablespoons chopped fresh dill weed,*
½ cup chopped green onion	*or 1 tablespoon dried*
2 cloves garlic, minced	*½ teaspoon salt*
½ cup chopped fresh parsley	*¼ teaspoon pepper*

Cook brown rice according to package directions. Set aside.

Pick over and wash lentils. Place in a saucepan and cover with water. Stir in whole garlic cloves and quartered onion. Cook lentils over medium-low heat until tender, about 10 minutes. Do not let lentils become mushy. Drain. Discard garlic and onion.

In a bowl, toss together brown rice, lentils, green onion, minced garlic, parsley, oil, lime juice, dill, salt, and pepper.

Cover lightly and refrigerate until serving time. Mix before serving.

…alories, 11.5 g fat, 1 g saturated fat, no cholesterol, 8 g dietary fiber, 282 mg sodium

GINGERED PINTO BEAN SALAD

Ginger tosses a little spicy-sweet-pungent flavor into this hearty salad. Always look for firm young ginger that's not too fibrous.

Makes 4 servings

2 cups cooked pinto beans, cooked from dry or canned, drained (see page 242)
¼ cup minced green onion
¼ cup sweet pickle relish
1 teaspoon brown, seeded mustard
1 jalapeño pepper, seeded and minced

¼ teaspoon salt
1 teaspoon minced fresh gingerroot
3 tablespoons reduced-fat mayonnaise
4 cups assorted lettuce pieces, such as oak leaf, Bibb, or watercress
4 hard-cooked egg whites, chopped (optional)

Put beans in a bowl. Toss with onion, relish, mustard, jalapeño, salt, gingerroot, and mayonnaise.

Place lettuce on chilled salad plates and top with bean salad. Scatter egg whites on top if using.

207 calories, 4.5 g fat, 1 g saturated fat, no cholesterol, 11 g dietary fiber, 402 mg sodium

Beans and Horses

Pinto is the Spanish word for "painted" and names both a bean and a horse. The term accurately describes the pretty mottled pink beans that are native to the Southwest and a staple in that region's cooking. Pintos, relative of the kidney bean, have an earthy flavor and mealy texture.

Two newer pinto hybrids carry names that evoke the romance of the West. The Appaloosa bean is slender and has black spots on a creamy background—just like the horse of the same name. Both are named for the Palouse, a major bean- and lentil-growing region that straddles western Idaho and eastern Washington.

The rattlesnake bean is pink and mottled like the common pinto but is somewhat more block-shaped. One can also imagine it has just a bit more bite.

BEAN BURRITOS WITH TOMATILLO SAUCE

It amazes us how so many of the southwestern recipes use the same ingredients and taste so different. Tomatillos, small green relatives of the tomato, are used in a variety of different-tasting sauces. The fruit, which is used green, is enclosed in a papery husk and tastes like a green tomato crossed with a tart apple. Tomatillos are available fresh in Hispanic food stores and in many supermarkets. Buy tomatillos that are firm. Peel off the outer husk and wash the fruits before using.

Makes 4 servings

Sauce:

1½ cups husked and chopped fresh
   tomatillos, or 1 can (10 ounces)
   tomatillos, drained and chopped

½ jalapeño pepper, or to taste, seeded
   and chopped

2 tablespoons minced fresh cilantro

1 clove garlic, minced

¼ teaspoon salt

Filling and tortillas:

1 tablespoon canola oil

2 cloves garlic, minced

½ cup chopped onion

1⅓ cups cooked and mashed pinto,
   black, or kidney beans (if using
   canned, drain and rinse well)

1 cup peeled and chopped tomatoes

¼ cup pine nuts

4 flour tortillas, preferably whole wheat

To make sauce: Chop all ingredients in a food processor fitted with the steel blade or in a blender. Or finely chop ingredients and toss them together. Cover lightly and refrigerate until serving time. Just before serving, simmer sauce for 10 minutes. Set aside.

Preheat oven to 350°.

To make filling: Spray a nonstick frying pan and heat oil over medium heat. Sauté garlic and onion about 5 minutes, until onion softens; stir occasionally. Mix in beans and tomatoes. Cook until heated through, stirring often. Stir in pine nuts.

Cover tortillas with aluminum foil and heat in the oven for 5 minutes, or until hot.

Spread filling down center of each tortilla and roll tightly. Place burritos on plates, seam side down. Ladle warm sauce on top and serve immediately.

288 calories, 9.4 g fat, 1 g saturated fat, no cholesterol, 12 g dietary fiber, 312 mg sodium

ENCHILADAS WITH ROASTED PEPPERS AND ONIONS

Enchiladas in fast-food restaurants tend to be gloppy with cheese. True enchiladas are really quite simple: tortillas dipped in a sauce, heated, and wrapped around a filling. This is a different variation on salsa verde (green sauce), in which the tomatillos are lightly cooked but the sauce is not.

Some brands of tortillas may tend to tear when they're dipped in salsa; if that's a problem, toast them in the skillet first, then dip in the sauce.

Makes 4 servings

4 large mild chile peppers (such as Anaheim or poblano)	**1 tablespoon nonfat yogurt**
1 large sweet onion, thinly sliced	**¼ cup finely chopped green onion**
1 tablespoon olive oil	**12 corn tortillas**
1 cup 1-percent cottage cheese	**Salsa Verde (recipe follows)**

Roast peppers (see page 14), remove cores and seeds, and cut into long strips.

Brush onion slices with oil and put under broiler. Cook until they begin to char, about 10 minutes.

Mix cottage cheese with yogurt and green onion. Set aside.

Heat a heavy, well-seasoned cast-iron skillet or griddle, or a nonstick frying pan that has been coated with nonstick cooking spray. Dip a tortilla in salsa verde, coating both sides. Add to pan and cook briefly over medium-high heat, turning once, until warmed and softened. Remove to a plate. Place several pieces of pepper and onion on tortilla, then top with about 1 tablespoon of cottage cheese mixture. Roll tortilla around filling and place on a plate, seam side down. Keep warm in a 200° oven while you heat, fill, and roll remaining tortillas.

Serve enchiladas with extra salsa verde on the side.

Without extra salsa: 320 calories, 7 g fat, 1 g saturated fat, 2.5 mg cholesterol, 6.5 g dietary fiber, 430 mg sodium

SALSA VERDE

Makes 2 cups

1 pound tomatillos
2 cups water
1 clove garlic, minced

⅓ cup finely diced green onion
¼ teaspoon salt
⅓ cup loosely packed cilantro leaves

Husk tomatillos and rinse well. Cook with water for 5 to 7 minutes, until they turn a moss-green color. Place tomatillos, ⅓ cup cooking water, and remaining ingredients in a blender or food processor and process until ingredients make a coarse puree.

This can be refrigerated for up to 2 days.

40 calories, 1 g fat, no saturated fat, no cholesterol, no dietary fiber, 136 mg sodium

PAN-FRIED TOFU WITH PICO DE GALLO AND GREEN PEPPERS

The marinade and accompaniments for this tofu dish draw inspiration from fajitas, the Texas specialty that grew into a national trend.

Makes 4 servings

Marinade:
½ cup fresh lime juice
1 tablespoon crushed fresh oregano, or
   1½ teaspoon dried
1 clove garlic, minced
1 teaspoon ground cumin

½ teaspoon Worcestershire sauce (see
   Note on page 112)
2 tablespoons dark brown sugar

1 cup drained strips of firm tofu

Pico de gallo (Tomato Relish):
1 cup finely chopped tomato
¼ cup finely chopped green onion
1 tablespoon minced fresh cilantro

1 small clove garlic, minced
½ to 1 jalapeño pepper, minced

Vegetables:

1 tablespoon canola oil
2 cups sliced green bell peppers
2 cloves garlic, minced
¾ cup sliced onion
½ cup cooked chick-peas (if canned,
   drain and rinse)
1 teaspoon ground cumin

½ cup chopped fresh cilantro

4 tablespoons nonfat sour cream
4 flour tortillas, wrapped in aluminum
   foil

Combine marinade ingredients in a bowl. Add tofu and marinate for 30 minutes, then drain. Reserve marinade.

Meanwhile, mix ingredients for *pico de gallo*. Cover and set aside.

Preheat oven to 350°.

Heat oil over medium heat in a nonstick frying pan that has been sprayed with nonstick cooking spray. Cook pepper slices, garlic, and onion about 5 minutes, or until tender, stirring occasionally.

Add tofu, chick-peas, and cumin. Stir lightly once or twice. Cook only until hot. Sprinkle with 2 tablespoons reserved marinade.

Heat covered tortillas in the oven about 5 minutes, or until warmed through.

Place tofu and vegetables on a warmed platter. Sprinkle with cilantro. Serve hot, accompanied by warm tortillas, sour cream, and *pico de gallo*.

182 calories, 7 g fat, 1 g saturated fat, no cholesterol, 4 g dietary fiber, 33 mg sodium

LAYERED BUCKWHEAT-RICOTTA CREPES WITH TOMATO-CHIVE SALSA

The sharpness of tomatoes and chives complement the earthiness of buckwheat. This resembles a layer cake and is cut into wedges the same way, but it's a savory main course. The crepes can be made in advance if desired; the salsa needs 1 to 4 hours in the refrigerator to let the flavors combine.

Makes 8 servings

Crepes:

⅔ cup all-purpose flour

⅓ cup buckwheat flour

¾ cup skim milk

¼ cup egg substitute

2 egg whites

1 tablespoon canola oil

1 tablespoon minced fresh sage leaves,
  or 1½ teaspoons dried

Filling:

15 ounces light ricotta cheese or
  1-percent cottage cheese

⅓ cup plain nonfat yogurt

1 teaspoon chili powder

½ teaspoon ground cumin

¼ cup minced fresh parsley or cilantro

¼ cup minced fresh chives

Tomato-Chive Salsa (recipe follows)

To make crepes: Combine flours, milk, egg substitute, egg whites, canola oil, and sage in a food processor or blender. Blend only a few seconds, until smooth. If mixing by hand, sift flour and use a whisk.

Let batter stand for 20 minutes. Stir before using.

Heat a nonstick 8-inch crepe pan that has been sprayed with nonstick cooking spray. Pour about 2½ to 3 tablespoons of batter into pan. Tilt pan so batter thinly coats the bottom; pour off any excess batter. Cook crepe until it is set and firm around the edges. Loosen edges with a knife. Flip crepe and cook only a few seconds on the other side. Continue cooking crepes until batter is used up, stacking the cooked crepes between sheets of foil or wax paper.

To make filling: Combine cheese, yogurt, chili powder, cumin, parsley, and chives in a small bowl.

To assemble: Set first crepe in the center of a serving plate. Spread with some of the filling. Top with a second crepe. Keep stacking crepes with filling until both are used up. Chill until serving time.

To serve, microwave crepe cake on high for 2 minutes, or just until heated through. Cut into wedges, set on plates, and spoon some of the salsa over. Serve remaining salsa on the side.

Without salsa: 153 calories, 4.5 g fat, 0.5 g saturated fat, 1 mg cholesterol, 1 g dietary fiber, 90 mg sodium

TOMATO-CHIVE SALSA

Makes 2½ to 2¾ cups; 8 servings

**2 cups peeled and chopped vine–ripened
   tomatoes
½ cup minced chives
3 cloves garlic, minced**

**½ cup chopped fresh cilantro or parsley
¼ teaspoon salt
2 jalapeño peppers (or to taste), seeded
   and chopped**

Toss all ingredients together in a deep bowl. Refrigerate for up to 4 hours. Let come
to room temperature and stir before serving.

13 calories, no fat, no cholesterol, 1 g dietary fiber, 72 mg sodium

FIRE-ROASTED SWEET AND WHITE POTATOES AND QUINOA, COUSCOUS, AND CHICKPEA PACKETS

This is the New Age equivalent of the cowboy campfire. Much of the West's open
range has now turned into subdivisions that frown on building backyard fires. That's
okay; suburban cowboy wannabes can tell jokes around the outdoor grill.

Cooking times for grilled foods vary depending on the temperature of the fire
and outdoor conditions. Foods cook much faster on a hot, dry day than on a cold,
damp one.

For more authenticity, use wood charcoal rather than briquettes (see Sources and
Resources, page 329).

Makes 4 servings

FIRE-ROASTED SWEET AND WHITE POTATOES

4 medium white baking potatoes,
scrubbed
4 small sweet potatoes, scrubbed
1 cup plain nonfat yogurt

¼ cup minced fresh cilantro
2 tablespoons chopped green chiles
4 teaspoons orange marmalade

Light wood charcoal on an outdoor grill.

Tear off 8 sheets of double-thickness aluminum foil (or 16 sheets of regular-thickness foil doubled), each large enough to enclose a potato. Spray the dull side of each sheet with butter-flavored nonstick cooking spray.

Pierce each potato in several places with the tip of a knife. Put each white potato and each sweet potato in the center of a sheet of foil. Bring up the ends of the foil, twisting them to seal the potato.

When the charcoal is hot, place the wrapped potatoes directly in the charcoal and bake about 40 minutes, or until tender, turning the potatoes every 15 minutes.

Mix the yogurt with the cilantro and green chiles. When the potatoes are baked, cut them in half. Serve the white potatoes with the yogurt mixture. Spread the sweet potatoes with marmalade.

370 calories, 0.5 g fat, no saturated fat, 1 mg cholesterol, 7.5 g dietary fiber, 75 mg sodium

QUINOA, COUSCOUS, AND CHICKPEA PACKETS

1 cup chopped onion
1 cup chopped green bell pepper
¼ cup dark raisins
2 cups cooked and drained chickpeas
½ cup grated carrots
1 cup cooked quinoa

½ teaspoon salt
¼ teaspoon pepper
¼ teaspoon ground nutmeg
½ cup vegetable stock (page 17) or
canned broth

Cut aluminum foil into four 12-by-9-inch pieces. Spray the dull side of each sheet of foil with olive oil–flavored nonstick cooking spray.

Toss all ingredients together in a bowl. Divide and spoon into prepared foil. Bring up the ends of the foil, twisting them to seal the food.

When the charcoal is hot, place the packets directly in the charcoal and bake about 20 minutes, until hot. Turn the packets once or twice during cooking.

Serve in the packets.

241 calories, 3.5 g fat, no saturated fat, no cholesterol, 8 g dietary fiber, 414 mg sodium

GRILLED PEPPERS WITH WHISKEY BLACK BEANS AND RADISH-JICAMA SALSA

Alcohol is a good "secret ingredient" in low-fat dishes because it carries flavors, much as fat does. Here we've added a spot of whiskey—the great social lubricant and leveler of the Wild West—to the black beans to heighten their flavor.

Jicama (HEE-kah-ma) looks like a large flattened globe with a tough brown skin. Its sweet, crunchy flesh is reminiscent of water chestnuts. Peel it with a potato peeler.

Make the beans and salsa ahead of time, then grill the peppers just before serving. The peppers can be prepared on a stovetop grill.

Makes 4 servings

Salsa:

2 cups grated radishes
½ cup peeled and finely diced jicama
1 cup chopped tomatoes

3 tablespoons sugar
3 tablespoons white vinegar
¼ cup minced fresh cilantro

Beans:

2 teaspoons canola oil
½ cup chopped onion
2 cloves garlic, minced
2 teaspoons chili powder
¼ teaspoon ground cumin
¼ teaspoon crushed red pepper

½ cup chopped tomato
2 cups cooked black beans or a mixture
*   of cooked black and kidney beans*
*   (rinse well and drain if canned)*
1 to 2 tablespoons whiskey, to taste

Grilled peppers:

1 tablespoon canola oil

1 teaspoon paprika

¼ teaspoon salt

½ teaspoon sugar

½ teaspoon ground cumin

¼ teaspoon black pepper

4 green bell peppers, seeded and sliced
    lengthwise into strips

To make salsa: Mix all ingredients in a medium bowl. Let stand for 1 hour or refrigerate until ready to serve. Drain before serving.

To make beans: Heat oil in a nonstick frying pan that has been sprayed with nonstick cooking spray. Sauté onion and garlic over medium heat until tender, covering pan if necessary to soften onion. Stir in remaining ingredients except whiskey. Cook until beans are heated through. Stir in whiskey. Serve immediately or refrigerate. Reheat before serving.

To grill peppers: Mix oil, paprika, salt, sugar, cumin, and black pepper in a small bowl.

Rub the spice paste evenly over the peppers. Transfer them to a sprayed grill rack and place over ashen coals. Grill for 3 to 5 minutes, turning once or twice, until charred and tender.

Serve immediately with beans and salsa.

270 calories, 7 g fat, 0.5 g saturated fat, no cholesterol, 8.5 g dietary fiber, 162 mg sodium

PAN-FRIED CHILES RELLENOS WITH MELON SALSA

Chiles rellenos are usually deep-fried, but we've cut the fat considerably by pan-frying them in a small amount of oil.

Makes 4 servings

Melon Salsa:

2 cups peeled and chopped ripe
   tomatoes
¾ to 1 cup chopped cantaloupe or
   honeydew
½ cup chopped onion

1 clove garlic, minced
⅓ cup chopped fresh cilantro or parsley
1 to 2 tablespoons freshly squeezed lime
   juice

1 jalapeño, seeded and chopped
8 poblano or Anaheim peppers or other
   large, mild chiles of your choice,
   roasted and peeled (page 14)
4 ounces reduced-fat Monterey Jack
   cheese, grated

Batter:

2 egg whites
¼ cup egg substitute
3 tablespoons all-purpose flour

½ teaspoon baking powder
¼ teaspoon salt
1 tablespoon canola oil

To make salsa: Combine all the ingredients in a bowl, cover lightly, and refrigerate for 1 hour or longer. Toss salsa before serving.

To prepare the peppers: Slit peppers lengthwise and discard stems and seeds. Carefully fill peppers with cheese. Set aside.

To make batter: Beat the egg whites until they form stiff, glossy peaks. Fold in egg substitute, flour, baking powder, and salt.

Roll chiles in the batter to coat evenly.

Heat canola oil in a large nonstick frying pan that has been sprayed with nonstick cooking spray. Add the chiles and cook over medium-high heat, turning as they cook, until golden brown on all sides.

Serve immediately, with salsa on the side.

With salsa: 284 calories, 10 g fat, 3.5 g saturated fat, 20 mg cholesterol, 5.5 g dietary fiber, 492 mg sodium

MASHED POTATO CAKES WITH BASQUE-STYLE TOMATO AND PEPPER SAUCE

When they came to Idaho, Utah, and Nevada to herd sheep, the Basques, whose homeland in the Pyrenees is now part of Spain, brought a bit of their signature Mediterranean cooking with them. Basque cooking features plenty of peppers, tomatoes, and beans, and is seasoned with lavish amounts of garlic.

This is the fancier presentation of this dish. For a quicker weeknight dish, just scoop the mashed potatoes (minus the egg substitute) onto a plate and spoon the sauce over them, gravy style.

Makes 4 servings

3 baking potatoes (about 1¾ pounds)
2 whole cloves garlic, peeled
1 cup water
¾ teaspoon salt
Freshly ground black pepper
2 tablespoons egg substitute or 1 egg white
6 medium plum tomatoes, fresh or canned

4 teaspoons olive oil
4 cloves garlic, minced
1 cup diced onion
1 red bell pepper, seeded and diced
1 tablespoon fresh thyme leaves or 1 teaspoon dried
¼ cup red wine or tomato juice
6 large pitted green olives, coarsely chopped

Peel potatoes and cut into chunks. Place potatoes and whole garlic cloves in a large saucepan with water. Bring to a boil, then reduce heat to medium, cover, and let cook about 20 minutes, or until potatoes have absorbed most of the liquid and are very tender. Check potatoes once or twice during cooking; if they look too dry, add a little water.

Remove from heat and mash potatoes and garlic cloves in their cooking liquid. Stir in ½ teaspoon of salt and pepper to taste. Let cool for 10 minutes, then stir in egg substitute. At this point, potatoes can be refrigerated for several hours or overnight.

Peel tomatoes and cut in half lengthwise. Discard seeds and cut tomatoes into ½-inch dice.

Heat 1 teaspoon of oil in a nonstick frying pan that has been sprayed with nonstick cooking spray. Add minced garlic, onion, and bell pepper, and sauté until onion softens. Add tomatoes, thyme, wine, and olives. Cook over medium heat for 3 to 5 minutes, until tomatoes begin to cook down into a sauce. Add remaining ¼ teaspoon of salt.

Heat remaining 1 tablespoon of oil in a clean nonstick 10- or 12-inch frying pan that has been sprayed with nonstick cooking spray. Drop cooled mashed potato mixture into pan in 4 mounds, using the back of a spoon to mold into 4 cakes. Cook over medium-high heat for 3 to 4 minutes, until golden. Spray tops of potato cakes lightly with nonstick cooking spray, then turn and cook until other side is golden, 3 to 4 minutes.

Place mashed potato cakes on plates. Spoon tomato-pepper sauce over them. Serve immediately.

209 calories, 6 g fat, 1 g saturated fat, no cholesterol, 4.5 g dietary fiber, 571 mg sodium

TEXAS CAVIAR SALSA ON A BAKED POTATO

Texas Caviar Salsa can also be served as part of a salad; for example, prepare a small bed of radicchio with Texas Caviar Salsa in the center and garnish with cantaloupe slices. Or it can be a dip for good-quality fat-free tortilla chips, or served rolled in a warm flour tortilla.

Makes 4 servings

Marinade:

2 cloves garlic, minced
½ cup minced onion
⅓ cup red wine vinegar
2 tablespoons canola oil
½ teaspoon salt

¼ teaspoon crushed red pepper

2 cups cooked black-eyed peas (drained and rinsed well if canned)

Salsa:

1 teaspoon canola oil

¼ cup chopped green onion

2 cloves garlic, minced

2 cups peeled and chopped tomatoes

1 teaspoon ground cumin

1 teaspoon fresh oregano, or
   ½ teaspoon dried

¼ teaspoon salt

⅓ cup chopped fresh cilantro or parsley

4 medium-large Idaho baking potatoes

To make marinade: Bring garlic, onion, and vinegar to a boil in a small saucepan. Stir in oil, salt, and crushed pepper.

Toss peas with marinade. Refrigerate for several hours or overnight.

To make salsa: Heat oil in a small nonstick saucepan that has been sprayed with nonstick cooking spray. Sauté onion and garlic over medium heat until soft, stirring occasionally. Add tomatoes, cumin, oregano, salt, and cilantro. Simmer for 3 to 4 minutes, stirring once or twice. Stir in peas. Set aside.

Bake or microwave potatoes until tender (see below). Split down the middle, squeeze open, and top with black-eyed pea salsa.

380 calories, 7 g fat, 0.5 g saturated fat, no cholesterol, 12 g dietary fiber, 403 mg sodium

The Perfect Baked Potato

A well-baked potato has a thick, crispy skin and fluffy flesh. There's really only one way to obtain such a potato: Bake it. Microwaving it does not count.

Preheat the oven to 400°.

Scrub good-size Idaho potatoes, then spray lightly with butter-flavored nonstick cooking spray. Do *not* wrap the potato in foil. Place the potatoes in the center of the oven on a cookie sheet or directly on the oven rack. Bake about 45 minutes, or until potatoes can be pierced easily with a fork.

Use the tines of the fork to poke a slit lengthwise down the center of each potato. Squeeze gently on the sides of the potato until it pops open.

For double-baked potatoes, cut 4 baked potatoes in half. Scoop out the potato, leaving a ½- to ¼-inch-thick shell. Mash the potato flesh with ½ cup of plain nonfat yogurt, ½ teaspoon salt, ¼ teaspoon freshly ground pepper, and ¼ cup of grated, reduced-fat Monterey Jack cheese.

Scoop this filling back into each potato shell. Spray lightly with nonstick cooking spray. Return to the oven for 10 to 15 minutes, until the top is crusty.

Since we live in the real world where no one seems to have any time, here's how to microwave a "baked" potato:

Pierce each potato in several places. Place a microwave-proof paper towel in the microwave (this absorbs moisture so the potatoes cook up fluffier). Place potatoes in a circle on the towel, with the thickest ends facing out. Microwave on high (100 percent) for 6 to 10 minutes, depending on the size of the potatoes. Let the potatoes stand for 5 minutes before handling them.

SCRAMBLED HUEVOS RANCHEROS WITH REFRIED BEANS

These spicy scrambled eggs can be served for breakfast or dinner.

Makes 4 servings

Ranchero sauce:

1 teaspoon canola oil
1 cup minced onion
1 green bell pepper, seeded and chopped
2 mild or hot finger peppers, seeded and chopped
3 cups peeled and chopped ripe tomatoes

1 cup vegetable stock (page 17), or ½ cup canned vegetable broth diluted with ½ cup water
1 teaspoon cumin seed
¼ teaspoon salt
Dash of crushed red pepper, or to taste

Eggs:

2 egg whites, at room temperature

2 teaspoons canola oil

¾ cup chopped onion

½ cup chopped fresh or canned mild
    green chiles

¼ teaspoon salt

¼ teaspoon pepper

1 cup egg substitute

4 corn tortillas

Refried Beans (recipe follows)

Sprigs of cilantro or parsley, or thinly
    sliced avocado

To make sauce: Heat oil in a nonstick saucepan that has been sprayed with nonstick cooking spray. Sauté onion and peppers over medium heat until soft, stirring occasionally. Mix in tomatoes, vegetable stock, cumin, salt, and red pepper. Simmer sauce about 5 minutes, stirring occasionally. Taste and adjust seasonings. Cool, then refrigerate until needed. Warm over low heat and stir before serving.

To prepare eggs: Beat egg whites until they form firm, glossy peaks, then set aside. Heat oil in a nonstick frying pan that has been sprayed with nonstick cooking spray. Sauté onion over medium heat for 4 to 5 minutes, stirring occasionally, until it softens. Mix in chiles, salt, and pepper. In a separate bowl, fold egg whites into egg substitute. Stir into vegetables in pan. Cook eggs, gently scrambling with a spatula, until set.

Spray a small nonstick frying pan with cooking spray. Heat over medium-high heat. Add 1 tortilla and cook for 30 seconds to 1 minute on each side, until heated through. Repeat with remaining tortillas.

To serve, set a warm tortilla on each plate and spoon warm eggs and sauce on it.

Serve warm refried beans on the side. Garnish the plate with cilantro, parsley, or a thin wedge of avocado.

243 calories, 7 g fat, 1 g saturated fat, 1 mg cholesterol, 5.5 g dietary fiber, 465 mg sodium

REFRIED BEANS

Makes 4 servings

2 tablespoons canola oil

½ cup chopped onion

1 jalapeño pepper, seeded and chopped

3 cups cooked, coarsely mashed pinto
    beans

1 teaspoon chili powder

½ teaspoon cumin seed

½ teaspoon salt

Heat oil in a nonstick frying pan. Sauté onion over medium heat until tender, about 5 minutes, covering pan to sweat onions if necessary. Stir in jalapeño pepper, beans, chili powder, cumin, and salt. Cook beans over medium heat, stirring only as necessary to prevent sticking, until hot. Beans may start to brown around the edges. Serve warm.

250 calories, 7.5 g fat, 0.5 g saturated fat, no cholesterol, 15 g dietary fiber, 277 mg sodium

VEGETABLE CHILI WITH AN HERBED CORNBREAD "HAT"

This is a fun dish for company or a family meal. You can make this in a 10-inch cast-iron or enameled frying pan and bring it directly to the table for serving.

Makes 6 servings

Chili:

1 tablespoon canola oil
2 cloves garlic, minced
1½ cups chopped onions
1½ teaspoons ground cumin
2 teaspoons ground chili powder
1 jalapeño pepper, seeded and chopped
2 cups chopped green or red bell peppers
½ cup grated carrot
1 cup chopped zucchini

2½ cups cooked kidney beans, drained
¾ cup cooked chickpeas (garbanzos), drained
2 cups chopped tomatoes
3 tablespoons tomato juice
¼ cup chopped fresh cilantro or parsley
½ teaspoon salt

Cornbread:

1 cup yellow or white cornmeal

¾ cup all-purpose flour

1½ tablespoons sugar

2 teaspoons baking powder

1 cup buttermilk

2 egg whites

1 cup fresh or frozen corn kernels

1 teaspoon finely chopped fresh
 marjoram, or ½ teaspoon dried

1 teaspoon finely chopped fresh thyme,
 or ½ teaspoon dried

¼ teaspoon salt

To make chili: Heat oil in a 10- to 12-inch ovenproof frying pan, preferably nonstick, that has been sprayed with nonstick cooking spray. Add garlic and onions, and cook, covered, over medium heat until tender. Stir occasionally. Stir in cumin, chili powder, jalapeño and bell peppers, carrot, zucchini, beans, chickpeas, tomatoes, tomato juice, cilantro, and salt. Cover and cook for 2 to 3 minutes. Stir.

Preheat oven to 425°.

To make cornbread: In a large bowl, mix together cornmeal, flour, sugar, and baking powder. Stir in buttermilk, egg whites, corn, marjoram, thyme, and salt. Do not overmix. Pour batter over chili, spreading it with the back of a spoon.

Bake in the center of the oven for 15 to 20 minutes, or until a tester inserted in the center comes out dry. Remove from oven, let stand a few minutes, then serve.

393 calories, 5.5 g fat, 1 g saturated fat, 1.5 mg cholesterol, 14.5 g dietary fiber, 563 mg sodium

Breads and Desserts

FLOUR TORTILLAS

Flour tortillas are indigenous to northern Mexico and the southwestern United States. They are best eaten right away, while still warm.

Makes 6 tortillas

1½ cups all-purpose flour

½ teaspoon salt

½ teaspoon baking powder

2 tablespoons vegetable shortening

½ cup hot water

Combine the flour, salt, and baking powder. Cut in the shortening using a pastry blender, a food processor, or an electric mixer on low speed. Stir in the water and mix just until the dough forms a ball.

Gather dough into a ball or knead dough a few times if not using a processor. Divide dough into 6 equal portions and shape into balls. Pat dough into rounds. On a lightly floured pastry cloth, roll out each round to a 6-inch circle. If using a tortilla press, follow manufacturer's directions.

Preheat an ungreased nonstick frying pan or heavy frying pan. Fry each tortilla about 30 to 45 seconds on each side, or until tortilla is cooked through and has brown spots.

Serve tortillas immediately or store in a plastic bag in the refrigerator. To reheat, wrap in foil and warm in a 325° oven for 5 minutes.

152 calories, 4.5 g fat, 1 g saturated fat, no cholesterol, 1 g dietary fiber, 178 mg sodium

BLUE-SPECKLED FLOUR TORTILLAS: Add 1 tablespoon of blue cornmeal (available in health-food stores and specialty shops) to the flour mixture.

WHOLE WHEAT TORTILLAS

Makes 8 tortillas

1 cup whole wheat flour

1 cup all-purpose flour

¼ teaspoon salt

2 tablespoons canola oil

¾ cup hot water

Using an electric mixer or food processor, or mixing by hand, stir together the flours and salt. Mix in the oil. Pour in the hot water and stir until dough holds together, or process a few seconds in the food processor until dough gathers into a ball.

Divide dough into 8 equal pieces and roll into balls. Flatten each ball into a round. Put each round, one at a time, on a lightly floured board or pastry cloth. Roll each dough ball into a thin tortilla about 6 inches wide.

Preheat an ungreased nonstick frying pan or heavy frying pan. Fry each tortilla about 30 to 45 seconds per side, or until tortilla is cooked through and has brown spots.

Serve tortillas immediately or store in a plastic bag in the refrigerator. To reheat, wrap in foil and warm in a 325° oven for 5 minutes.

138 calories, 4 g fat, 0.5 g saturated fat, no cholesterol, 2.5 g dietary fiber, 68 mg sodium

CORN TORTILLAS

For easy handling when using a tortilla press (available at gourmet food shops and Mexican grocery stores), set a sheet of wax paper about 8 inches square, or a wax paper sandwich bag, directly on the press. Shape a ball of dough and place it just slightly off center, toward the back hinge. Again place a piece of wax paper or bag on top of the dough. Press the lid down firmly to make a 5- or 6-inch circle. Open the press and peel the wax paper from the tortilla.

Makes 4 tortillas

1 cup masa harina　　　　　　　　**1 tablespoon vegetable shortening**
¼ teaspoon salt　　　　　　　　　**⅓ cup hot water**

Using an electric mixer or food processor, or mixing by hand, mix masa harina, salt, and vegetable shortening in a bowl. Stir in water. Gather dough into a ball.

Divide dough into 4 equal pieces. Flatten each dough ball into a round. Put each round, one at a time, on a lightly floured board or pastry cloth. Roll into a thin tortilla, about 6 inches wide.

Preheat an ungreased nonstick frying pan. Fry each tortilla until cooked through on both sides, about 30 to 45 seconds per side.

Serve tortillas immediately or store in a plastic bag in the refrigerator. To reheat, wrap in foil and warm in a 325° oven for 5 minutes.

132 calories, 4.5 g fat, 1 g saturated fat, no cholesterol, 4 g dietary fiber, 135 mg sodium

LAYERED CANYON CORNBREAD WITH DRIED TOMATO BUTTER

This cornbread, layered in hues of yellow, orange, and grayish blue, reminds us of canyon walls at sunset. Its pleasantly coarse texture and earthy corn flavor add to the illusion. Serve it with a terra-cotta–colored tomato spread (see facing page).

Cornmeals range from very coarse (including stone-ground) to fine and floury. For best results choose blue and yellow cornmeals with a similar, preferably fairly coarse, grind.

Makes 1 loaf; about 14 slices

Yellow and orange layers:
2 cups coarsely ground yellow cornmeal
½ cup whole wheat flour
2 tablespoons sugar
2 teaspoons baking powder
½ teaspoon baking soda
½ teaspoon salt

½ cup egg substitute or 4 egg whites, lightly beaten
2 tablespoons olive oil
1 cup buttermilk
1 tablespoon tomato paste

Blue layer:
¾ cup blue cornmeal
¼ cup whole wheat flour
2 teaspoons sugar
½ teaspoon baking powder
½ teaspoon baking soda
¼ teaspoon salt

¼ cup egg substitute, or 2 egg whites
1 tablespoon olive oil
½ cup buttermilk

Dried Tomato Butter (page 263)

Preheat oven to 350°. Spray a 9-by-5-inch loaf pan with nonstick cooking spray.

To make yellow and orange layers: Mix yellow cornmeal, whole wheat flour, sugar, baking powder, baking soda, and salt in a large mixing bowl. Stir in egg substitute, oil, and buttermilk just until blended.

Pour half of the batter into the prepared pan and smooth out with the back of a spoon. Stir tomato paste into remaining batter, then spoon that over the yellow layer. Smooth out with the back of a spoon.

To make blue layer: In the same mixing bowl, mix blue cornmeal with whole wheat flour, sugar, baking powder, baking soda, and salt. Stir in egg substitute, oil, and buttermilk just until blended. Spoon blue batter evenly over orange batter and smooth out with the back of a spoon.

Bake for 45 to 55 minutes, or until bread is golden and a tester inserted into the center comes out completely clean. Look carefully and wipe the tester with your finger; it may look clean at first glance but still have some moist batter clinging to it.

Let cool, then turn out of pan and slice. Serve with tomato butter.

166 calories, 4.5 g fat, 1 g saturated fat, 1 mg cholesterol, 3.5 g dietary fiber, 270 mg sodium

DRIED TOMATO BUTTER

Makes about ¾ cup

6 dried, oil-packed tomatoes, drained
⅓ cup nonfat cream cheese
1 clove garlic, minced

1 tablespoon pitted and coarsely
chopped flavorful black olives
2 tablespoons cilantro leaves

Place all ingredients in a food processor or blender and process until creamy, adding 1 to 2 tablespoons of water if necessary.

Per tablespoon: 18 calories, 0.5 g fat, no saturated fat, 1.5 mg cholesterol, no dietary fiber, 74 mg sodium

WHOLE WHEAT SOURDOUGH BREAD

Although Americans everywhere used to make sourdough bread and pancakes, romance links sourdough with the West. It was the food of Alaskan prospectors, Montana miners, and Oklahoma housewives. For more information on sourdough, see Self-Starters (page 265).

Purists don't taint their sourdoughs with commercial yeast, but we find that adding a little yeast gives much more consistent results. The bread still has a full body and a fine, slightly tart flavor.

Makes 1 loaf; 12 servings

Starter:
½ cup cool water
Pinch of active dry yeast

1 cup bread flour

Dough:
½ cup starter
1 cup cool water
1½ teaspoons salt
1½ cups bread flour, plus more as needed

1½ cups whole wheat flour, plus more as needed
2 tablespoons egg substitute or ½ egg beaten with 2 teaspoons water

To make starter: In a glass or ceramic bowl or large jar, mix water, yeast, and flour together to make a sticky dough. Cover loosely with a damp towel and let sit at room temperature for 48 to 72 hours, dampening the towel now and then. Starter should be bubbly and have a pleasantly sour smell.

To finish the dough: Place ½ cup starter in the large bowl of a heavy-duty electric mixer fitted with the dough hook. Reserve remaining starter for your next batch of bread (see page 265). Add water and squeeze starter in water with your fingers to break up lumps. Stir in salt, then bread flour. Add enough whole wheat flour to make a soft, fairly sticky, dough.

Knead dough with mixer for about 5 minutes, then turn out onto a floured board and knead for a minute by hand. Dough should be soft, pillowy, and slightly sticky. Or knead dough completely by hand for 10 to 15 minutes.

Cover dough with a damp towel and let rise at cool room temperature for 6 to 10 hours, or until doubled. Punch down and shape into a round loaf. Place in an oiled 8-inch-round cake pan and let rise 3 to 4 hours, or until light.

Preheat oven to 425°.

Brush loaf with egg substitute or egg-water mixture. With a razor blade or sharp knife, make 3 or 4½-inch-deep slashes in the top of the loaf. Bake in the cake pan for 15 minutes. Turn loaf out of pan and place directly on oven rack. Continue baking for 10 to 15 minutes, or until loaf is golden brown, has a crunchy crust, and sounds hollow when tapped on the bottom.

Place on a wire rack. Let cool completely before slicing. Unsliced, this bread will keep up to 3 or 4 days.

146 calories, 0.5 g fat, no saturated fat, no cholesterol, 2.5 g dietary fiber, 268 mg sodium

Self-Starters

Legend has it that the wagon trains heading west revived the art of sourdough at a time when much of the country was discovering the consistent joys of commercially made yeast. The pioneers, it is said, wanted something that would keep on the trail and allow their families to enjoy the bread they liked "back home." Some of those sourdoughs—not to mention a few from Nefertiti's Egypt—are still alive today, sourdough aficionados claim.

All we can say is, those folks must have extremely conscientious descendants. We've tried on several occasions to keep a sourdough starter—the blend of flour, liquid, and yeast (sometimes)—alive for a couple of weeks. We always forget to feed it, and it gets pushed to the back of the refrigerator, where it eventually will knock your socks off with the ammonia smell.

Romance holds that sourdoughs keep their unique character wherever they may live. Professional bakers say that isn't so. Common sense holds that if you transport some wild Tanzanian sourdough culture to Fort Collins, Colorado, eventually the Coloradoan yeasts will Americanize it. Still, we love all the sourdough stories. They illustrate a true passion for bread that fortunately is beginning to revive in America.

As for feeding a starter, that's easy—once you remember the stuff is in the refrigerator. Add at least as much flour as there is starter, then enough water to make a soft, sticky dough. Keep the starter at room temperature for about 8 to 12 hours if you're going to make bread, or refrigerate it for up to 2 or 3 days; then either use it or feed it. If the starter begins to get too voluminous, throw most of it away and feed what's left.

You can also use the "old dough" method: Simply pinch off a piece from the dough you're turning into bread and save and feed that as your starter.

CINNAMON ROLLS

Although cinnamon rolls, a Montana favorite, fall into the "health food" category only if you're discussing psychological health, our rolls are not as laden with fat as some of their more decadent cousins, and they're low in saturated fat.

Makes 15 rolls

Dough:

4 teaspoons active dry yeast
½ cup warm water (110° to 115°)
3 tablespoons sugar
1 teaspoon salt
1 tablespoon canola oil

¾ cup plain low-fat yogurt, at cool
    room temperature
1½ cups bread flour, plus more as
    needed
1½ cups whole wheat flour

Filling:

2 tablespoons melted unsalted butter
    (browned butter is especially nice)

½ cup sugar
1 tablespoon cinnamon

Glaze:

½ cup confectioners' sugar
1 teaspoon lemon juice

1 teaspoon vanilla extract
1 teaspoon water

To make dough: Dissolve yeast in warm water in the bowl of a heavy-duty electric mixer fitted with the dough hook. Stir in sugar, salt, oil, and yogurt. Stir in flours to make a soft, fairly sticky dough. Knead until smooth and elastic, about 5 minutes, working in just enough additional flour as needed to keep dough from sticking all over the bowl. (Or mix and knead dough by hand, working in just enough flour to keep dough from sticking all over your hands and the board.)

Place dough in a clean, oiled bowl, cover, and let rise in a warm place until doubled in bulk, about 1 to 1½ hours.

Punch dough down and roll on a lightly floured surface to a rectangle about 12 by 20 inches. Brush evenly with melted butter. Mix sugar and cinnamon and sprinkle evenly over dough. Roll up dough the long way, as tightly as possible. Pinch edges to seal.

Cut into 15 slices. Place slices about an inch apart on a baking sheet that has been sprayed with nonstick cooking spray. Cover loosely with a thin towel or plastic wrap and let rise in a warm place until light, about 45 minutes to 1 hour.

Preheat oven to 375°.

Bake cinnamon rolls about 15 minutes, or until golden. Let cool on baking sheet for 5 to 10 minutes.

Meanwhile, make the glaze: Mix confectioners' sugar with lemon juice, vanilla extract, and water. Drizzle over rolls while still hot.

Remove rolls to a wire rack to finish cooling.

167 calories, 3 g fat, 1 g saturated fat, 5 mg cholesterol, 2 g dietary fiber, 152 mg sodium

TRAIL MIX TRUFFLES

Hikers, mountain bikers, and others engaged in vigorous outdoor exercise often rely on quick sugar to give a jolt of energy and calories. These "truffles" taste better than most granola bars. Keep them cool.

Makes 4 servings; 8 small balls

2 tablespoons golden raisins
¼ cup light peanut butter
2 tablespoons apple butter

1 cup nonfat granola
2 tablespoons water
¼ cup toasted wheat germ

Using a food processor, pulse raisins with peanut butter and apple butter a few times, until raisins are chopped. Stir in granola and water, and process in 3 or 4 pulses until mixture sticks together slightly.

With a tablespoon, shape granola mixture into 8 balls. Spread wheat germ in a small bowl. Roll each ball in wheat germ. Put on a plate and chill until firm.

243 calories, 8.5 g fat, 1 g saturated fat, no cholesterol, 3 g dietary fiber, 121 mg sodium

HUCKLEBERRY YOGURT PIE

At the end of summer, the northern woods of the West start crawling with men, women, and children carrying baskets, and the newspaper classifieds abound with ads for huckleberries. The huckleberry is a distant, wild cousin to the blueberry.

You can use 1 envelope of gelatin, which is not vegetarian, in place of the agar in the pie filling.

Makes 6 servings

Filling:
1 large container (16 ounces) plain
*   nonfat yogurt*
2 tablespoons agar flakes
6 tablespoons frozen unsweetened apple
*   juice concentrate, thawed*

1 cup nonfat cream cheese
2 teaspoons vanilla extract

Crust:
1⅓ cups finely crushed low-fat or fat-
*   free graham crackers*
½ teaspoon ground cinnamon

2 tablespoons frozen unsweetened apple
*   juice concentrate, thawed*

Topping:

1 pint (2 cups) fresh or frozen
   huckleberries, or blueberries
½ cup frozen apple juice concentrate,
   thawed

1 tablespoon cornstarch
⅛ teaspoon ground cinnamon
⅛ teaspoon grated nutmeg
1 teaspoon vanilla extract

Place the yogurt in a sieve or funnel lined with a coffee filter or 2 thicknesses of cheesecloth. Set the sieve or funnel over a wide-mouthed measuring cup. Let yogurt drain about 30 minutes, or until ½ cup liquid has drained into the cup. If you will not be using the drained yogurt immediately, refrigerate.

While yogurt drains, make the crust: Spray a 9-inch pie pan with nonstick cooking spray. Preheat oven to 350°.

With a fork, mix graham cracker crumbs with cinnamon and apple juice concentrate just until crumbs are moistened. Lightly oil or spray the fork and use it to gently press the crumbs evenly over bottom and up sides of the pie pan. Crust will be crumbly.

Bake for 6 to 8 minutes, until crust is toasted and seems firm. Let cool completely before filling.

To make filling: Sprinkle agar over apple juice concentrate in a small saucepan. Stir. Bring to a simmer and cook over medium heat for 5 to 10 minutes, stirring frequently, until agar is completely dissolved. Set aside to cool. (If using gelatin, sprinkle over apple juice concentrate, let stand for 5 minutes, then heat over low heat until gelatin dissolves. Let cool.)

Place drained yogurt in a food processor or mixing bowl with cream cheese and vanilla extract. Process or beat until smooth. Stir in cooled apple concentrate. Pour into cooled crust. Refrigerate for several hours or until set.

At least 2 hours before serving, make topping: Place berries and apple juice concentrate in a saucepan with cornstarch, cinnamon, nutmeg, and vanilla extract. Stir well. Cook over medium heat, stirring often, until filling clears and thickens and berries begin to cook down, about 5 minutes. Let cool completely, then spread over filling. Refrigerate at least 1 hour, or until topping is set.

Serve pie cold.

310 calories, 3 g fat, 0.5 g saturated fat, 5 mg cholesterol, 2 g dietary fiber, 449 mg sodium

5

The Pacific Coast

San Francisco Chinese-style Birthday Party

Seaweed Soup

Vegetable Packets

Jade Broccoli

Hoisin Noodles with Bean Curd

Almond Jelly with Gingered Pineapple

Pacific Northwest Harvest Dinner

Riesling-poached Asian Pears with Tillamook Cheddar

Chanterelle-Filbert Tart with Phyllo Crust

Stir-fried Autumn Greens

Low-fat Chocolate Raspberry Soufflés

A Sixties Reunion

Tofu-Mushroom Burgers

Brown Rice, Fruit, and Walnut Salad

Steamed Squash, Peppers, and Fennel with Gremolata

Orange-scented Tofu Carrot Cake

Appetizers, Salads, and Side Dishes

California Maki with Avocado,
Cucumber, and Green Onion

Sweet-Sour-Hot Slaw

Salads in Rice Paper

Soups

Simmered Vegetables with Buckwheat Noodles

Won Ton Soup

Cold Swirled Tomato and Spinach Soup

Entrées

Artichoke Pizza with Dried Tomatoes and Pine Nuts

Couscous with Pistachios, Blood Oranges, and Snow Peas

Quinoa with Three Peppers

Quinoa and Couscous with Spinach

Mu Shu Vegetables in a Chinese Pancake

All-American Chow Mein

Black Bean Tostadas

Tangerine-perfumed Crepes with Shiitake Mushrooms and Juice

Soba (Buckwheat Noodles) with a Light Peanut Sauce

Grilled Vegetables with Lemon Sage Polenta

Stir-Fry Primavera

Saffron Angel Hair with Asparagus and Red Pepper Pesto

Potato and String Bean Salad with Roasted Garlic Dressing

Roasted Garlic

Breads and Desserts

Olive-Fennel Bread

Bread with Many Grains

Buckwheat Focaccia with Dried Tomatoes

Fruit and Oatmeal Scones

Amaranth Blackberry Muffins

Cider-poached Apples

Peach and Chardonnay Soup with Roasted Plums

Europe has the Mediterranean. We have the Pacific Coast.

The warm breezes off the Pacific moderate the climate along the coast, allowing growers to produce olives, wine grapes, almonds, walnuts, pistachios, filberts (hazelnuts), blood oranges and regular oranges, lemons, garlic, and artichokes. These "Mediterranean" products join an endless list of other edibles from California, Washington, and Oregon, including asparagus, peaches, plums, sweet cherries, raspberries, blackberries, blueberries, pears, apples, cheeses, butter, tofu, tomatoes, spinach, lettuce, wild mushrooms, seaweed, and rice (most of the Japanese rice sold in the United States comes from California).

The single state of California exports more produce than many states—and countries—grow, period. The Gold Rush of 1849 may have brought the state fame, but agriculture is its gold today. The rest of the country sometimes grimly predicts California's falling into the ocean, but if it did, the rest of us would go a little hungrier—and thirstier.

Hawaii has an even milder climate and grows the ingredients that thrive in the tropics: ginger, pineapples, mangos, macadamia nuts, and coffee. Recently, it has become the first place in the United States to grow cocoa beans.

From the seventies on, California has enjoyed a reputation as the capital of "health food" and deserved much of the blame when every second-rate eatery in the United States started topping sandwiches with alfalfa sprouts. But when Americans started to become more interested in nutrition and healthful eating, California quickly emerged as the leader of the new and improved American cuisine.

Chefs such as Alice Waters, Jeremiah Tower, Deborah Madison, Annie Sommerville, Wolfgang Puck, Barbara Tropp, Ken Hom, and Joyce Goldstein helped define the new direction in American cooking, toward ingredients that were valued for their intrinsic flavors and ethnic roots rather than the sauces they were drowned in.

For many, the Pacific Coast represents paradise, and cities large and small support melting pots of every imaginable ethnicity, from the Scandinavians and Native Americans of Oregon and Washington to the Italians and Chinese of San Francisco to the Koreans and Mexicans of Los Angeles to the Filipinos, Japanese, and native Hawaiians of Hawaii. The flavors that most infuse the food along this stretch, however, are Mediterranean, Latino, and Asian.

The architects of the new cuisine used these flavors and ingredients to embellish their creations: lemongrass, ginger, wasabi, hoisin sauce, baby bok choy, Asian pears, black beans, jicama, chiles, cilantro, extra-virgin olive oil, dried tomatoes, goat cheese, rosemary.

They paired these new compositions with some of the world's finest wines, from California and, increasingly, from Oregon and Washington. And they topped them off with espresso, which spread from Seattle and the Italian neighborhoods of the coastal cities to captivate the nation.

California was also the first state to set a standard for certifying produce as organically grown and one of the first to encourage and support organic farming on a large scale.

Much of the Pacific Northwest enjoys a growing season as long as California's—if somewhat cooler. And Seattle has its own crop of talented, newly discovered chefs. Half of California, it now seems, lives in Seattle and Portland these days—or so the natives of Washington and Portland grumble—so why shouldn't the center of the food world move with them?

Stay tuned.

• SAN FRANCISCO CHINESE-STYLE BIRTHDAY PARTY •

Tourists in San Francisco wouldn't dream of leaving without wandering through the city's famous Chinatown, a jumble of tea shops, restaurants, noodle factories, grocery stores, and endless souvenir shops selling dolls, tai chi slippers, fans, and chopsticks.

Behind the tourist glitz, the Chinese in San Francisco, like the Italians and Irish in New York and the Germans and Poles in Chicago, have roots that go generations deep in American soil. Chinese-Americans are a potent economic force in San Francisco—and a culinary one. There's still no better city in the United States to order a really good Chinese lunch for next to nothing.

This Chinese-American birthday menu pays homage to the long tradition of using foods to represent wealth, happiness, and luck. The vegetable packets—little presents for each diner—

need no explanation. Broccoli is green, the color of jade and dollar bills. Noodles are long, and so, it is hoped, will be the celebrant's life.

Suggested Wines: Champagne can stand up to the flavors in this menu, and bubbly seems best for a birthday party. But tea is an even better bet. Choose a delicate green tea, an oolong, or a black tea, as you wish.

Seaweed Soup

Nori, or dried laver, comes in pliable sheets in Asian markets and some supermarkets. Pleasantly briny, it is one of the milder tasting seaweeds. It's most easily cut with scissors.

Makes 8 servings

*7 cups vegetable stock (page 17) or
4 cups canned vegetable broth diluted
with 3 cups water*
1 cup shredded nori
¼ teaspoon pepper
*2 tablespoons light (reduced-sodium)
soy sauce*

½ teaspoon grated fresh gingerroot
2 green onions, minced
1 cup drained and diced firm tofu
½ teaspoon dark sesame oil
4 egg whites
1 egg

Heat vegetable stock in a large saucepan over medium-high heat. Stir in nori, pepper, soy sauce, and ginger, and simmer for a minute, then stir in green onions, tofu, and oil.

Lightly beat egg whites and egg with a fork in a small bowl. Bring soup to a boil. In a slow, steady stream, stir eggs into boiling soup. Turn off heat immediately and let soup sit for 1 minute; do not stir.

Ladle into bowls and serve hot.

61 calories, 3 g fat, 0.5 g saturated fat, 27 mg cholesterol, 0.5 g dietary fiber, 676 mg sodium

Vegetable Packets

This Chinese technique of frying without really frying is similar to the French technique of baking in parchment. Since people in China did not have ovens, everything was cooked on the stovetop—and that tradition continues in this country. The small amount of food in the packets is just a bonus. The real reason for this course is the fun of opening the packets at the table.

Makes 16 packets; 8 servings

Marinade:

2 teaspoons minced fresh gingerroot

3 tablespoons light (reduced-sodium) soy sauce

3 tablespoons dry white wine

1 teaspoon sugar

½ teaspoon dark sesame oil

¼ teaspoon pepper

½ teaspoon powdered mustard

Filling:

2 small, evenly shaped sweet potatoes, peeled and thinly sliced into 16 circles

4 green onions, trimmed, cut in half lengthwise, and then cut into 4

pieces each to make 32 pieces about 1 inch long

16 snow peas, trimmed

2 cups canola oil

Mix marinade ingredients in a shallow glass bowl. Add sweet potatoes, green onions, and snow peas. Marinate at room temperature for 1 hour. Drain.

Have ready 16 wax paper sandwich bags or wax paper cut into sixteen 6-inch squares.

To make a packet, put 1 slice sweet potato, 2 pieces green onion, and 1 snow pea in a sandwich bag or on a sheet of wax paper. Roll edges together and seal with a little water to make an envelope-style packet. Repeat until you have 16 packets. This can be done ahead of time and packets refrigerated for several hours.

When ready to serve, heat oil in a wok or deep-frying pan to 375°. Deep-fry vegetable packets, 3 or 4 at a time, turning once, for a few minutes, or until vegetables are cooked through.

Put 2 packets on each plate. Guests unwrap the packages at the table.

47 calories, 1 g fat, no saturated fat, no cholesterol, 1.5 g dietary fiber, 69 mg sodium

Jade Broccoli

This unusual but tasty combination of ingredients illustrates again how alcohol can enhance the flavors of other ingredients. This would make a good side dish for nearly any meal.

Makes 8 servings

1 ½ *pounds broccoli*
1 *tablespoon canola oil*
1 *teaspoon grated fresh gingerroot*
3 *cloves garlic, minced*
¼ *teaspoon pepper*
½ *cup sliced water chestnuts (fresh or canned, drained and rinsed)*

3 *tablespoons light (reduced-sodium) soy sauce*
3 *tablespoons dark brown sugar*
½ *teaspoon dark sesame oil*
3 *tablespoons gin or dry white wine*

Cut broccoli heads into florets. Peel and thinly slice stems. Blanch broccoli for 2 to 3 minutes in lightly salted boiling water. Drain and rinse under cold running water. Set aside.

Heat oil in a nonstick wok or frying pan that has been sprayed with nonstick cooking spray. Add ginger and garlic, and sauté until fragrant. Add pepper, broccoli, and water chestnuts. Mix together soy sauce, brown sugar, and sesame oil, and add to broccoli. Add gin, cover, and cook for 1 minute. Transfer vegetables to a serving bowl and serve immediately.

76 calories, 2 g fat, no saturated fat, no cholesterol, 3 g dietary fiber, 217 mg sodium

Hoisin Noodles with Bean Curd

This colorful pyramid is an impressive centerpiece for a festive occasion. The long, unbroken strands of noodles symbolize longevity.

Hoisin, a thick, dark brown sauce made from fermented soybeans, garlic, chiles and other spices, is spicy, salty, and sweet. If your Chinese stir-fries don't taste as good as those you've had in restaurants, the fault may lie in that supermarket sauce, which often is mostly sugar. If possible, buy hoisin and other Chinese sauces in a Chinese market.

Makes 8 servings

4 cups cooked and drained Asian-style thin egg noodles

1 teaspoon dark sesame oil
½ cup minced green onion

Sauce:

1 tablespoon light (reduced-sodium)
   soy sauce

1 tablespoon dry white wine

1 tablespoon rice vinegar

½ teaspoon sugar

2 tablespoons hoisin sauce

½ teaspoon salt

2 tablespoons vegetable stock
   (page 17)

2 eggs

2 egg whites

¼ teaspoon white pepper

1 large cucumber, peeled, seeded, and
   thinly sliced

8 ounces firm bean curd (tofu), drained
   and diced

½ cup trimmed snow peas

¼ cup chopped cilantro

In a bowl, toss noodles with sesame oil and green onion. In a separate small bowl, stir sauce ingredients together. Toss sauce with noodles. Spread noodles out on a large, flat plate, making a bed for the remaining ingredients.

Beat eggs and egg whites with pepper. Scramble eggs in a nonstick frying pan that has been sprayed with nonstick cooking spray.

Mound ingredients on top of noodles in this order, making increasingly smaller mounds to create a pyramid shape: cucumber, bean curd, scrambled eggs, snow peas, then cilantro.

Serve warm or at room temperature. As you serve with chopsticks or two forks, mix the ingredients together.

170 calories, 4 g fat, 1 g saturated fat, 79 mg cholesterol, 3 g dietary fiber, 236 mg sodium

●━━━◆━━━●

Almond Jelly with Gingered Pineapple

Almond jelly is a white, almond-flavored set dessert. Unusual for a classic Chinese dish, it contains milk. You can easily prepare this dish the day before serving.

If you are not a strict vegetarian, you can make the dessert with gelatin instead of agar. Soften 2 envelopes of gelatin in ½ cup of water, then microwave on high for 30 seconds or until gelatin dissolves. Stir in remaining ingredients.

Makes 8 servings

1½ *cups cold water*
2 *cups 2-percent milk*
1½ *tablespoons agar flakes*
⅓ *cup sugar*
1 *teaspoon almond extract*

2 *cups chopped fresh pineapple or*
  canned and drained crushed
  pineapple packed in juice
2 *tablespoons minced candied ginger*

Stir water and milk together in a saucepan. Stir in agar, then sugar. Bring to a boil over medium heat, reduce heat to low, and simmer about 5 minutes, or until agar dissolves; stir occasionally. Remove from heat and stir in almond extract.

Pour mixture into an 8-inch-square pan. Refrigerate for 3 hours or longer, until very firm.

Using a small, sharp knife, cut almond jelly into 1-inch cubes. Toss pineapple with candied ginger and stir into jelly. Ladle into shallow dessert dishes. Serve chilled.

83 calories, 1.5 g fat, 1 g saturated fat, 4.5 mg cholesterol, no dietary fiber, 31 mg sodium

• PACIFIC NORTHWEST HARVEST DINNER •

Thanks to the mild Pacific climate and the legendary constant rain or threat of it, the Pacific Northwest is one of the greenest spots in the United States. That means it's a good place for mushrooms—a good share of the wild mushrooms sold in this country come from the Northwest, and armed "turf wars" have even broken out over the matsutake, a fungus highly prized by the Japanese.

The charitable climate also blesses agricultural pursuits such as raspberry growing—Washington State is the red raspberry capital—and winemaking.

In the fall, Pikes Place in Seattle and other markets lure food-lovers with golden chanterelles, trumpet-shaped golden orange mushrooms with a fruity-woodsy flavor, and Oregon and Washington filberts—or hazelnuts, as they're more commonly (and erroneously) called. Bell peppers, salad and cooking greens, raspberries, radicchio, apples, and pears only intensify the wish that autumn would last forever.

Suggested Wines: A Riesling, of course, is the perfect partner for the Riesling poached pears and Cheddar. The chanterelle tart requires a richer wine, such as a Chardonnay, champagne, or white Bordeaux.

Riesling-poached Asian Pears with Tillamook Cheddar

Asian pears, or apple pears, look like greenish russet apples, but have a granular-juicy flesh, like pears. They're crisper than standard pears, however, and stay crisp when cooked. They're available in some supermarkets from summer through early spring. Unlike pears, they're hard when ripe; choose Asian pears that are fragrant and refrigerate them.

Those who have access to it can use Tillamook Cheddar—the cheese from Oregon's famous cooperative—but any good Cheddar will do.

Makes 8 servings

4 firm but ripe Asian pears or Bartlett pears
¾ cup Johannisberger Riesling
¼ cup water
1 long strip orange peel
½ teaspoon whole cloves

½ teaspoon juniper berries (optional)
½ teaspoon whole coriander seed
2 ounces good-quality Cheddar, shaved into very thin slices
Cracked black pepper
Low-fat, unsalted crackers

Peel pears, core, and thinly slice. In a stainless steel skillet or one with a nonstick coating, bring wine, water, orange peel, cloves, juniper berries, and coriander seed to a simmer. Add pears. As soon as liquid returns to a simmer, remove from heat and let cool. Bartlett pears will discolor and should be served immediately after cooling. Asian pears can be refrigerated in liquid until serving time. Drain well before serving.

Arrange on plate, alternating with Cheddar slices. Sprinkle with pepper. Serve with crackers.

Without crackers: 59 calories, 2.5 g fat, 1.5 g saturated fat, 7.5 mg cholesterol, 1 g dietary fiber, 44 mg sodium

Chanterelle-Filbert Tart with Phyllo Crust

If you're lucky enough to live in the Pacific Northwest, you can buy a bagful of chanterelles, those lovely mushrooms, and musky-sweet filberts (hazelnuts) and make this lovely special-occasion dish. If you live elsewhere, you may be able to find fresh chanterelles (for a hefty price) in gourmet supermarkets in the fall. Or use oyster mushrooms and dried tomatoes for a different—but equally good—tart.

Phyllo dough, also sometimes labeled strudel or fillo dough, is available frozen in many supermarkets. The paper-thin sheets turn very crisp when baked.

Makes 8 servings

1 pound fresh chanterelles or oyster
    mushrooms
3 dried apricot halves, or 6 dried
    tomato halves (not packed in oil)
1 tablespoon unsalted butter
½ cup minced red onion
1 tablespoon minced fresh basil or
    marjoram, or 1 teaspoon dried

2 tablespoons white wine or water
3 tablespoons light sour cream
Salt and pepper to taste
5 sheets phyllo dough, thawed
2 tablespoons extra-virgin olive oil
⅓ cup finely chopped filberts
    (hazelnuts)

Cut mushrooms lengthwise into halves or quarters depending on size. Cut apricots or dried tomatoes into slivers.

Heat butter in a large nonstick skillet. Add onion and sauté until soft. Add mushrooms, apricots or tomatoes, and basil or marjoram; sauté until mushrooms are softened and most of the liquid has evaporated, 8 to 10 minutes. Stir in wine and sour cream. Season with salt and pepper.

Preheat oven to 400°. Lightly oil a 10- to 11-inch tart pan. Gently peel off 1 sheet of phyllo dough and lay on a clean work surface. Keep remaining phyllo sheets under a damp towel to keep them from drying out.

Dab the sheet of phyllo very lightly with oil. Lay another sheet of phyllo atop the first, dabbing lightly with oil. Continue until you have stacked all 5 phyllo sheets.

Gently transfer stacked sheets of dough to the tart pan. Smooth dough to edges of pan. Turn under overhanging edges of dough and press into rough ruffles to form a rim.

Sprinkle 2 tablespoons nuts evenly over bottom of crust. Bake crust for 8 to 10 minutes, until edges begin to turn golden. Reduce oven temperature to 375°. Spoon mushroom mixture evenly over crust. Sprinkle remaining nuts over mushrooms.

Return to oven for 10 to 15 minutes, until pastry is a deep golden brown.

Cut into wedges while still warm.

138 calories, 8.5 g fat, 2 g saturated fat, 6 mg cholesterol, 2 g dietary fiber, 121 mg sodium

Stir-fried Autumn Greens

This is basically a warm salad suitable for the cooler days of autumn. If you can find young, tender radicchio and like its bitter edge, you can use 1 cup of shredded radicchio instead of 1 cup of cabbage.

Makes 8 servings

1½ pounds bok choy, preferably baby
*   bok choy*
½ pound red cabbage
2 teaspoons canola oil
1 tablespoon finely minced fresh
*   gingerroot*
2 medium leeks, cut in half lengthwise,
*   thoroughly rinsed, and cut into shreds*

1 orange bell pepper, seeded and slivered
2 tablespoons low-sodium soy sauce
3 tablespoons apple cider or juice
2 teaspoons cornstarch or arrowroot
*   mixed with 1 tablespoon water*
½ teaspoon sugar
¼ teaspoon salt, or to taste
Pinch or 2 of red pepper

Trim the bok choy and cabbage and cut into thin shreds.

Heat oil in a wok or deep-frying pan that has been sprayed with nonstick cooking spray. Add ginger and leeks, and stir-fry for 1 minute. Add bok choy, cabbage, and bell pepper. Stir-fry over high heat just until greens are wilted, about 3 to 4 minutes.

Remove from heat and place in a large bowl. Place soy sauce, apple juice, cornstarch mixture, sugar, salt, and red pepper in a pan. Bring to a simmer and cook, stirring, until sauce thickens and clears. Pour over greens and toss to coat. Serve warm.

46 calories, 1.5 g fat, no saturated fat, no cholesterol, 2 g dietary fiber, 256 mg sodium

◆━━◆

Low-fat Chocolate Raspberry Soufflés

The soufflé is still one of the most elegant of desserts. We've trimmed the fat in these soufflés to practically nothing and have offset their sweetness with tart raspberries.

You can use any nonfat chocolate sauce in this, but we like the sauce from Washington-based Wax Orchards, which is sweetened with fruit juice and has a bitter chocolate flavor that's a good counterpoint to sweet ingredients. It's available in health-food stores and gourmet shops, or can be ordered by mail (see Sources and Resources, page 329).

Makes 8 servings

4 cups fresh raspberries

10 tablespoons sugar

8 egg whites, at room temperature

½ teaspoon cream of tartar

2 cups nonfat chocolate sauce

Press 1 cup of the raspberries through a strainer to make a smooth puree. Set aside.

Spray 8 individual soufflé dishes (ramekins) with canola oil nonstick cooking spray. Sprinkle insides of ramekins with 4 tablespoons sugar, shaking out excess sugar. Preheat oven to 375°.

Beat egg whites in a mixer on high speed until foamy. Sprinkle cream of tartar and remaining 6 tablespoons sugar over egg whites and continue beating until firm, glossy peaks form. Using a whisk, gently fold in 1 cup chocolate sauce and raspberry puree.

Spoon egg white mixture into prepared ramekins. Bake in the center of the oven for 10 to 12 minutes, until soufflés have risen and tops are firm.

Put each soufflé on a dessert plate. Sprinkle remaining raspberries around soufflés and drizzle remaining chocolate sauce over them. Serve at once.

213 calories, 1 g fat, 0.5 g saturated fat, no cholesterol, 4 g dietary fiber, 70 mg sodium

• A SIXTIES REUNION •

It was the best of times and the worst of times. Soaring guitar solos, free love, Beatles playing dead, the mudfest at Woodstock, clunky beads, silly pants, drug overdoses, and assassinations that left the country stunned and drained.

Were the sixties really that long ago?

In those days, California—especially the University of California at Berkeley and San Francisco's Haight Ashbury neighborhood—was a hotbed of radical activity and "hippie food" such as brown rice, tofu, breads that weighed a ton and a half, brown rice, sprouts, steamed vegetables, and brown rice.

Like so much in the 1960s, that oh-so-brown diet changed the culinary landscape. It may have taken a while, but many of today's Establishment parent types actually enjoy tofu now that they've learned not to drown it in soy sauce.

This menu is suitable for a gathering of old college friends, staying up into the night (or at least beyond when the kids have gone to bed), and reminiscing about sit-ins, campus takeovers—and brown rice before everybody was eating it.

Suggested wines: Nothing you drank in college, that's for sure. However, a decent white Zinfandel would actually go with the menu and remind you, however fleetingly, of the days when wine—and much of life—was sweet. For a more sophisticated choice, choose a light red such as Merlot, Chianti, or Pinot Noir.

Tofu-Mushroom Burgers

Eating burgers is a ritual as American as shooting baskets, grousing about the IRS, and forming communes. But you no longer have to eat meat to join in the fun.

Although there are a number of good vegetarian burgers on the market, we still prefer homemade ones when we have time to prepare them. These burgers are chewy and moist, and have a fresh, vegetable-herb flavor.

For best results chop the vegetables, one at a time, in the food processor.

Makes 8 servings

2 tablespoons olive oil

4 cups very finely chopped mushrooms

2 cups finely grated carrots

1½ cups very finely chopped onions

3 to 4 large cloves garlic, minced

1 tablespoon dried mixed herbs, such as Italian seasoning, or 2 tablespoons fresh minced herbs

¾ cup fine bulgur

8 ounces extra-firm tofu, mashed

1 cup dry bread crumbs, plus more if needed

½ teaspoon salt

8 Fluffy Buns (page 136) or whole wheat hamburger buns

Heat oil in a nonstick frying pan that has been sprayed with nonstick cooking spray. Add mushrooms, carrots, onions, garlic, and herbs. Cook over medium heat, stirring often, until vegetables no longer give off liquid.

Remove from heat. Add bulgur, tofu, bread crumbs, and salt. Mix thoroughly. Mixture should be thick and pasty; if it seems too wet, add more bread crumbs.

Form into 8 patties using a generous ½ cup for each. Place on a wax paper–lined plate, cover loosely with wax paper or plastic wrap, and refrigerate at least 1 hour and up to 24 hours.

To cook, heat a large nonstick skillet that has been coated with nonstick cooking spray. Add burgers and cook in 2 batches over medium heat, turning once, until golden and heated through, 5 to 7 minutes. Or grill burgers on a lightly oiled grid over hot coals, turning once, until nicely browned on both sides and heated through.

Serve between buns with accompaniments of your choice. These are nice with mustard, tomato, grilled onions, and yogurt or nonfat mayonnaise.

180 calories, 6 g fat, 1 g saturated fat, no cholesterol, 5 g dietary fiber, 257 mg sodium

Brown Rice, Fruit, and Walnut Salad

Brown rice was the quintessential "hippie" food of the sixties. Often it was teamed up with soy sauce—lots of soy sauce.

This brown rice salad is just as tied to the earth, Mother Nature, and good vibrations but is light, bright, and New Age in its trendy combining of ingredients.

Wehani is a lovely mahogany-colored rice developed by Lundberg Farms in Richvale, California (see page 332). It has a toasty-musky flavor that is especially nice with fruit.

Makes 8 servings

1 cup long-grain brown rice
½ cup Wehani or long-grain brown rice
2½ cups water
½ teaspoon salt
⅓ cup coarsely chopped walnuts, preferably toasted
2 tablespoons extra-virgin olive oil
2 tablespoons balsamic or raspberry vinegar

1 medium nectarine, pitted and diced
1 cup peeled and diced jicama or cucumber
1 cup halved seedless green grapes
1 kiwi fruit, peeled and diced
1 to 2 tablespoons finely chopped fresh rosemary, to taste
Freshly ground black pepper to taste
Leaf lettuce

Cook rices together in water until cooked through but still firm, 35 to 45 minutes. Let cool.

Place rice in a bowl and toss with remaining ingredients except lettuce. Line a plate or bowl with the lettuce and spoon rice salad onto lettuce. Serve at cool room temperature.

Although the rice can be cooked up to 2 days ahead of time and refrigerated, the salad itself should be assembled shortly before serving.

168 calories, 7 g fat, 1 g saturated fat, no cholesterol, 2 g dietary fiber, 137 mg sodium

Steamed Squash, Peppers, and Fennel with Gremolata

To add pizzazz to steamed vegetables, we've borrowed gremolata—a mix of parsley, lemon, and garlic—from its standard use as a condiment for veal shanks.

Makes 8 servings

1 zucchini, cut into strips

2 yellow squash, cut into strips

2 California red bell peppers, seeded
 and cut into strips

2 bulbs fennel, cored and cut into strips

½ cup Italian parsley leaves

Zest of 1 medium lemon, grated

2 to 3 cloves garlic, chopped

Juice of 1 lemon

Salt and freshly ground pepper to taste

Place zucchini, yellow squash, bell peppers, and fennel in a large colander or steamer. Set over boiling water, cover tightly, and steam, tossing once, for 10 minutes, or until cooked through but still crisp.

Meanwhile, chop parsley with lemon zest and garlic until finely minced.

Toss vegetables with gremolata. Season with lemon juice, salt, and pepper. Serve warm.

24 calories, no g fat, no cholesterol, 1.5 g dietary fiber, 96 mg sodium

Orange-scented Tofu Carrot Cake

Makes 8 servings

Carrot Cake:

8 ounces firm tofu, drained

¼ cup canola oil

½ cup honey, preferably orange
 blossom

1 tablespoon vanilla extract

1 tablespoon grated orange zest

1½ packed cups finely grated carrots

½ teaspoon salt

1½ teaspoons baking soda

1½ cups whole wheat flour

1 teaspoon ground cinnamon

¼ teaspoon ground nutmeg

½ cup raisins

⅓ cup chopped walnuts

Frosting (optional):

3 ounces light cream cheese

2 tablespoons nonfat sour cream

2 tablespoons honey, preferably orange
  blossom

½ teaspoon orange extract

⅛ teaspoon vanilla extract

Preheat oven to 350°. Spray a 9-inch-square cake pan with nonstick cooking spray.

To make cake: In a large mixing bowl, beat tofu with oil, honey, and vanilla extract until well blended. Beat in orange zest and carrots. Beat in salt, baking soda, flour, cinnamon, and nutmeg until well blended. Stir in raisins and walnuts.

Pour into prepared pan and bake for 35 to 40 minutes, until a tester inserted in the center comes out clean. Let cool in pan.

When the cake is cool, make frosting if desired: Beat cream cheese and sour cream together until smooth. Beat in honey and orange and vanilla extracts to make a soft icing. Refrigerate to firm up slightly, then spread over cooled cake. Refrigerate until shortly before serving time. This cake keeps well for up to 3 days.

With frosting: 336 calories, 14 g fat, 2.5 g saturated fat, 10 mg cholesterol, 4.5 g dietary fiber, 346 mg sodium

Without frosting: 301 calories, 11 g fat, 1 g saturated fat, no cholesterol, 4.5 g dietary fiber, 300 mg sodium

Appetizers, Salads, and Side Dishes

CALIFORNIA MAKI WITH AVOCADO, CUCUMBER, AND GREEN ONION

The seaweed (nori), wasabi (Japanese powdered horseradish), and pickled ginger are available at Asian food stores and most health-food stores. The rice mixture used in this maki (hand-rolled sushi) is so delicious that we recommend using it in other dishes as well.

You can make this with long-grain rice or the shorter-grain Japanese rice. Use 1⅓ cup Japanese rice and 1¾ cup water.

Makes 4 servings (1 roll per person)

1 cup uncooked long-grain rice

2 cups water

6 tablespoons Japanese rice vinegar

2 tablespoons sugar

¼ teaspoon salt

4 sheets (7 × 8 inches) sushi nori (pressed, toasted seaweed)

1 tablespoon wasabi powder, reconstituted with 1 tablespoon water

1 small cucumber, peeled, cut lengthwise, seeded, and cut in slivers

1 small ripe avocado, peeled and cut in thin wedges

2 tablespoons fresh lemon juice

2 green onions, cut in 1-inch pieces and slivered

¼ cup low-sodium soy sauce

2 tablespoons dry white wine

½ cup pickled ginger

Put rice in a small saucepan with water. (Or use an electric rice cooker according to manufacturer's directions.) Bring to a boil over medium heat and cook about 7 to 8 minutes. Cover pan and remove from heat. Let stand for 5 minutes.

Mix together vinegar, sugar, and salt in a small saucepan. Cook over medium heat, stirring often, until sugar has dissolved. Using a wooden spoon or rice paddle, sprinkle vinegar over hot rice and stir to combine.

Spoon rice into a bowl. Set aside.

Set seaweed in front of you on the counter on a cloth napkin or small bamboo mat. Spoon about ¾ cup of rice in the center and smooth it the length of the seaweed. Using a spoon, smear a thin line of wasabi down the center of the rice; use sparingly because it is very hot. Put ¼ of the cucumber, ¼ of the avocado sprinkled with lemon juice, and ¼ of the onion over rice.

Working quickly, roll up the maki into a tight roll. Cut the maki roll into 1-inch pieces with a very sharp knife, using a sawing motion. Roll and fill remaining sheets of seaweed.

Serve 1 roll per person. Serve with the small bowl of soy sauce mixed with white wine and the pickled ginger. Dip the maki into the soy sauce. Put a slice of pickled ginger on top of the maki.

300 calories, 8 g fat, 1 g saturated fat, no cholesterol, 2.5 g dietary fiber, 534 mg sodium

SWEET-SOUR-HOT SLAW

This slaw is based on the hot-sour-sweet dipping sauces that show up on tables in Thai and Vietnamese restaurants across the United States. This makes a good potluck dish if you double the recipe. For a cross-cultural experience, serve it with buckwheat noodles.

Makes 4 servings

½ small head (about ½ pound) green cabbage

1 small carrot, cut into long strips (use a vegetable peeler or citrus zester)

½ cup very thinly sliced red onion

½ cup cider vinegar

2 tablespoons water

¼ cup sugar

1 clove garlic, minced

½ teaspoon salt

Pinch of hot red pepper flakes, or to taste

1½ teaspoons cornstarch

1 tablespoon finely chopped fresh cilantro (optional)

Core cabbage half and cut in half. Slice cabbage into very thin shreds. Place in a large bowl with carrot and onion.

Mix vinegar, water, sugar, garlic, salt, and red pepper flakes in a small non-aluminum saucepan. Stir in cornstarch until smooth. Cook over medium heat, stirring, until dressing turns clear and thickens. Remove from heat and let cool. Stir in cilantro.

Pour dressing over vegetables and toss to coat. Refrigerate until serving. The slaw tastes best if it marinates for at least 1 hour before serving.

76 calories, no fat, no cholesterol, 2 g dietary fiber, 281 mg sodium

SALADS IN RICE PAPER

This is a fun way to lift the standard salad out of the ordinary. It's inspired by fresh Vietnamese spring rolls. Make it easy on yourself by buying assorted, trimmed, already washed lettuce in the bag.

Rice paper wrappers can be found in most stores that carry Southeast Asian ingredients. Although fish sauce gives this a more authentic flavor, it is not vegetarian. Soy sauce makes a suitable substitute.

Makes 4 servings (2 packets per serving)

8 rice paper wrappers
About 3 ounces mixed lettuce
Handful of fresh basil or mint leaves
½ seedless cucumber, or 1 small regular cucumber, cut in half lengthwise and thinly sliced

2 carrots, cut into strips
3 green onions, cut into strips
2 tablespoons finely chopped peanuts
Edible flowers, such as pansies, rose petals, or marigolds (optional)

Dipping sauce:

3 tablespoons orange juice
3 tablespoons rice vinegar
2 teaspoons sugar
1 tablespoon fish sauce or soy sauce

1 small red chile pepper, seeded and finely chopped
1 tablespoon finely chopped fresh basil or mint

Fill a shallow bowl or pie plate with warm water. Lay a damp towel on the work surface next to you. Place 1 rice paper wrapper in the warm water. Let it soak for 30 to 45 seconds, or until softened. Lay the softened rice paper out flat on the damp towel.

Mix lettuce with mint or basil leaves. Place a small handful of lettuce down the center of the rice paper. Lay a row of overlapping cucumber slices on top of the lettuce. Add a few strips of carrot, a few strips of green onion, and just a few peanuts. Wrap bottom of rice paper over filling, then fold in sides. Continue rolling to enclose salad. Place bundle, seam side down, on a plate.

Repeat with remaining rice paper wrappers and salad. Refrigerate rolls up to 4 hours. Before serving, garnish with edible flowers.

Shortly before serving, make the dipping sauce by mixing all ingredients.

Diners eat these with their hands, dipping them in the sauce.

67 calories, 2.5 g fat, 0.5 g saturated fat, no cholesterol, 2.5 g dietary fiber, 266 mg sodium

Soups

SIMMERED VEGETABLES WITH BUCKWHEAT NOODLES

Wasabi is a very potent green Japanese horseradish made from the root of the wasabi plant. It comes in powdered form and is available at Asian food markets and in some supermarkets. It is mixed with water to make a paste.

Makes 4 to 6 servings

Sauce and wasabi:

¼ *cup low-sodium soy sauce*

¼ *cup dry white wine*

2 tablespoons fresh lemon or lime juice

2 tablespoons wasabi powder

Warm water

Noodle soup:

6 cups vegetable stock (page 17) or 4 cups canned vegetable broth diluted with 2 cups water

1 sheet nori (toasted seaweed), cut into small strips with scissors

2 cups finely shredded cooked cabbage

2 cups trimmed and cooked spinach, drained

4 green onions, minced

4 white or shiitake mushrooms, cleaned and trimmed

½ cup grated carrot

½ cup diced firm tofu

2 cups cooked Japanese buckwheat noodles (soba)

To make the sauce and wasabi: Combine soy sauce, wine, and juice in a bowl. Set aside at room temperature.

Mix wasabi powder with just enough warm water to form a thick paste. Let mixture stand for 6 to 8 minutes, cover, and set aside.

To make soup: Bring stock and nori to a boil in a large saucepan or pot. Discard nori. Add vegetables, tofu, and noodles to stock. Simmer until heated through.

Ladle soup into bowls. Put sauce in small sauce dishes, one for each diner. Put a dab of wasabi on the side of each sauce dish. Diners add sauce and wasabi to soup as they desire.

Serve immediately.

4 servings: 189 calories, 2.5 g fat, 0.5 g saturated fat, no cholesterol, 5 g dietary fiber, 817 mg sodium

WON TON SOUP

Won ton wrappers (wheat-based Chinese square noodles) can be purchased at large supermarkets and in Asian grocery stores. Put extra won tons in self-sealing freezer bags and freeze for up to three months.

Makes 8 servings

Filling:

2 green onions, minced
½ cup drained water chestnuts, minced
4 dried shiitake mushrooms, reconstituted in boiling water, trimmed, and minced

½ cup bean sprouts (that have been rinsed in hot water, drained, and chopped)
½ teaspoon grated fresh gingerroot
1 egg white, lightly beaten

24 won ton wrappers
4 green onions, minced
½ teaspoon dark sesame oil
8 cups vegetable stock (page 17), or 5 cups canned broth diluted with 3 cups water

½ cup chopped watercress
1 teaspoon honey
1 teaspoon low-sodium soy sauce
⅛ teaspoon pepper

Keep won ton wrappers under a damp towel so they do not dry out.

Mix all filling ingredients in a bowl.

Bring a pot of lightly salted water to a boil. Have a small bowl of water handy to seal won tons. Place a won ton on the table with one point facing you. Put about 1 teaspoon of filling on bottom half of wrapper. Working quickly so won ton does not dry out, brush edges with water. Fold top of wrapper over filling, pressing edges of wrapper together to seal it securely. Bend won ton as though you were going to fold it in half again and press the remaining 2 points together.

Lightly flour a cookie sheet. Set won tons on flour to keep from sticking and cover with plastic wrap. Repeat filling and folding won tons until wrappers and filling are used up. Cook as quickly as possible to keep from drying out. Slide won tons into a pot of boiling water and cook over medium-high heat about 6 minutes. With a slotted spoon remove won tons to a large, shallow bowl. Add onions and oil.

Bring stock to a boil, then reduce to simmer. Add won tons just to heat through.

Ladle soup and won tons into individual soup bowls. Sprinkle with watercress and serve warm.

118 calories, 1.5 g fat, no saturated fat, 3 mg cholesterol, 1 g dietary fiber, 826 mg sodium

COLD SWIRLED TOMATO AND SPINACH SOUP

With its green-white puree swirled through russet, this lovely soup reminds us of Italian marble. The spinach mixture does not keep well, so serve the soup the same day you make it.

Makes 4 servings

Tomato soup:

1 tablespoon olive oil

2 cloves garlic, minced

2 pounds fresh, very ripe tomatoes, cored and diced

1 tablespoon tomato paste

¼ cup dry red wine

2 teaspoons minced fresh oregano or thyme

1 teaspoon snipped chives

½ to 1 teaspoon sugar (optional)

¼ teaspoon salt

Freshly ground pepper to taste

Spinach soup:

1 cup cooked, drained, and chopped spinach

1 tablespoon chopped fresh basil

Pinch of ground nutmeg

½ cup nonfat sour cream

½ cup skim milk

¼ teaspoon salt

To make tomato soup: Heat oil in a large saucepan. Add garlic and sauté until fragrant. Add tomatoes, tomato paste, and wine; stir well. Bring to a simmer. Reduce heat to low and cook, loosely covered, for 20 minutes, or until tomatoes have cooked down and are pulpy.

Puree soup in a food processor or blender until smooth. Push soup through a sieve to remove tomato skins and seeds. Return to pan and stir in oregano, chives, sugar, salt, and pepper.

To make spinach soup: Put spinach in a food processor or blender with basil, nutmeg, sour cream, milk, and salt. Process until smooth.

Chill tomato and spinach soups separately. Just before serving, spoon about ½ cup spinach soup into the center of each soup bowl. Ladle about ¾ cup tomato soup around the spinach soup. Then run a spoon gently through the spinach soup to swirl with the tomato soup. Serve cold.

136 calories, 4.5 g fat, 0.5 g saturated fat, no cholesterol, 4.5 g dietary fiber, 397 mg sodium

Entrées

ARTICHOKE PIZZA WITH DRIED TOMATOES AND PINE NUTS

By definition a California pizza is an individual pie with unconventional toppings. This pizza sports a sunny medley of artichokes, dried tomatoes, and pine nuts.

Makes 6 (7-inch) pizzas

Crust:

1 scant cup warm water (105° to 115°)
½ teaspoon honey
1 package (2¼ teaspoons) active dry yeast

¾ cup whole wheat flour
2 to 2½ cups all-purpose flour
½ teaspoon salt
1 tablespoon olive oil

Topping:

1 tablespoon plus 1 teaspoon olive oil
2 large shallots, minced
6 ounces (about ⅔ cup) goat cheese
1 cup chopped dried tomatoes (that have been soaked in hot water until softened)

1 (12-ounce) jar marinated artichokes, drained and quartered
2 tablespoons pine nuts

Pour water into measuring cup or small bowl. Mix in honey and yeast. Let mixture stand in warm area for 3 to 5 minutes, until yeast begins to bubble.

While yeast is proofing, use an electric mixer or food processor to mix whole wheat flour and 2 cups all-purpose flour with salt and oil.

Mix in yeast and process only until a sticky, soft dough is formed, about 8 seconds in a processor or 3 to 5 minutes with the mixer. Turn dough out onto a lightly floured board and knead until smooth, working in additional flour as needed. Place the dough in a deep ungreased bowl; cover lightly with a kitchen towel. Allow dough to rise until it doubles in bulk, about 1 hour. Punch dough down; let stand for 5 minutes. On a lightly floured pastry cloth, divide dough into 6 pieces. Stretch dough by hand or roll into 7–inch circles.

Preheat oven to 425°.

Heat 1 teaspoon oil in a nonstick frying pan that has been sprayed with nonstick cooking spray. Sauté shallots until soft, stirring occasionally.

With a spatula, place crusts on pizza tiles (available at cookware stores) that are set on cookie sheets. If you do not have pizza tiles, place pizzas directly on cookie sheets. Brush very lightly with 1 tablespoon oil. Dot cheese over crusts and spread slightly. Sprinkle crusts with shallots, tomatoes, artichokes, and pine nuts.

Bake for 20 minutes, or until crust is a light golden brown.

462 calories, 18 g fat, 5.5 g saturated fat, 13 mg cholesterol, 7.5 g dietary fiber, 768 mg sodium

COUSCOUS WITH PISTACHIOS, BLOOD ORANGES, AND SNOW PEAS

Couscous—a tiny relative of pasta—has become very popular in the last few years, with very good reason. The kind sold in the United States has been presteamed so that it needs no real cooking, just steeping in hot liquid.

Blood oranges are grown in California now and increasingly are showing up in supermarkets. Their flesh ranges from deep orange to a marvelous crimson. They're more sweet than tart. You can substitute regular oranges.

Makes 4 servings

3 cups fresh orange juice (from regular oranges)
2 cups couscous
¼ cup chopped fresh mint
½ teaspoon salt

¼ teaspoon white pepper
½ cup chopped pistachios
2 blood oranges, peeled and sliced with the slices cut in half again
2 cups fresh snow peas, trimmed

Bring orange juice to a boil in a large nonaluminum saucepan. Stir in couscous, mint, salt, and pepper. Cover pan tightly, remove from heat, and let stand 5 to 7 minutes, until couscous has absorbed liquid. Fluff couscous with a fork. Mix in pistachios.

While couscous is standing, heat a nonstick frying pan that has been sprayed with nonstick cooking spray, or use a stovetop grill according to manufacturer's directions. Add orange pieces and snow peas, and cook over medium heat about 2 to 3 minutes, turning once or twice.

Mound couscous on plates. Surround it or cover it with orange pieces and snow peas. Serve hot.

474 calories, 8.5 g fat, 1 g saturated fat, no cholesterol, 5.5 g dietary fiber, 274 mg sodium

Nuts

California grows more nuts than any other state in America, and in fact more than any country in the world. Almonds, walnuts, and pistachios bring in nearly $1 billion a year for the state's growers.

California grows 70 percent of the world's supply of almonds (and all of America's). The state's seven thousand almond growers export two-thirds of the crop. America's number one customer for almonds is Germany, where almonds are turned into marzipan and a host of other confections. Almonds still in the shell go mostly to India.

Diamond Walnut, a cooperative in Stockton, represents about half of California's five thousand walnut growers. A third of the crop goes overseas; walnuts are especially popular in the Mediterranean and Middle East. Ninety percent of the walnuts sold in the United States are shelled.

Our pistachios used to come from Iran, but now they're grown on about fifty thousand acres in California's San Joaquin Valley.

Unlike the red pistachios you may remember from your youth, today's pistachios are plump and tan. California growers remove the thin red skins from the nuts within forty-eight hours of picking them. When the skin is not removed, it dyes the shell the familiar rose color.

QUINOA WITH THREE PEPPERS

To cook quinoa, rinse and drain. Place in a heavy saucepan with water to cover by 1 inch. Bring to a boil, then reduce heat to low. Cook for 15 to 20 minutes, until quinoa has absorbed the water. Fluff with a fork.

Makes 4 servings

1 tablespoon canola oil
¾ cup chopped green onion
3 cloves garlic, minced
2 cups sliced red or green bell pepper
¾ cup roasted, peeled, and sliced
   poblano pepper (page 14)

2 jalapeño peppers, seeded and chopped
2 cups cooked quinoa
1 teaspoon fresh oregano, or
   ½ teaspoon dried
½ teaspoon cumin seed
½ teaspoon salt

Heat oil over medium heat in a nonstick frying pan that has been sprayed with nonstick cooking spray. Cook onion and garlic, covered, about 3 minutes, stirring once or twice. Stir in all 3 peppers and cook, partially covered, until tender. Stir in quinoa, oregano, cumin, and salt. Cook until heated through. Serve hot.

175 calories, 6 g fat, 0.5 g saturated fat, no cholesterol, 4.5 g dietary fiber, 290 mg sodium

QUINOA AND COUSCOUS WITH SPINACH

Couscous and quinoa may seem very similar at first, but couscous cooks up light and fluffy, while quinoa has a distinctive crunch. Although most quinoa is still imported from South America, a small amount is grown in California.

Makes 4 servings

1 tablespoon canola oil

¾ cup chopped white onion

3 cloves garlic, minced

½ cup uncooked quinoa

6 cups cleaned and trimmed spinach

¼ cup vegetable stock (page 17) or
   canned broth

2 cups cooked couscous, cooled

½ teaspoon crushed fresh thyme leaves,
   or ¼ teaspoon dried

½ teaspoon salt (use less with canned
   broth)

¼ teaspoon pepper

1 cup chopped ripe tomatoes

Heat oil in a large nonstick frying pan that has been sprayed with nonstick cooking spray. Sauté onion, garlic, and quinoa about 3 minutes, stirring once or twice. Stir in spinach and vegetable stock. Cook, covered, until spinach is soft. Stir in couscous and seasonings, and heat through. Mix in tomatoes. Serve hot or warm.

285 calories, 2 g fat, no saturated fat, no cholesterol, 5 g dietary fiber, 347 mg sodium

MU SHU VEGETABLES IN A CHINESE PANCAKE

Mu Shu Vegetables are served in a Chinese pancake, which are available frozen at Asian grocery stores and large supermarkets if you prefer not to make your own. You can substitute a flour tortilla in a pinch.

   Spicy and sweet, hoisin sauce is frequently used in mushroom dishes.

Makes 4 servings

½ cup egg substitute

¼ teaspoon salt

1 egg white, beaten until firm, glossy
     peaks form

2 teaspoons canola oil

4 green onions, cut in half lengthwise,
     then into 1½-inch pieces

3 cloves garlic, minced

1 teaspoon minced fresh gingerroot

2 cups thinly shredded Chinese cabbage
     or green cabbage

1 cup drained bamboo shoots, shredded

⅓ cup cloud ear mushrooms,
     reconstituted in warm water, sliced
     thin

½ cup dried shiitake mushrooms,
     reconstituted in warm water, sliced
     thin

3 tablespoons homemade vegetable
     stock mixed with 2 tablespoons
     cornstarch

2 tablespoons dry white wine

2 tablespoons low-sodium soy sauce

½ teaspoon sugar

¼ teaspoon salt

¼ teaspoon pepper

½ cup hoisin sauce

Chinese pancakes (recipe follows)

Gently mix the egg substitute and salt into beaten egg white. Heat a nonstick frying
pan that has been sprayed with nonstick cooking spray and cook the egg mixture over
medium heat, scrambling eggs until they set. Remove from pan and set aside.

Heat oil in a nonstick wok or frying pan that has been sprayed with nonstick
cooking spray. Cook onions, garlic, and gingerroot, covered, on high heat for about 1
minute, stirring once.

Add cabbage and cook, covered, 2 to 3 minutes. Remove cover and add bamboo
shoots, cloud ears, and mushrooms; stir-fry for 1 to 2 minutes. Stir in vegetable stock–
cornstarch mixture, wine, soy sauce, sugar, salt, and pepper. Continue stir-frying
until sauce thickens, 1 to 2 minutes. Stir in eggs.

Spread hoisin sauce down center of a heated pancake. Put ½ cup of egg filling over
sauce and roll pancake, tucking bottom of pancake over. Repeat with remaining
filling and pancakes. Direct guests to eat pancake with their hands.

352 calories, 9 g fat, 1.5 g saturated fat, 53 mg cholesterol, 3 g dietary fiber, 1,098 mg sodium

CHINESE PANCAKES

Makes 12 to 16 pancakes

2 cups all-purpose flour
1 cup minus 2 tablespoons boiling
  water

Dark sesame oil

Using a food processor or an electric mixer with a dough hook, mix flour with water until smooth and soft. Gather dough into a ball. Cover dough with plastic wrap and let rest for 20 minutes.

Roll out dough to ¼-inch thickness, then cut into 2½- or 3-inch circles. Lightly brush the circles with ¼ to ½ teaspoon oil each. Set an oiled round on top of a second oiled round, pressing them together. Roll into a 5- to 6-inch circle. Repeat with remaining rounds. Do not turn dough over.

Heat a nonstick frying pan. On medium-high heat, cook each pair of pancakes 35 to 45 seconds on first side and 10 to 15 seconds on second side.

Separate pancakes by pulling them apart when hot. Stack and wrap pancakes in aluminum foil or plastic wrap. These are best used the same day, but you can freeze them or refrigerate for 2 days. Steam pancakes or microwave on high for 30 seconds (depending on your microwave) to serve.

50 calories, 1 g fat, no saturated fat, no cholesterol, 0.5 g fiber, no sodium

ALL-AMERICAN CHOW MEIN

This longtime Chinese-American carryout favorite reportedly originated in the San Francisco area, and for better or worse, was the first encounter many of us had with Chinese-style food. Still, the basic idea is sound: a stir-fry of bits and pieces (chow mein). Chop suey is served on rice; chow mein on fried noodles. Stir-frying the noodles makes them nice and crisp on the outside and chewy inside.

Makes 4 servings

½ pound dried Asian-style egg noodles
(such as ramen)

⅓ cup vegetable stock (page 17) or
water

1 tablespoon cornstarch

3 tablespoons canola oil

2 cloves garlic, minced

1 teaspoon minced fresh gingerroot

6 green onions, minced

1 (5-ounce) can sliced water chestnuts,
drained

2 cups sliced celery

2 green bell peppers, seeded and thinly
sliced

3 cups fresh bean sprouts, rinsed

¼ teaspoon salt

¼ teaspoon pepper

2 tablespoons low-sodium soy sauce

3 tablespoons ketchup

1 tablespoon dry white wine

Cook noodles in a large pot of lightly salted boiling water for 4 to 5 minutes (or according to package directions), just until tender. Drain and put in a bowl of very cold water until ready to use.

Mix stock or water with cornstarch and set aside.

Heat 1 tablespoon oil in a wok or nonstick frying pan. Add garlic, gingerroot, and green onions; stir-fry for a few seconds. Add water chestnuts, celery, peppers, bean sprouts, salt, and pepper. Stir-fry about 2 minutes; vegetables should be heated but still crisp. Add soy sauce, ketchup, wine, and stock-cornstarch mixture. Stir-fry for 2 minutes, or until sauce thickens slightly. Remove to a bowl.

Working quickly, drain noodles. Heat remaining 2 tablespoons oil in the same wok. Stir-fry noodles just until heated through.

Place noodles on a serving dish. Spoon cooked vegetables over noodles and serve at once.

400 calories, 13 g fat, 1 g saturated fat, 50 mg cholesterol, 8 g dietary fiber, 858 mg sodium

BLACK BEAN TOSTADAS

Some foods never go out of style. The tostada, a salad heaped on a crisp tortilla, is still one of California's best cheap lunches. To make this dish especially quick, use canned beans and a bottled salsa.

Seasoning the beans with a sauce made of chipotles, smoked jalapeños, will give them an intriguing hint of smokiness.

Makes 4 servings

1 tablespoon olive oil

1 clove garlic, minced

1½ to 1¾ cups cooked black beans
(drain and rinse well if canned)

½ teaspoon ground cumin

¼ teaspoon salt (omit if using canned
beans)

Splash of chipotle chile sauce or regular
hot red pepper sauce

1 cup finely diced zucchini

1 cup finely diced ripe tomato

1 tablespoon minced fresh cilantro

8 corn tortillas

½ cup salsa of your choice

½ cup nonfat sour cream

4 cups shredded romaine lettuce

Heat oil in a small nonstick frying pan. Add garlic and sauté until fragrant, then add beans and cumin. Cook, coarsely mashing beans with the back of a wooden spoon, until heated through. Remove from heat and add salt and hot pepper sauce. Set aside.

Preheat oven to 425°.

Mix zucchini, tomato, and cilantro in a small glass bowl; set aside.

Spray tortillas on both sides with nonstick cooking spray. Place in the oven directly on the rack and toast for 3 to 5 minutes, until crisp. Watch carefully so they don't burn.

Place 2 tortillas on each plate. Spread each tortilla with 1 tablespoon salsa, then top with 2 to 3 tablespoons beans and 1 tablespoon sour cream. Spoon zucchini-tomato salad over beans and sour cream, then top with lettuce. Serve immediately.

319 calories, 6 g fat, 1 g saturated fat, no cholesterol, 9.5 g dietary fiber, 463 mg sodium

TANGERINE-PERFUMED CREPES WITH SHIITAKE MUSHROOMS AND JUICE

Shiitake mushrooms are now being cultivated in California and other states. Available both dried and fresh, this meaty, plump, full-bodied mushroom can be steamed, sautéed, or juiced. When reconstituted, save the flavorful liquid; use in soup or as a juice, as we do here.

Both the juice and filling can be prepared the day before serving, and the crepes can be frozen or prepared the day before and refrigerated.

Makes 4 servings (2 crepes per serving)

Shiitake juice:

1 cup dried shiitake mushrooms
2 cups boiling water
1 seedless tangerine, chopped

2 tablespoons brandy or orange liqueur, or to taste

Shiitake filling:

1 tablespoon canola oil
½ cup minced shallots
2 cups sliced fresh shiitake mushroom caps
½ cup reconstituted shiitake mushrooms (reserved from juice), caps only, sliced

½ cup chopped reconstituted dried tomatoes
1 tablespoon minced fresh basil or tarragon or 1½ teaspoons dried
¼ teaspoon salt
¼ teaspoon freshly ground black pepper

Tangerine crepes:

1 tablespoon finely grated tangerine zest
2 eggs
2 egg whites
1 cup skim milk
1 cup water

¼ cup tangerine juice
1 cup all-purpose flour
½ teaspoon salt
1½ tablespoons canola oil
1 tablespoon minced fresh basil or tarragon, or 1½ teaspoons dried

To make juice: Wash mushrooms and put them in a heatproof bowl. Pour boiling water over mushrooms. Add chopped tangerine and brandy. Let mushrooms stand for 45 minutes, or until very soft. Drain mushrooms, reserving juice. Set aside ½ cup mushrooms for filling; reserve remainder for another use. Trim stems from mushrooms. Strain juice.

Put juice in a small pan. Cook over medium heat until reduced slightly and very flavorful. Remove from heat. You can refrigerate the juice for up to a day if desired. Reheat to serve, adding a little more brandy if desired to intensify flavors.

To make filling: Heat oil in a nonstick saucepan. Cook shallots, covered, about 1 minute. Stir in mushrooms and tomatoes. Cook, partially covered, until mushrooms are soft, stirring occasionally. Season with basil, salt, and pepper. Cool, cover, and refrigerate until needed. Reheat at serving time.

To make crepes: Batter can be made in a blender or food processor, or in a bowl using a whisk. Put all ingredients in a processor or blender. Mix only a few seconds, or until batter is smooth. Or sift flour and whisk ingredients. Let batter stand for 20 minutes.

Spray a heated 6-inch nonstick crepe pan or frying pan with nonstick cooking spray. Pour about 2½ to 3½ tablespoons batter into pan, tilting pan so batter covers bottom. Pour off any excess batter.

Crepe is ready when it is set and firm around the edges. Loosen edges with a knife. Turn it over using a spatula; cook only a few seconds. Stack crepes between sheets of aluminum foil or wax paper. Cover; if not using immediately, refrigerate or freeze. Defrost (see Crepe Magic, page 60) and rewarm in a 300° oven.

To serve: Heat shiitake juice and spoon some onto plates. Put about 3 tablespoons of heated, drained mushroom filling in the center of each crepe. Roll crepes, then place on plates, seam side down. Serve immediately.

338 calories, 12 g fat, 1.5 g saturated fat, 107 mg cholesterol, 4.5 g dietary fiber, 637 mg sodium

SOBA (BUCKWHEAT NOODLES) WITH A LIGHT PEANUT SAUCE

Makes 4 servings

8 ounces Japanese buckwheat noodles
   (soba)
2 teaspoons canola oil
2 cloves garlic, minced
¾ teaspoon grated fresh gingerroot
4 green onions, including tops, minced
1½ tablespoons reduced-fat peanut
   butter

2 tablespoons low-sodium soy sauce
½ teaspoon dark sesame oil
2 tablespoons white wine vinegar
2 tablespoons dry white wine
2 teaspoons honey
1 cup cooked green peas, drained

Cook soba noodles in lightly salted water according to package directions, about 7 to 8 minutes, or until tender. Drain. Put in a serving bowl and set aside.

Heat canola oil in a nonstick wok or frying pan that has been sprayed with nonstick cooking spray. Sauté garlic and gingerroot about 1 minute, stirring so they do not burn. Stir in green onions and continue cooking for 2 minutes. Mix in peanut butter, soy sauce, sesame oil, vinegar, wine, and honey. Remove from heat.

Toss noodles with sauce and peas. Serve warm or cold.

309 calories, 5.5 g fat, 0.5 g saturated fat, no cholesterol, 2 g dietary fiber, 735 mg sodium

GRILLED VEGETABLES WITH LEMON SAGE POLENTA

Outdoor grilling has captivated the summer food scene. We like to grill this particular recipe with grapevines added to the coals as an aromatic. In California, grapevines abound. So if you have grapes in your backyard or know where to find wild ones, this is a good use for the vines. In other parts of the country, you might be able to find dried grapevines in specialty shops. Otherwise, toss some sprigs of fresh sage or some apple or cherry wood chips onto the coals.

Makes 4 servings

2 tablespoons canola oil

¼ to ½ teaspoon ancho chile dust (see page 313)

½ pound thin asparagus, trimmed

1 cup yellow or green beans, trimmed

1 large tomato, sliced

1 cup sliced yellow summer squash or peeled butternut squash

1 red onion, sliced

1 small eggplant, peeled and sliced

3 handfuls dried grapevines in 6-inch pieces, soaked in water 30 minutes and drained

Lemon Sage Polenta (recipe follows)

Mix oil and ancho chile dust in a shallow bowl.

Wash vegetables. Blanch asparagus in boiling water for 1 minute; drain well and rinse under cold water. Put vegetables on a tray and brush with ancho chile oil.

When coals are hot, add soaked grapevines. Spray or lightly oil a grill rack and set on grill. Place vegetables on rack in a single layer and cook for 2 to 4 minutes, until lightly browned. Squash, onion, and eggplant should take longer to cook, so put them on the grill first, followed by the asparagus, beans, and tomatoes.

Serve with polenta.

LEMON SAGE POLENTA

Makes 4 servings

1¾ cups water

¾ cup yellow or white cornmeal

2 tablespoons minced fresh sage, or 1 tablespoon dried and crumbled

1 tablespoon grated lemon zest

¼ teaspoon salt

¼ teaspoon white pepper

Bring water to a boil in a saucepan. Whisk in cornmeal, sage, lemon zest, salt, and pepper. Reduce heat to medium and continue cooking, whisking constantly, until thick. Make sure to whisk out any lumps.

Pour polenta into an 8-inch-square nonstick baking pan that has been sprayed with nonstick cooking spray. Cool, then refrigerate until firm.

Cut polenta into 8 rectangles, 4 by 2 inches. Set them on a sprayed grill rack over hot coals. Cover and grill about 4 minutes on each side, or until lightly browned.

Vegetables and polenta: 215 calories, 7.5 g fat, 0.5 g saturated fat, no cholesterol, 6 g dietary fiber, 143 mg sodium

Chile Dust

With its raisiny-hot flavor, the ancho chile—a dried poblano—makes a good partner for many dishes. You can dry and finely grind just about any dried chile, however, to make a "dust" that can be used to flavor chiles, beans, and soups, or used as part of a rub or basting mixture for grilled or pan-fried foods.

To make ancho chile dust, place ancho chiles on a baking sheet and toast in a 225-degree oven for 35 to 40 minutes, until brittle. Remove stems and seeds, and grind chiles in a food processor or spice grinder to make a fine powder.

Keep, tightly covered, for up to six months in a cool, dry place. A medium-size ancho chile will yield about 1 tablespoon of powder.

To give barbecued vegetables a smokier flavor, toast and grind chipotle, smoked jalapeño, peppers. They are smaller, so you will not have to toast them as long.

You also can buy specialty chile powders in some specialty shops or by mail (see Sources and Resources, page 329).

STIR-FRY PRIMAVERA

The area around Stockton, California, is asparagus country. It's the area that produces most of the spears that excite so many of the shoppers around the United States. (Michigan is also a major asparagus producer, but most of its crop is canned or frozen.) When asparagus shows up in the supermarket, you know spring is finally on the way.

Makes 4 servings

1 bunch asparagus, cut diagonally in
   1-inch pieces (about 2 cups)
2 tablespoons olive or canola oil
2 large cloves garlic, minced
1½ teaspoons grated fresh gingerroot
4 green onions, cut into 1½-inch pieces
¼ pound fresh green beans, cut into
   1½-inch pieces

2 carrots, grated
1 pound mushrooms, thinly sliced
1 large yellow or red pepper, seeded and
   thinly sliced
1½ teaspoons minced fresh oregano
1 teaspoon minced fresh basil
Salt and pepper to taste

Blanch asparagus in boiling water to cover for 1 minute; drain.

   Heat oil in a wok or deep nonstick frying pan over high heat. Stir-fry garlic, gingerroot, and onions quickly, about 2 minutes. Add asparagus, beans, and carrots. Continue stir-frying about 3 minutes. Stir in remaining ingredients and stir-fry only until heated through. The vegetables should stay crisp.

   Serve immediately with rice or noodles.

142 calories, 7.5 g fat, 1 g saturated fat, no cholesterol, 5.5 g dietary fiber, 155 mg sodium

SAFFRON ANGEL HAIR WITH ASPARAGUS AND RED PEPPER PESTO

Makes 4 servings

4 teaspoons extra-virgin olive oil
3 cloves garlic, finely minced
¼ teaspoon saffron threads
¼ cup white wine or vegetable stock
   (page 17)
2 tablespoons blanched almonds
Vegetable stock or water
2 roasted red peppers, seeded and
   coarsely chopped (page 14)

2 teaspoons minced fresh basil
2 teaspoons balsamic vinegar
Salt
¾ pound asparagus, snapped into
   2-inch pieces
Pepper
12 ounces angel hair pasta

To make pesto: Heat 3 teaspoons oil in a small pan and sauté garlic until fragrant. Add saffron and wine, and bring to a simmer, crushing saffron lightly with the back of a spoon. Remove from heat and set aside.

Place almonds in a food processor with 2 tablespoons stock or water; grind until almonds are finely chopped. Add saffron-garlic mixture, peppers, basil, vinegar, 1 teaspoon oil, and ¼ teaspoon salt. Process until finely minced, adding more stock or water if necessary. Set aside.

Bring a pot of water to a boil for pasta.

Place asparagus in a colander or steamer and steam, tightly covered, over boiling water for 3 to 5 minutes, until tender-crisp. Remove steamer from pan. Season asparagus lightly with salt and pepper, and set aside.

Meanwhile, cook pasta in boiling water until al dente, about 2 to 3 minutes. Drain well. Toss pasta with roasted pepper pesto, season with salt and pepper, and mound on a platter. Make a "nest" of pasta, using forks to pull pasta away from center. Mound asparagus in the center.

Serve warm.

418 calories, 11 g fat, 1.5 g saturated fat, 79 mg cholesterol, 8 g dietary fiber, 286 mg sodium

POTATO AND STRING BEAN SALAD WITH ROASTED GARLIC DRESSING

This is a French-style salad and is wonderful made with those skinny, crisp little French-style green beans. We also like to add some color by tossing in a little roasted red pepper or a handful of currant tomatoes (tiny cherry tomatoes that grow in clusters, like grapes).

Makes 4 servings as a main course

2 pounds small thin-skinned boiling potatoes
½ pound fresh string beans, preferably French, snapped into 2 or 3 pieces

⅓ cup chopped fresh parsley

Dressing:

1 head roasted garlic (see below)
2 tablespoons white wine vinegar with
  tarragon
½ to ¾ teaspoon salt, to taste

¼ cup extra-virgin olive oil
Freshly ground black pepper
Diced roasted red pepper (page 14) or
  red currant tomatoes (optional)

Cook whole, unpeeled potatoes and beans in a large pot of boiling water. Use a slotted spoon to remove beans after 3 to 5 minutes, or when tender-crisp. Rinse under cold running water, drain well, and place in a large bowl. Continue cooking potatoes until they can be easily pierced with a knife but are still fairly firm. This will take a total of 10 to 20 minutes depending on the size of the potatoes.

Peel potatoes under cold running water. Cut into thick slices and place in bowl with beans. Add parsley.

To make dressing: In a blender or small food processor, puree roasted garlic with vinegar, salt, and oil until smooth.

Pour dressing over warm vegetables. Toss gently to coat. Season generously with black pepper. If desired, add a handful of diced roasted red pepper or red currant tomatoes.

Serve immediately or refrigerate. Bring to room temperature before serving.

349 calories, 14 g fat, 2 g saturated fat, no cholesterol, 6 g dietary fiber, 416 mg sodium

ROASTED GARLIC

Roasting tames garlic, turns it into a spreadable puree, and brings out its normally hidden caramel nature. Roasted garlic can be used in salad dressings, sauces, soups, dips, and spreads—wherever you want a dose of garlic without the pungency.

This recipe can also be made in the microwave. Cut off the top half inch of the garlic before cooking. Set the garlic on a microwave-proof dish. Cook on high for 5 minutes or until soft.

Makes 4 servings

4 large bulbs garlic
2 teaspoons olive oil

¼ teaspoon freshly ground pepper

Preheat oven to 350°.

Remove loose outer skin from garlic bulbs. Brush the whole garlic with oil. Set garlic, stem side up, in a baking dish.

Bake until garlic is very soft when pressed, about 35 to 45 minutes. With a sharp knife, cut off top ½ inch of bulb. Sprinkle with pepper.

Serve hot with crusty bread. To eat, squeeze garlic from skins, much the same as you would toothpaste.

A Breath of Pungent Air

The air around Gilroy, California, reeks—especially the last weekend in late July when the town throws the biggest, smelliest food festival in the United States. It began modestly in 1979, but now the Gilroy Garlic Festival draws more than 150,000 people who are happy to breathe, cook, and eat the odiferous bulb, which is harvested in June and July. Ninety percent of the U.S. crop is grown within a ninety-mile radius of Gilroy.

Like most festivals, Gilroy's has a reigning queen and king and arts, crafts, memorabilia, and food from garlic wine to garlic jewelry to garlic ice cream.

Perhaps its most famous event is the recipe contest, which draws nearly one thousand entries from around the United States—remarkable when you consider that finalists have to pay their own way to Gilroy and compete for a mere $200 in prize money. The official rules require that at least three cloves of garlic be used. That seems to pose little problem for the winners, who often include such instructions as: "Take 6 heads of garlic . . ."

One of our favorite tips from the Gilroy Garlic Festival organizers, who have published four cookbooks, is how to de-scent your fingers after chopping garlic: Rub your fingers under the bowl of a stainless steel teaspoon while holding it under running water for a few minutes.

We tried it. It really works.

Breads and Desserts

OLIVE-FENNEL BREAD

Try to find full-flavored black olives for this—either imported ones, or truly ripe California olives, available in specialty shops, some health-food stores, and by mail (see Sources and Resources, page 329).

Makes a 2-pound loaf; 16 servings

3 cups plus 1 tablespoon bread flour
2 packages (4½ teaspoons) active dry yeast
1½ cups warm water (105° to 115°)
3 tablespoons olive oil
⅓ cup coarsely chopped black olives

1 tablespoon wildflower honey
½ teaspoon salt
1 tablespoon fennel seeds
1 egg white, beaten
2 tablespoons fennel seeds or sunflower seeds

Mix 2 cups of flour and the yeast in the large bowl of a heavy-duty mixer. Stir in water. Using the dough hook, run the mixer about 15 seconds. Add 1 cup flour and mix 1½ to 2 minutes. Add oil, olives, honey, salt, and seeds. Run mixer only until all ingredients are mixed in; dough will be very sticky. Sprinkle with remaining 1 tablespoon flour, cover, and let rise in a warm place until doubled, about 50 to 60 minutes.

Punch dough down. Grease a cookie sheet. Using a scraper, scrape dough onto cookie sheet; it will be very sticky. Gently shape into a large round. Cover lightly with plastic wrap and let rise in a warm place until light, about 30 minutes.

Preheat oven to 325°.

Brush top of dough with egg white. Sprinkle with fennel or sunflower seeds. Bake in the center of the oven for 25 minutes. Raise the temperature to 350°—don't open the oven door—and bake another 15 minutes, or until bread is a deep golden brown and sounds hollow when tapped. Cool bread on a rack.

121 calories, 3 g fat, 0.5 g saturated fat, no cholesterol, 1.5 g dietary fiber, 85 mg sodium

BREAD WITH MANY GRAINS

This bread is very robust and healthful. Unlike many of its hippie ancestors, however, it will not double as a doorstop.

Makes 1 loaf; about 12 servings

1 cup plus 2 tablespoons warm
*   water*
3 tablespoons wildflower (or other)
*   honey*
1 package (2¼ teaspoons) active dry
*   yeast*
1½ cups bread flour
1½ cups whole wheat flour
½ teaspoon salt

2 tablespoons canola oil
½ cup millet
¼ cup nonfat granola
¼ cup All-Bran or 100% Bran cereal
¼ cup old-fashioned oats, plus some for
*   sprinkling on top of bread*
1 egg white, lightly beaten

In a small bowl, mix 2 tablespoons warm water with ½ teaspoon of honey. Add yeast and let stand for 5 minutes, until foamy.

Put flours, salt, oil, millet, granola, bran cereal, 1 cup water, and remaining honey in the large bowl of a heavy-duty electric mixer fitted with the dough hook. Stir in yeast mixture and mix well. Dough will be very sticky.

Place dough in a greased or sprayed bowl, cover, and set aside in a warm place to rise until doubled in bulk, about 1½ hours.

Punch dough down. Batter will feel more like a dough. Knead about 2 minutes on a pastry cloth or board without any flour.

Spray an 8-inch-round cake pan with nonstick cooking spray. Toss a handful of oats into pan and shake pan so oats adhere to sides and bottom of pan. Set dough in pan, pushing lightly with floured fingers so it fills the pan. Cover and let rise 1 hour, or until light.

Preheat oven to 375°. Brush bread with egg white and sprinkle with a few additional oats. Bake in the center of the oven for 45 minutes, or until bread sounds hollow when turned out of the pan and lightly tapped on the bottom. Return the loaf, without the pan, to the oven for 5 minutes. This is a dense bread and needs to be cooked completely through.

Place bread on a rack and let cool completely before slicing.

191 calories, 3 g fat, 0.5 g saturated fat, no cholesterol, 4 g dietary fiber, 119 mg sodium

BUCKWHEAT FOCACCIA WITH DRIED TOMATOES

This full-flavored, pungent Italian flat bread is best served hot right from the oven. We bake it in a cast-iron frying pan and serve it directly from the pan, but it can be rolled out into a round or rectangular shape and baked on a sprayed baking sheet sprinkled with cornmeal.

For a wonderful luncheon, make focaccia sandwiches. Cut the focaccia into wedges, then cut each wedge in half to make 2 layers. Fill with grilled vegetables.

Makes 8 servings

1 package (2¼ teaspoons) active dry
*   yeast*
1⅓ cups warm water
2½ cups all-purpose flour
½ cup buckwheat flour
⅓ cup minced fresh thyme, or
*   3 tablespoons dried*
2 tablespoons plus 1 teaspoon olive oil
½ teaspoon salt

Cornmeal
1 cup chopped onion
3 cloves garlic, minced
2 tablespoons reconstituted and
*   chopped dried tomatoes*
½ teaspoon kosher (coarse) salt
½ teaspoon ground black pepper

Sprinkle yeast over warm water in a mixing cup. Stir to mix yeast and let stand about 5 minutes. While yeast is proofing, put flours in a bowl or in an electric mixer fitted with the dough hook. Mix in thyme. Add yeast, 1 tablespoon oil, and salt.

Knead dough on medium speed about 6 minutes, or until an elastic dough is formed. Turn out onto a lightly floured board and knead 1 minute.

Place dough in an oiled bowl, turning to coat with oil. Cover with plastic wrap or a damp kitchen towel. Let dough rise in a warm area for 1 hour.

Preheat oven to 450°. Spray two 8-inch-round cake pans with nonstick cooking spray and sprinkle cornmeal evenly over bottom of pans.

Heat 1½ teaspoons oil in a nonstick frying pan that has been sprayed with nonstick cooking spray. Cook onion and garlic, covered, over medium heat about 5 minutes, stirring occasionally. Set aside.

Punch dough down again. Put on a lightly floured board. Cut dough in half. Place half of dough in each prepared pan and pat dough into pan, covering pan completely. With a fork or your fingertips, poke indentations in dough. Brush remaining oil lightly over dough. Sprinkle evenly with sautéed garlic and onion, tomatoes, kosher salt, and pepper.

Bake in the center of the oven (on baking tiles, if you have them) for 15 to 20 minutes, until focaccia is golden brown.

Serve hot or warm.

215 calories, 5 g fat, 1 g saturated fat, no cholesterol, 3 g dietary fiber, 258 mg sodium

FRUIT AND OATMEAL SCONES

The recipe for this breakfast treat is from Starbucks, king of the Pacific Northwest coffee retailers. Naturally, these scones go well with coffee.

Makes 6 large scones

½ cup dried tart cherries

5 dried apricot halves, cut into
   ¼-inch dice

½ cup buttermilk

1 egg, or ¼ cup egg substitute

1 cup old-fashioned or quick-cooking
   (not instant) oats

1 cup plus 3 tablespoons flour

2½ tablespoons brown sugar

1½ teaspoons baking powder

½ teaspoon baking soda

¼ teaspoon salt

4 tablespoons cold unsalted butter, cut
   into pieces

Preheat oven to 350°.

Soak cherries and apricots in hot tap water for 15 minutes.

Place buttermilk and egg in a mixing bowl. Add oatmeal (do not stir) and let soak for 10 minutes.

Drain fruit well and add to buttermilk mixture. Do *not* stir.

In the bowl of a food processor equipped with the steel blade, combine flour, brown sugar, baking powder, baking soda, salt, and butter. Process until very well blended. Gently fold flour mixture into buttermilk mixture; do not overstir.

Turn dough onto a floured surface and pat it into a round about 1 inch thick. The dough will be very sticky. Do not add flour and do not knead. Lightly flour a knife to keep it from sticking to dough and cut into 6 equal wedges. Place wedges on an ungreased cookie sheet.

Bake for 20 to 30 minutes on the middle or top shelf of the oven, until golden brown.

275 calories, 10 g fat, 5.5 g saturated fat, 57 mg cholesterol, 2.5 g dietary fiber, 307 mg sodium

The Daily Grind

Thanks to Starbucks, the Pacific Northwest—and now, a good portion of the rest of the country—boasts an espresso bar on nearly every corner.

Inspired by a trip to Italy, which long has enjoyed a passionate love affair with coffee, the chief executive officer of Starbucks, Howard Schultz, decided to try to kindle a similar romance in America. Starbucks, named for the first mate in *Moby-Dick*, had been founded in 1971. Its first store was in Seattle's Pike Place Market. The coffee bar was an idea tailor-made for drizzly Seattle, and the idea took off like a shot of espresso. Starbucks is the largest specialty coffee retailer in the United States.

Espresso lies at the heart of most of the specialty drinks sold by Starbucks and its many competitors. It is made by shooting water at high pressure through deep-roasted, very finely ground coffee beans. Properly made espresso is intensely flavored but not bitter, and wears a topping of creamy tan froth.

"Short," "tall," and "grande" refer to the size of the cup, not the strength of the espresso.

Cappuccino, a popular beverage at coffee bars, is made of roughly equal parts of espresso and hot steamed and foamed milk. Wet cappuccino has more milk than foam, while dry cappuccino is the opposite.

A caffe latte consists of one part espresso to two parts steamed milk, with a bit of foam on top.

Macchiato is espresso with a dollop of milk, frothed or not. Caffe Americano is espresso diluted with water to produce a more typically American-style beverage.

Caffe mocha consists of chocolate syrup, a shot of espresso, and steamed milk, and is topped with whipped cream and a dusting of cocoa. You'd better think of this one as a dessert splurge; it weighs in at about 400 calories and 30 grams of fat—without the cream.

You can reduce the calories and fat considerably in any of these specialty drinks by asking for skim milk and skipping the cream.

What about the health effects of coffee? Although doctors generally counsel pregnant women to avoid caffeine, most research indicates a daily cup or two of coffee—regular or decaffeinated—poses little risk to most people. One study did find that coffee-drinking women run a greater risk of osteoporosis, but the effect was offset by drinking milk. Latte, anyone?

AMARANTH BLACKBERRY MUFFINS

Amaranth, held sacred by the Incas, has recently become popular because it is a rich source of protein. It is grown in the Plains states.

Oregon is a prime source of blackberries, which stand up better than raspberries in cooking.

Makes 12 muffins

¼ cup canola oil

⅓ cup sugar

½ cup egg substitute

1½ cups all-purpose flour

½ cup amaranth flour

4 teaspoons baking powder

½ teaspoon salt

1 tablespoon grated lemon zest

¾ cup lemon fat-free yogurt

¾ cup fresh blackberries or raspberries

Topping:

½ cup sugar

2 tablespoons all-purpose flour

½ teaspoon ground cinnamon

Line a muffin tin with paper liners. Preheat oven to 400°.

Beat oil and sugar in the large bowl of an electric mixer or in a deep mixing bowl. Beat in egg substitute. Mix 1¼ cups flour with amaranth, baking powder, salt, and lemon zest. Add dry ingredients to egg mixture alternately with yogurt.

Wash and pat berries dry with paper towels. Toss berries with remaining ¼ cup flour. Spoon berries lightly into batter.

Spoon batter into paper-lined muffin tins, filling cups about ¾ full.

Mix topping ingredients together and sprinkle over muffins.

Bake in the center of the oven for 25 minutes, or until muffins are firm to the touch and a tester inserted in the center comes out dry. Cool muffins 5 minutes, then turn out of pan. Cool on wire rack.

185 calories, 5.5 g fat, 0.5 g saturated fat, 1 mg cholesterol, 1 g dietary fiber, 268 mg sodium

CIDER-POACHED APPLES

An alternative sauce idea is to drizzle poached apples with maple syrup.

Makes 4 servings

Poached apples:

*4 large, firm cooking apples, such as
    Granny Smith or Pippin*

2 tablespoons lemon juice

*6 cups apple cider, or enough cider to
    cover apples*

⅛ teaspoon grated nutmeg

Filling:

2 tablespoons chopped walnuts

¼ cup currants

⅛ teaspoon ground cinnamon

2 teaspoons light brown sugar

Cider sauce:

1 cup reserved poaching liquid

⅛ teaspoon grated nutmeg

¼ teaspoon vanilla extract

Core and peel apples using a vegetable peeler. Reserve apples in a bowl of water mixed with lemon juice to prevent apples from turning color.

Heat cider and nutmeg to a boil in a heavy saucepan over medium heat. Lower apples into liquid and reduce heat to simmer. Continue cooking for 15 or 20 minutes, or until apples are tender but not mushy. Turn apples occasionally. Remove apples with a slotted spoon to individual deep dessert bowls; reserve liquid.

Toss nuts, currants, cinnamon, and sugar together. Fill apple cavities.

Strain 1 cup reserved poaching cider into a small saucepan. Add nutmeg and vanilla extract. Cook over high heat until liquid is reduced to ½ cup. Add any remaining filling. Drizzle sauce over and around apples.

Serve warm.

173 calories, 3 g fat, 0.5 g saturated fat, no cholesterol, 3.5 g dietary fiber, 5 mg sodium

PEACH AND CHARDONNAY SOUP WITH ROASTED PLUMS

The next time you have the remains of a buttery, apricot-scented Chardonnay to use, try it in this positively luxurious sweet soup. With its golden brown and scarlet hues, this is a lovely dessert for fall. In the spring and early summer, try it with apricots, using 1½ pounds of apricots as the base for the soup and roasting 3 medium apricots for the garnish. You may not need as much sugar.

Makes 4 servings

Roasted plums:

3 medium plums, preferably Santa Rosa

4 teaspoons sugar mixed with ½ teaspoon cinnamon

Soup:

4 teaspoons unsalted butter

4 large or 5 medium peaches (1½ pounds), peeled and diced

2 tablespoons light brown sugar

2 tablespoons granulated sugar, or to taste

1½ cups California Chardonnay, preferably a very buttery one

1 teaspoon vanilla extract

1 cinnamon stick, broken in two

⅛ teaspoon Chinese five-spice powder

Topping (optional):

⅓ cup light ricotta cheese

2 tablespoons nonfat sour cream

1 teaspoon light brown sugar

¼ teaspoon vanilla extract

To roast plums: Preheat oven to 250°. Cut plums in half along crease and remove pits. Thinly slice. Lay plum slices in a single layer on a wire rack set on a foil-lined cookie sheet. Sprinkle with half the cinnamon sugar.

Bake for 1 hour. Turn, sprinkle with remaining cinnamon sugar, and bake another 30 minutes to 1 hour, or until plums are nicely glazed and tender and skins are beginning to look leathery. Plums should be moist and sticky, but not juicy. Let cool on rack, then cover and keep refrigerated until ready to use.

While plums roast, make the soup: Heat butter in a heavy-bottomed saucepan. Add peaches and sugars, and cook for 5 minutes over medium heat. Stir in wine, vanilla extract, cinnamon, and five-spice powder. Simmer, loosely covered, over low heat for 45 minutes, until peaches have cooked down a bit and soup is syrupy. Let cool slightly, then remove cinnamon sticks and puree soup in a blender or food processor until smooth. Chill for at least 2 hours.

To make optional topping: Mix ricotta, sour cream, brown sugar, and vanilla extract in a food processor until smooth. Drop a spoonful in the center of each bowl of soup.

Without topping: 232 calories, 5 g fat, 2.5 g saturated fat, 11 mg cholesterol, 2.5 g dietary fiber, 11 mg sodium

Topping: 28 calories, 1 g fat, no saturated fat, no cholesterol, no dietary fiber, 6 mg sodium

Sources and Resources

Information About Vegetarianism

The North American Vegetarian Society offers booklets, recipes, and lists of vegetarian resources and clubs. Send a self-addressed, stamped business-size envelope to North American Vegetarian Society, P. O. Box 72 L, Dolgeville, NY 13329.

The Vegetarian Resource Group provides useful information on eating vegetarian. Send a self-addressed, stamped business-size envelope to Vegetarian Resource Group, P. O. Box 1463, Baltimore, MD 21203.

Vegetarian Times, a monthly magazine published in Oak Park, Illinois, features celebrity profiles, news briefs of interest to vegetarians, recipes (vegan and otherwise), and articles on current events and issues. A one-year subscription costs $24.95. For subscription orders and information, call (800) 435-9610.

The Practical Vegetarian is a bimonthly newsletter aimed at making vegetarian cooking and eating easy, and it rates cookbooks and convenience foods. A one-year subscription costs $16.95. Write to *The Practical Vegetarian*, P. O. Box 6253, Evanston, IL 60204.

Assorted Food Products

American Spoon Foods
1668 Clarion Avenue
P. O. Box 566
Petoskey, MI 49770
(800) 222-5886 OR (616) 347-9030

Dried tart cherries, dried cranberries, dried wild and domestic blueberries, dried persimmons; wild black walnuts, butternuts, hickory nuts, pecans, and chestnuts; dried morels; Minnesota wild rice; Michigan maple syrup and cream; preserves, including Spoon Fruit preserves made without sugar; salad dressings, sauces; gift baskets.

Dean & DeLuca
560 Broadway
New York, NY 10012
(800) 221-7714 OR (212) 431-1691

New York City's famous deli and specialty grocery store deluxe sells just about any specialty food you'd want, from beans to tea. Catalog $3.

Walnut Acres
Penns Creek, PA 17862
(717) 837-0601

Pennsylvania-style soups, granola, grains and flours, pasta, condiments, and many other items made from organically grown foods.

Beans

Bean Bag
818 Jefferson Street
Oakland, CA 94607
(800) 845-BEAN

All kinds of beans, including unusual varieties, harvested within the past year. Catalog $1.

Chiles and Southwestern Ingredients

Casados Farms
P.O. Box 852
San Juan Pueblo, NM 87566
(505) 852-2433

Chiles, ristras (chiles strung in wreaths), blue and white cornmeal, pozole, pine nuts, spices. Call or write for brochure.

Chocolate Sauces

Wax Orchards
22744 Wax Orchards Road, S.W.
Vashon Island, WA 98070
(800) 634-6132

Fat-free, fruit-sweetened chocolate sauces. Products are available in health-food stores and some specialty shops.

Equipment

Chef's Catalog
3215 Commercial Avenue
Northbrook, IL 60062
(800) 967-CHEF

Wide range of cooking equipment. Catalog $3.

Flours and Grains

Arrowhead Mills
P.O. Box 2059
Heresford, TX 79045

Blue cornmeal, buckwheat flour, quinoa, teff, amaranth, and a wide range of other grains and flours. Products also widely available in health-food stores. Write for catalog.

Black Duck Company
10932 Glen Wilding Place
Bloomington, MN 55431
(612) 884-3472

Wild rice at reasonable prices. Ask for brochure.

Falls Mill and Country Store
134 Falls Mill Road
Belvidere, TN 37306
(615) 469-7161

Stone-ground grits, white cornmeal, whole wheat flour, buckwheat flour, rye meal, and rice flour. Ask for price list.

King Arthur Flour
P.O. Box 876
Norwich, VT 05055
(802) 649-3717
(800) 827-6836

High-quality patent flours. Unbleached all-purpose, cake, and pastry, whole-grain flours, grains, a high-protein flour for bread baking, multipurpose white wheat, and a whole wheat flour that bakes like a white flour.

Lundberg Family Farms
P.O. Box 369
Richvale, CA 95974
(916) 882-4551

Brown and exotic rices and rice mixes, including the mahogany-colored Wehani and the black Japonica. Products also available in health-food stores.

White Lily Foods Co.
P.O. Box 871
Knoxville, TN 37901
(615) 546-5511 (no phone orders)

Milled from soft red wheat, White Lily flour is widely available in southern supermarkets and hardly anywhere else. It's *the* flour to use for biscuits. The company will ship to individuals; ask for an order and information sheet.

Herbs and Spices

Penzey's Spice House
P.O. Box 1448
Waukesha, WI 53187
(414) 574-0277

Top-quality spices hand-ground on the premises, including many hard-to-find spices.

Key Lime Juice

The Cook's Bazaar
516 Fleming Street
Key West, FL 33040
(305) 296-6656

Mushrooms

Aux Delices des Bois
4 Leonard Street
New York, NY 10013
(800) 666-1232 OR (212) 334-1230

Dried and fresh wild mushrooms, including morels, porcini, and chanterelles.

Nuts

Missouri Dandy Pantry
414 North Street
Stockton, MO 65785
(800) 872-6879

Black walnuts and black walnut products.

Olives

Santa Barbara Olive Company
3280 Calzada Road
Santa Ynez, CA 93460
(800) 4SB-OLIVE

Plain and flavored green and ripe olives; including some organically grown and certified.

Natural Charcoal for Grilling

People's Gourmet Woods
75 Mill Street
Cumberland, RI 02864
(800) 729-5800

Contributors of Recipes for This Book

Rick Moonen, Oceana, 55 East Fifty-fourth Street, New York, NY 10022; (212) 759-5941.

Pat Tillinghast, New Rivers Restaurant, 7 Steeple Street, Providence, RI 02903; (401) 751-0350.

Carl Jerome, Cooking and Hospitality Institute of Chicago, 361 West Chestnut, Chicago, IL 60610; (312) 944-0882.

Thiérry LeFeuvre, Froggy's French Cafe and Catering, 306 Greenbay Road, Highwood, IL 60040; (708) 433-7800.

Starbucks Coffee Company, 2203 Airport Way South-SMK-1, Seattle, WA 98134; (800) 782-7282 for catalog.

Bibliography

Allen, James Paul, and Eugene James Turner. *We the People: An Atlas of America's Ethnic Diversity.* New York: Macmillan, 1988.

American Journal of Clinical Nutrition. "Vegetarian Nutrition." Proceedings of symposium in Arlington, Virginia, June 28–July 1, 1992.

Bradford, William. *The History of Plymouth Colony: A Modern English Version.* New York: D. Van Nostrand Co., 1948.

Caffrey, Kate. *The Mayflower.* New York: Stein and Day, 1974.

Griggs, Barbara. *The Food Factor: An Account of the Nutrition Revolution.* London: Penguin, 1988.

Grunes, Barbara. *The Heartland Food Society Cookbook.* Santa Rosa, Ca.: Cole, 1993.

Havala, Suzanne, and Joanne Dwyer. "Position of the American Dietetic Association: Vegetarian Diets." *Journal of the American Dietetic Association* (November 1993): 1317–19.

Kimball, Marie. *Thomas Jefferson's Cookbook.* Charlottesville: University Press of Virginia, 1976.

Mayo, Bernard. *Jefferson Himself: The Personal Narrative of a Many-Sided American.* New York: Houghton Mifflin, 1942.

Nestle, Marion. "The Politics of Dietary Guidance—a New Opportunity." *American Journal of Public Health* (May 1994): 713–14.

Parsons, Russ. "To Soak or Not to Soak, It's No Longer a Question." Los Angeles: *Los Angeles Times,* February 24, 1994.

Raichlen, Steven. *Miami Spice.* New York: Workman, 1993.

Sahni, Julie. *Classic Indian Vegetarian and Grain Cooking.* New York: Morrow, 1985.

Sass, Lorna J. *Recipes from an Ecological Kitchen.* New York: Morrow, 1992.

Schneider, Elizabeth. "Whole Grains Explained," *Food Arts* (August/September 1994): 90–94.

———. *Uncommon Fruits and Vegetables: A Commonsense Guide.* New York: Harper & Row, 1986.

Sifakis, Carl. *American Eccentrics.* New York: Facts on File Publications, 1984.

Tufts University Diet and Nutrition Letter. "Healthier and Wealthier, the Wise Eater" (April 1994): 3–6.

Van Vynckt, Virginia. "Eat Like the Chinese, Study Finds." *Chicago Sun-Times,* November 21, 1991.

Voeltz, Jeanne, and Caroline Stuart. *The Florida Cookbook.* New York: Knopf, 1993.

Weaver, William Woys. *Pennsylvania Dutch Country Cooking.* New York: Abbeville Press, 1993.

Willett, Walter, M.D. "*Trans* Fatty Acids: Are the Effects Only Marginal?" *American Journal of Public Health* (May 1994): 722–24.

Index

Acadians, 91
Adams, Abigail, 105
African-American cooking, 91
Agar, 113–14, 269, 282
Alcohol
  enhancing flavors, 250, 279
Allspice, 92
Almond jelly
  with Gingered Pineapple, 281–82
Almonds, 4, 14, 275, 302
  Toasted Almond Tabbouleh, 188–89
Amaranth, 2, 215
  Amaranth Blackberry Muffins, 323–24
Amino acids, 3
Anaheim chile, 239
Ancho (chile), 239, 313
Angel hair
  Saffron, with Asparagus and Red Pepper Pesto,
    314–15
Animal foods, 1, 2, 3
Annatto seeds (achiote), 69
Antipasto, 42–43
Appetizers, 183
  Midwest and Heartland, 144, 165–69
  Northeast, 20, 48–53
  Pacific Coast, 272, 292–99
  the South, 88, 110–14
  the West, 212, 232–35
  Zucchini and Celery Sticks with Blue Cheese
    Dip, 52–53
Apple butter, 27
Apples, 207, 275, 283
  Apple Bran Muffins, 202
  Apple Currant Crisp, 206
  Apple Upside-down Gingerbread, 32–33
  Cider-poached, 324–25
  Slow-baked Sauerkraut with Carrots and, 191
Appleseed, Johnny, 207
Après-ski Party, 211, 226–31
Armstrong, Louis, 121
Aromatics, 52
Artichokes, 275
  Artichoke and Spinach Frittata, 102–3
  Artichoke Pizza with Dried Tomatoes and Pine
    Nuts, 300–1
  Garlicky Sautéed, 45–46
Asiago (cheese), 42
Asian pears, 276
  Riesling-poached, with Tillamook Cheddar,
    283–84
Asparagus, 148, 275
  Large Pumpkin Ravioli with, and Tomato-
    Chive Sauce, 175–76
  Risotto with, and Morels, 186–87

Asparagus (cont'd)
  Saffron Angel Hair with, and Red Pepper
    Pesto, 314–15
  Stir-fry Primavera, 313–14
Avocados, 2
  California Maki with Avocado, Cucumber, and
    Green Onion, 292–93

Bagels, 216
Baked goods, 5
Bananas, 92, 98
Barbecue, 91
  Barbecued Bean Sandwiches, 179–80
Barbecue sauce
  Tofu Sandwiches with, and Tangy Slaw, 128–30
Barley
  Quinoa and, and Brown Mushroom Soup,
    235–36
Basil, 13
  Bruschetta with Tomatoes and, 42–43
Bean curd
  Hoisin Noodles with, 280–81
  see also Tofu (bean curd)
Beans, 2, 4, 6, 10–11, 23, 148, 215, 216
  Appaloosa, 240, 242
  baked, 74
  Baked, with a Pumpernickel Crust, 64
  Barbecued Bean Sandwiches, 179–80
  basic southwest, 232–33
  Bean and Carrot Pâté with Watercress Sauce,
    36–38
  Bean Burritos with Tomatillo Sauce, 242–43
  fresh, 53
Great Northern, 10
  navy, 10
  rattlesnake, 242
  Red, and Rice, 121
  refried, 225, 232, 257–58
  and rice, 91, 92
  Scrambled Huevos Rancheros with Refried,
    256–58
  sources of, 330
  in Two-Corn Succotash, 48
  Warm Bean and Tomato Salad with Honey-
    Mustard Dressing, 185–86
  White Bean and Yellow Pea Soup, 171
  see also Black beans; Pinto beans

Beer, 93, 106, 153, 159, 227
Beet greens, 57, 134
Beets
  Cold Beet Soup with Dill, 56–57
  Sweet-and-Sour, 26–27
  Wilted Kale and Beet Salad, 132–33
Benne
  Benne Wafers, 140–41
Berries, 5, 23, 216
  Berry and Cherry Compote with White
    Cheese Mousse, 207–8
  Four-Berry Summer Pudding, 83–84
Beta-carotene, 1, 4–5, 134
Betty Crocker (co.), 148
Bettys, 82
Biryani
  Cauliflower and Cashew, 159–61
Biscotti
  Orange-Chocolate, 46–47
Biscuits
  Whole Wheat, 138
Black beans, 232–33, 276
  Black Bean Crepes with Salsa Cruda, 224–25,
    232–33
  Black Bean Tostados, 307–8
  Grilled Peppers with Whiskey, and Radish-
    Jicama Salsa, 250–51
  Lemon-scented Black Bean Soup, 95–96
Black walnuts, 148
  Black Walnut and String Bean Spread with Pita
    Bread, 165–66
  Green Salad with Dried Cranberries and, 167–
    69
Blackberries, 275
  Amaranth Blackberry Muffins, 323–24
Blackening, 130
Blood oranges, 8, 275
  Couscous with Pistachios and, and Snow Peas,
    301–2
Blueberries, 23, 148, 275
  Chilled Blueberry Soup, 55–56
Blue cheese
  Winter Vegetable Soup with Blue Cheese
    Croutons, 227–28
Boiled Dinner
  New England Red, with Honey-Mustard
    Sauce, 67

Bok choy, 276

Borscht, 170

Boston Brown Bread, 74

Botulism, 73

Bradford, William, 33

Bread machine(s), 24, 76, 77

Bread pudding
  Silky, with Bourbon Sauce, 104–5

Bread(s), 24, 147
  Apple Bran Muffins, 202
  Baked Boston Brown, 74
  Braided Egg (Challah), with Wheat Germ, 75–76
  brown, 24
  Buckwheat Focaccia with Dried Tomatoes, 320–21
  Cinnamon Rolls, 266–67
  Fluffy Buns, 136
  French, 137
  Irish Soda, 79–80
  with Many Grains, 319–20
  Midwest and Heartland, 145, 199–209
  Milwaukee Potato, 199–200
  Northeast, 21, 74–85
  Olive-fennel, 318
  Onion Rye, 68, 78–79
  Pacific Coast, 273, 318–27
  Pinto Quick, with dates, 220
  rye, 23
  Semolina Rolls with Parmesan and Pepper, 200–1
  Soft Pretzels, 76–77
  the South, 89, 136–42
  Sweet Potato–Pecan, with Sherried Fig Spread, 139–40
  twisted, 78
  the West, 213, 215, 259–69
  Whole Wheat Biscuits, 138
  Whole Wheat Pita, 204
  Whole Wheat Sourdough, 264–65

Broccoli, 4, 23, 234, 277
  Jade, 279–80
  and Raisin, and Sunflower Seed Salad, 154
  and Roasted Pepper Risotto, 117–18

Brown rice, 287
  and Fruit, and Walnut Salad, 289–90
  Salad of Orange Lentils and, 240

Bruschetta
  with Tomatoes and Basil, 42–43

Buckles, 82

Buckwheat
  and Bows, and Mushrooms, 63
  Buckwheat Focaccia with Dried Tomatoes, 320–21
  Buckwheat Pancakes with Apple Cider Sauce, 80–81
  Layered, –Ricotta Crepes with Tomato-Chive Salsa, 246–48

Buckwheat noodles (Soba)
  Japanese, with a Light Peanut Sauce, 311
  Simmered Vegetables with, 296–97

Bulgur, 188

Burbank, Luther, 216

Burgers, vegetarian, 288–89

Burritos
  Bean, with Tomatillo Sauce, 242–43

Butter, 1, 5, 6, 8, 12, 23, 275
  browned, 30
  clarified, 30
  -flavored cooking spray, 18

Buttermilk, 18

C. W. Post (co.), 203

Cabbage
  Pepper, 26
  red, 67
  Sweet-and-Sour Stuffed Cabbage Rolls, 195–96
  Whole, Stuffed with Spinach and Wild Rice, 194–96

Cabbage family, 5

Cacti, 221

Cactus pears, 221–22

Caffe latte, 323

Caffe mocha, 323

Cajuns, 91

Cake
  Minty Fudge Snack, 157–58
  Orange-scented Tofu Carrot, 291–92

Calcium, 3–4, 134

Canola oil, 6, 8, 12

Capers, 11

Cappuccino, 323

Carambola (starfruit), 92, 98, 99

Caraway, 23
Carbohydrates, 227
Caribbean cooking, 91, 92
Carotenoids, 5
Carrots, 17, 67
  Bean and Carrot Pâté with Watercress Sauce, 36–38
  Carrot Soup with Matzo Balls, 172
  Orange-scented Tofu Carrot Cake, 291–92
  Roasted Carrot and Potato Casserole, 192
  Slow-baked Sauerkraut with, and Apples, 191
  Zucchini, Carrot, and Potato Pancakes, 151–52
Carver, George Washington, 117
Cashews
  Cauliflower and Cashew Biryani, 159–61
Cauliflower, 4, 234
  and Cashew Biryani, 159–61
Celery
  Zucchini and Celery Sticks with Blue Cheese Dip, 52–53
Cepes, 229
Cereals, 23, 203
Challah, 75–76
Chanterelles, 282
  Chanterelle-Filbert Tart with Phyllo Crust, 284–85
Chard, 133
Cheddars, 23, 178
  Open-face Cheddar and Farmstand Tomato Sandwiches, 177
  Riesling-poached Asian Pears with Tillamook, 283–84
Cheeses, 148, 178, 275
  Colby, 178
  Honeyed Cheese Pudding with Fresh Fruit, 164–65
  Parmesan, 42, 200–1
  Swiss and Sauerkraut Sandwich on Homemade Onion Rye, 68–69
  Whole Wheat Crepes Filled with Herbed, 173–74
  see also Blue cheese; Cheddars; Goat cheese
Cherries, 216, 275
  Berry and Cherry Compote with White Cheese Mousse, 207–8
  Montmorency, 148, 150
Chicago, 158–59

Chickpeas, 166
  Cherry Tomatoes Stuffed with Hummus, 166–67
  Quinoa, Couscous, and Chickpea Packets, 249–50
Chile dust, 313
Chiles, 2, 215, 216, 238–39, 276
  sources of, 330–31
Chiles rellenos
  Pan-fried, with Melon Salsa, 251–52
Chili, 215
  Four-way, 196–97
  Two-Chile Lentil and Shiitake, 237–38
  Vegetable, with an Herbed Cornbread "Hat," 258–59
Chinese-Americans, 276
Chipotle, 239, 313
Chives
  Layered Buckwheat-ricotta Crepes with Tomato-chive Salsa, 246–48
Chocolate, 2, 215
  Chocolate Cinnamon Meringue Peaks, 231
Cholesterol, 1
Chop suey, 306
Chow Mein
  All-American, 306–7
Cilantro, 13, 14, 58, 216, 276
Cinnamon, 215, 216
Citrus fruits, 5, 11
Cobblers, 82
Coffee, 149, 225, 275, 321, 322–23
  Coffee Flan, 225–26
Colcannon, 70
Collard greens
  Slow-roasted Vidalia Onions with, 110, 133–34
Compotes
  Peach and Nectarine, with Mango-Ginger Frozen Yogurt, 84–85
Convenience foods, 7
Cookies
  bar, 147, 153
  Benne Wafers, 140–41
  Orange-Chocolate Biscotti, 46–47
Cooking
  low-fat, 6
  vegetarian, 2

Cooking and Hospitality Institute, Chicago, 207

Cooking spray, 18

Coriander; see Cilantro

Corn, 2, 8, 23, 33, 36, 215, 216
Fresh Corn Chowder, 169
in Midwest and Heartland, 148
in southern cooking, 92
tortillas, 4, 261–62
Two-Corn Succotash, 48–49
White Corn Sticks, 34–35
Yellow Corn Relish, 34–35

Cornbread, 34, 35, 91, 92
Layered Canyon, with Dried Tomato Butter, 262–63
Vegetable Chili with an Herbed Cornbread "Hat," 258–59

Cornmeal
Soft Cornmeal Loaf (Mamaliga) Four Ways, 65–66
White Cornmeal and Grits Spoonbread, 110–11

Corn on the cob, 148

Country Pie
Free-form, 181–83

Couscous, 6, 147
with Pistachios, Blood Oranges, and Snow Peas, 301–2
Quinoa and, and Chickpea Packets, 249–50
Quinoa and, with Spinach, 303–4

Cranberries, 2, 150
Cranberry-apple relish, 38
Green Salad with Dried, and Black Walnuts, 167–69

Cranberry relish, 24

Crepes, 44, 240
Black Bean, 232–33
Black Bean, with Salsa Cruda, 224–25
cooking, 60–61
Layered Buckwheat-ricotta, with Tomato-chive Salsa, 246–48
Ratatouille-filled Corn, with Dill, 126–27
Rye-Caraway, with Glazed Onions, 24, 59–60
tangerine, 309
Tangerine-perfumed, with Shiitake Mushrooms and Juice, 309–10

Whole Wheat, Filled with Herbed Cheese, 173–74

Crespelle
Double-Spinach, 43–45

Crisps (crunches), 82

Cruciferous vegetables, 4

Cucumbers, 91
Boiled New Potatoes and, with Sour Orange Sauce, 131–32
California Maki with Avocado and, and Green Onion, 292–93
Chilled Yogurt Soup with, and Tomatoes and Dill, 149–50
Greengrocer's, with Vegetable Shreds, 50–51

Cumin, 215, 216

Dairy products, 3–4, 5, 8, 148

Dark leafy greens, 4, 5, 91, 134

Dates, 216
Pinto Quick Bread with, 220

Desserts, 2
Almond Jelly with Gingered Pineapple, 281–82
Apple Currant Crisp, 206
Apple Upside-down Gingerbread, 32–33
Berry and Cherry Compote with White Cheese Mousse, 207–8
Chocolate Cinnamon Meringue Peaks, 231
Coffee Flan, 225–26
Cornflake-topped Noodle Pudding, 205
Dark and Spicy Pumpkin Pie, 40–41
Dried Fruit Compote, 230
Four-Berry Summer Pudding, 83–84
Hasty Pudding with Maple Syrup, 39–40
Honeyed Cheese Pudding with Fresh Fruit, 164–65
Huckleberry Yogurt Pie, 268–69
Key Lime Ice and Assorted Tropical Fruits, 98
Low-fat Chocolate Raspberry Soufflés, 286–87
Maple-scented Tropical Fruits Délice, 208–9
Midwest and Heartland, 145, 199–209
Minty Fudge Snack Cake, 157–58
Northeast, 21, 74–85
Orange-chocolate Biscotti, 46–47
Orange-scented Tofu Carrot Cake, 291–92
Pacific Coast, 273, 318–27

Desserts (*cont'd*)
   Peach and Chardonnay Soup with Toasted Plums, 325–27
   Peach and Nectarine Compote with Mango-Ginger Frozen Yogurt, 84–85
   Peach Custard Rice Pudding, 141–42
   Peach Ice Cream, 110
   Pinto Quick Bread with Dates, 220
   Plum Custard Bake, 152–53
   the South, 89, 136–42
   Strawberry Grunt, 81–82
   the West, 212, 259–69
Diamond Walnut (co.), 302
Diet, 4, 5
Diet for a Small Planet (Moore Lappé), 3
Dill
   Chilled Yogurt Soup with Cucumbers, Tomatoes, and, 149–50
   Cold Beet Soup with, 56–57
   Ratatouille-filled Corn Crepes with, 126–27
Dinner in the Desert, 211, 221–26
Dips
   Blue Cheese, 53
Disease prevention, 1, 4–5
Dressings, 103–4, 132, 154
   Basil Vinaigrette, 156–57
   Cranberry Vinaigrette, 168
   Honey-Mustard, 185–86
   roasted garlic, 316
   Sesame and Pickled Ginger, 234–35
   Thousand Island, 68
Dumplings, 147

Ecological Kitchen, The (Sass), 119
Eggplant, 12, 91, 92
   with Cumin and Black Pepper, 163–64
   Louisiana Rice and, 120
   Ratatouille-filled Corn Crepes with Dill, 126–27
   Whole Wheat Pasta with, and Toasted Pine Nuts, 62
Eggs, 8
   Artichoke and Spinach Frittata, 102–3
   Bernice's Radish and Egg Sandwiches, 181
   Denver-style Egg White Omelet, 218–19
   Pepper and Egg Sandwiches, 180–81
   Scrambled Huevos Rancheros with Refried Beans, 256–58

Egg substitutes, 11
Enchiladas
   with Roasted Peppers and Onions, 243–45
Endive
   Egg Lemon Soup with, and Orzo, 57–58
Energy bars, 215
Entrées
   Midwest and Heartland, 144–45, 173–98
   Northeast, 20–21, 59–72
   Pacific Coast, 272–73, 300–17
   the South, 88, 117–35
   the West, 212–13, 240–59
Equipment, 331
Escarole, 57
Espresso, 276, 322–23
Exercise, 3

Fajitas, 245
Farmers' markets, 6, 53
Fats, 1, 2, 8, 9, 12
   and flavor, 18
   good/bad, 5–6
Fatty acids, omega-3, 12
Fennel
   Steamed Squash, Peppers and, with Gremolata, 290–91
Fettucini
   with Creamy Porcini-Sage Sauce, 229–30
Fiber, 1, 14, 18, 203
Fiddlehead ferns
   Lemon-steamed, 51–52
Figs
   Sherried Fig Spread, 140
   Warm Fig Salad with Pine Nuts, 222
Filberts (hazelnuts), 275, 282
   Chanterelle-Filbert Tart with Phyllo Crust, 284–85
Filé, 101
Fish, 1, 2
Fish sauce, 189, 295
Flan
   Coffee, 225–26
Flavors, 8, 275, 276
Flavor enhancement, 18
   by alcohol, 250, 279
Flours, 12–13, 138
   sources of, 331–32

Focaccia
  Buckwheat, with Dried Tomatoes, 320–21
Folic acid, 1
Food poisoning, 7
Food products, sources of, 329–35
Fools, 82
Fritters
  Parsnip, and Cranberry-apple Relish, 38–39
Froggy's (cafe), 208
Frosting, 158, 292
Fruit(s), 2, 5
  Brown Rice and, and Walnut Salad, 289–90
  citrus, 5, 11
  Dried, Compote, 230
  exotic, 99–100
  healing power of, 4, 5
  Honeyed Cheese Pudding with Fresh, 164–65
  Key Lime Ice and Assorted Tropical, 98
  Maple-scented Tropical, Délice, 208–9
  and Oatmeal Scones, 321–22
  in southern cooking, 92
  tropical, 91, 98
Fu Fu, 94

Garlic, 13, 23, 91, 134, 215, 216, 275
  Gilroy Garlic Festival, 317
  healing power of, 4
  Minted, Tortilla Soup, 223
  Roasted, 316–17
  -Spiked Potato Soup, 58
Garlic toast, 102, 137
Gazpacho
  Shimmering, 113–14
Gelatin, 114, 269, 282
General Mills (co.), 148
Genistein, 119
Gilroy Garlic Festival, 317
Gingerbread
  Apple Upside-down, 32–33
Gingerroot, 84, 275, 276
  Gingered Pinto Bean Salad, 241
  pickled, 234, 292
Glycogen, 227
Goat cheese, 108, 276
  Pasta Torte with, and Tomatoes, and Olives, 106–7
Goldstein, Joyce, 275

Grains, 2, 6
  Bread with Many, 319–20
  healing powers of, 4, 5
  sources of, 331–32
Grapes, wine, 275
Gravy
  Carrot-miso, 197–198
Greens, 134
  Stir-fried Autumn, 285–86
  in stock, 17
  see also Collard greens; Dark leafy greens
Gremolata
  Steamed Squash, Peppers and Fennel with, 290–91
Grilling, 248, 311
  Grilled Medley of Garden Vegetables, 108–9
  natural charcoal for, 334
Grits, 92, 124
  Fried, and Cheese Finger Sandwiches, 125
  Souffléd, with Red Peppers, 123–24
  White Cornmeal and Grits Spoonbread, 110–11
Grunts, 82
  Strawberry, 81–82
Gumbo
  Green and Red, 101–2

Habañero (Scotch bonnet), 92
Hancock Village, 71
Health-food stores, 6
Hemings, James, 105
Henry, Patrick, 105
Herbs, 13–14, 18, 53, 71
  sources of, 333
  in vinegars, 73
Hoisin sauce, 276, 280, 281, 304
Hom, Ken, 275
Hominy, 215, 236
Huckleberries
  Huckleberry Yogurt Pie, 268–69
Hummus
  Cherry Tomatoes Stuffed with, 166–67

Ice cream
  Light Strawberry, 109–10
  Peach, 110
Icing(s); see Frosting

Immigrants, 2, 23–24, 147, 148–49, 159
Indians, 158–59, 162, 163
Ingredients, 10–18
Italian-American cooking, 42

Jalapeño, 238–39, 313
Jazz Brunch, 87, 100–5
Jefferson, Thomas, 105–6, 109
Jeffersonian Fourth, A, 87, 105–10
Jerk, 96
Jerome, Carl, 207
Jicama, 250, 276
Juice, calcium-fortified, 4

Kale, 134, 227
    Mashed Potatoes with, 70–71
    Wilted, and Beet Salad, 132–33
Kasha, 63
Kellogg, John Harvey, 203
Kellogg's (co.), 148
Key lime juice, 333
Key limes
    Key Lime Ice and Assorted Tropical Fruit, 98
Korma, 159

Lacto-ovo vegetarians, 1
Lactose intolerance, 134
Leafy Greens Council, 134
LeFeuvre, Thiérry, 208
Legumes, healing power of, 4
Lemongrass, 2, 276
Lemons, 11, 275
Lentils, 10, 216
    orange, 240
    Salad of Orange, and Brown Rice, 240
    Two-Chile Lentil and Shiitake Chili, 237–38
Lettuce, 216, 275, 295
    Warm Winter, with Sesame and Pickled Ginger Dressing, 234–35
Lima beans
    "Barbecued" Baby Limas, 111–12
Limes, 11, 92
    see also Key limes
Lingonberries, 150
Lundberg Farms, 289
Lychee, 99–100

Macadamia nuts, 275
Macaroni pie, 106–7
Macchiato, 323
Madison, Deborah, 275
Maki
    California, with Avocado, Cucumber, and Green Onions, 292–93
Malt, 78
Mamaliga, 65–66
Mangos, 84, 92, 98, 275
Manicotti
    Double-Spinach Crespelle, 43–45
Maple pudding, 24
Maple syrup, 2, 23, 208
    Hasty Pudding with, 39–40
Margarine, 1, 5, 6, 8
Masa, 158
Massasoit, Chief, 33
Matsutake, 282
Matzo Balls, 172–73
Mayflower, 33, 36
Meat, 1, 2
Mediterranean-style diet, 5
Meringue, 232
    Chocolate Cinnamon Meringue Peaks, 231
Mexican cooking, 215
Microwave, 10, 119, 256, 316
Midwest and Heartland, 143–209
Midwest Family Reunion, 143, 153–58
Millet, 27
Minerals, 4, 5
Mirlitons
    Savory Stuffed, 112–13
Miso, 2, 4, 134, 197, 199
Molasses, 23
Monounsaturated fats, 6, 12
Moonen, Rick, 83
Moore Lappé, Frances, 3
Morels, 187–88
    Risotto with Asparagus and, 186–87
Muffins
    Amaranth Blackberry, 323–24
    Apple Bran, 202
Mulato (chile), 239
Mushrooms, 17, 216, 282–83
    Buckwheat, Bows, and, 63
    Free-form Country Pie, 181–83

Mu Shu Vegetables in a Chinese Pancake, 304–6
Pickled, 25–26
porcini, 229
Quinoa, Barley, and Brown Mushroom Soup, 235–36
sources of, 333
Tofu-Mushroom Burgers, 288–89
wild, 2, 148, 229, 275
see also Shiitake
Mu Shu Vegetables, 304–6
Mustard, 178
Baked Potato Wedges with, and Rosemary, 233–34
Mustard greens, 134

Nam pla, 189
Native Americans, 23, 33, 36, 48, 215
New Age farmers, 216
New England cooking, 67
New Orleans, 91, 100, 102, 137
New Rivers (restaurant), 84
Noodles, 147, 277
buckwheat, 294
Cornflake-topped Noodle Pudding, 205
fried, 306
Hoisin, with Bean Curd, 280–81
Pad Thai, 189–90
Saffron Noodle Squares, 28
soba, 294
see also Buckwheat noodles (Soba)
Nopales (nopalitos), 221
Nori, 277, 292
North American Vegetarian Society, 329
North End Italian Dinner Party, 19–20, 41–47
Northeast, 19–85
Nutrition, 5–6, 8
vegetarian, 3–4
Nutritional analysis, 8–9
Nuts, 8, 14, 302
sources of, 333

Oatmeal
Fruit and Oatmeal Scones, 321–22
Oils, 12
infused with herbs, 73
soybean, 199

Okra, 91, 92, 101
Olive oil, 5, 6, 8, 12, 276
Olives, 275
Olive-fennel Bread, 318
Pasta Torte with Goat Cheese, Tomatoes, and, 106–7
Omelet(s)
Denver-style Egg White, 218–19
Onions
California Maki with Avocado, Cucumber, and Green, 292–93
Enchiladas with Roasted Peppers and, 243–45
Rye-caraway Crepes with Glazed, 59–60
see also Vidalia onions
Oranges, 11, 92, 275
Orange and Grapefruit Salad with Pecans, 103–4
see also Blood oranges
Organic farming, 276

Pacific Coast, 271–327
Pacific Northwest Harvest Dinner, 271, 282–87
Pad Thai, 189–90
Pancakes, 147
Buckwheat, with Apple Cider Sauce, 80–81
Chinese, 304, 306
Swedish, with Cherry Sauce, 150–51
Zucchini, Carrot, and Potato, 151–52
Parmesan cheese, 42
Semolina Rolls with, and Pepper, 200–1
Parsley, 13, 14
Parsnips
Parsnip Fritters and Cranberry-apple Relish, 38–39
Pasilla (chile), 239
Passion fruit, 92, 98, 99
Pasta, 2, 6
Fettucine with Creamy Porcini-sage Sauce, 229–30
Garden Pasta Salad with Basil Vinaigrette, 156–57
Pasta Torte with Goat Cheese, Tomatoes, and Olives, 106–7
Whole Wheat, with Eggplant and Toasted Pine Nuts, 62
Pasties, 147
Root Vegetable, with Saffron Crust, 183–84

Pâté
  Bean and Carrot, with Watercress Sauce, 36–38
Peaches, 148, 275
  Peach Custard Rice Pudding, 141–42
  Peach Ice Cream, 110
Peanut butter, 134
Peanuts, 91, 92, 117
  Pea and Peanut Salad, 155
  Sweet Potato–Peanut Soup, 116
Pears, 275, 283
Peas
  Bisque of Fresh, 115
  black-eyed, 10, 122
  dried, 10–11
  Hoppin' John Bake (Black-eyed, and Rice), 122
  Pea and Peanut Salad, 155
  split, 10
  White Bean and Yellow Pea Soup, 171
Pecans, 2
  Orange and Grapefruit Salad with, 103–4
Pennsylvania Dutch, 24, 28, 30, 48
Pennsylvania Dutch Sunday Dinner, 19, 24–33
Peppers, 14–15, 91, 134, 282–83
  Broccoli and Roasted Pepper Risotto, 117–18
  Enchiladas with Roasted, and Onions, 243–45
  Grilled, with Whiskey Black Beans and Radish-Jicama Salsa, 250–51
  Holland, 14
  Pan-fried Tofu with Pico de Gallo and Green, 245–46
  Pepper and Egg Sandwiches, 180–81
  Quinoa with Three, 303
  Souffléd Grits with Red, 123–24
  Steamed Squash and, and Fennel with Gremolata, 290–91
Pesto
  Red Pepper, 315
Phyllo dough, 284
Phytochemicals, 4–5
Pico de Gallo (Tomato Relish), 245–46
Pie(s)
  Dark and Spicy Pumpkin, 40–41
  Huckleberry Yogurt, 268–69

Pie crust, 40, 182, 268
  saffron, 183–84
Pigeon peas
  Savory Rice with, 69–70
Pilaf
  Cauliflower and Cashew Biryani, 159–61
Pilgrims, 33
Pillsbury (co.), 148
Pine nuts, 215
  Artichoke Pizza with Dried Tomatoes and, 300–1
  Warm Fig Salad with, 222
  Whole Wheat Pasta with Eggplant and Toasted, 62
Pineapples, 275
Pinto beans, 10, 232, 242
  Gingered Pinto Bean Salad, 241
  Pinto Quick Bread with Dates, 220
Pistachios, 275, 302
  Couscous with, and Blood Oranges, and Snow Peas, 301–2
Pita
  Black Walnut and String Bean Spread with, 165–66
  Whole Wheat, 204
Pizza, 216
  Artichoke, with Dried Tomatoes and Pine Nuts, 300–1
Plantain, 92
  Plantain Chips or Fu Fu, 93–94
Plums, 148, 275
  Plum Custard Bake, 152–53
  roasted, 326
Poblano, 239
Polenta, 24, 65
  Lemon Sage, 312
Popcorn, 148
Porcini
  Fettucini with Creamy Porcini-sage Sauce, 229–30
Post (co.), 148
Potatoes, 2, 8, 15, 24, 67, 148
  baked, 255–56
  Baked Potato Wedges with Mustard and Rosemary, 233–34
  Boiled New, and Cucumbers with Sour Orange Sauce, 131–32

Fire-roasted Sweet and White, and Quinoa, Couscous, and Chickpea Packets, 248–50
Garlic-spiked Potato Soup, 58
Hot German-style Potato Salad, 193–94
Idaho, 216
Mashed, with Kale, 70–71
Mashed Potato Cakes with Basque-style Tomato and Pepper Sauce, 253–54
Milwaukee Potato Bread, 199–200
Potato and String Bean Salad with Roasted Garlic Dressing, 315–16
Potato Soup with Pickle and Horseradish, 170
Roasted Carrot and Potato Casserole, 192
Savory Potato Pudding, 193
Spicy Hashed Brown, 219
Texas Caviar Salsa on a Baked, 254–55
Zucchini, Carrot, and Potato Pancakes, 151–52
Potpie
Vegetable, with Saffron Noodle Squares, 28–29
Poultry, 1, 2
Pozole, 236–37
Practical Vegetarian, The (newsletter), 329
Preserved foods, 23
Pressure cooker, 10, 119
Pretzels, 24, 78
Soft, 76–77
Preventive medicine, 2
Proteins, 1, 3, 4
Puck, Wolfgang, 275
Pudding(s)
bread, 137
Cornflake-topped Noodle, 205
cream, 91
Four-berry Summer, 83–84
Hasty, with Maple Syrup, 39–40
Honeyed Cheese, with Fresh Fruit, 164–65
Peach Custard Rice, 141–42
Savory Potato, 192, 193
Silky Bread, with Bourbon Sauce, 104–5
Pumpkin, 24, 215
Dark and Spicy Pumpkin Pie, 40–41
Large Pumpkin Ravioli with Asparagus and Tomato-chive Sauce, 175–76

Quajillo (chile), 239
Quaker Oats (co.), 148

Quesadillas
with Tomato-Mango Salsa, 217–18
Quinoa, 2, 8, 215, 216
and Barley, and Brown Mushroom Soup, 235–36
and Couscous, and Chickpea Packets, 249–50
and Couscous with Spinach, 303–4
with Three Peppers, 303

Radicchio, 283, 285
Radishes
Bernice's Radish and Egg Sandwiches, 181
Raisins
Broccoli, Raisin, and Sunflower Seed Salad, 154
Raspberries, 275, 282, 283
Low-fat Chocolate Raspberry Soufflés, 286–87
Ratatouille
-filled Corn Crepes with Dill, 126–27
Ravioli, 147
Large Pumpkin, with Asparagus and Tomato-chive Sauce, 175–76
Red beans and rice, 3, 121
Redenbacher, Orville, 148
Relish(es)
cranberry, 24
Cranberry-apple, 38
sweets and sours, 25–27
Rhubarb, 81
Rice, 2, 92, 275
arborio, 117–18
basmati, 2, 120, 159, 160
beans and, 91, 92
Hoppin' John Bake, 112
Japanese, 292, 293
Louisiana, and Eggplant, 120
Red Beans and, 3, 121
Savory, and Pigeon Peas, 69–70
Valencia, 118
Wild Pecan, 120
see also Brown rice; Wild rice
Rice Paper, Salads in, 295–96
Risotto, 119
with Asparagus and Morels, 186–87
Broccoli and Roasted Pepper, 117–18
Rolls

Rolls (*cont'd*)
  Cinnamon, 266–67
  Whole Grain Icebox, 25, 27–28
Root vegetables, 23
  Root Vegetable Pasties with Saffron Crust, 183–84
Rosemary, 13, 276
  Baked Potato Wedges with Mustard and, 233–34
Rosewater, 164
Roux, 101
Rum, 23
Rush, Benjamin, 105
Rutabaga, 67
Rye bread doughs, 78

Saffron, 28, 31, 75
  Root Vegetable Pasties with Saffron Crust, 183–84
Salad(s), 131, 147, 153, 307
  Broccoli, Raisin, and Sunflower Seed, 154
  Brown Rice, Fruit, and Walnut, 289–90
  Garden Pasta, with Basil Vinaigrette, 156–57
  Gingered Pinto Bean, 241
  Green, with Dried Cranberries and Black Walnuts, 167–69
  Hot German-style Potato, 193–94
  Midwest and Heartland, 144, 165–69
  Northeast, 20, 48–53
  Orange and Grapefruit, with Pecans, 103–4
  of Orange Lentils and Brown Rice, 240
  Oscar's Waldorf, 49
  Pacific Coast, 272, 292–99
  Pea and Colby, 155, 156
  Pea and Peanut, 155
  Potato and String Bean, with Roasted Garlic Dressing, 315–16
  in Rice Paper, 295–96
  Shimmering Gazpacho, 113–14
  the South, 88, 110–14
  Tarragon-scented String Bean, Shaker Style, 71–72
  Warm Bean and Tomato, with Honey-Mustard Dressing, 185–86
  Warm Fig, with Pine Nuts, 222
  the West, 212, 232–35, 254

Wilted Kale and Beet, 132–33
  see also Dressings
Salmonella, 7, 11
Salsa
  Cruda, 224–25
  Mango, 217
  Melon, 252
  Radish-Jicama, 250
  Texas Caviar, 254–55
  Tomato-chive, 246–48
Salsa verde, 243, 245
Sandwiches, 147
  Barbecued Bean, 179–80
  Bernice's Radish and Egg, 181
  focaccia, 320
  Fried Grits and Cheese Finger, 125
  Open-face Cheddar and Farmstand Tomato, 177
  Pepper and Egg, 180–81
  on pretzels, 76
  Swiss and Sauerkraut, on Homemade Onion Rye, 68–69
  Tofu, with Barbecue Sauce and Tangy Slaw, 128–30
San Francisco Chinese-style Birthday Party, 271, 276–82
Sangria, 216
Sass, Lorna, 119
Saturated fats, 1, 5, 8, 9, 12
Sauces, 44, 296
  Apple Cider, 80–81
  Barbecue, with Beer, 180
  Boiled New Potatoes and Cucumbers with Sour Orange, 131–32
  Bourbon, 104–5
  Cherry, 150
  chocolate, 286, 331
  Cider, 325
  dipping, 295
  fish, 189, 295
  Hoisin, 276, 280, 281, 304
  honey-mustard, 67
  hot-sour-sweet dipping, 294
  Mashed Potato Cakes with Basque-style Tomato and Pepper Sauce, 253–54
  Peanut, 311
  Porcini-sage, 229–30

Ranchero, 256–57
Shiitake, 66
Tomatillo, 242, 243
tomato, 195
Tomato-chive, 175–76
Watercress, 37
Worcestershire, 112
see also Barbecue sauce; Soy sauce
Sauerkraut
Slow-baked, with Carrots and Apples, 191
Swiss and Sauerkraut Sandwich on Homemade
Onion Rye, 68–69
Scandinavian-style Brunch, 143, 148–53
Schultz, Howard, 322
Scones
Fruit and Oatmeal, 321–22
Seasonings, 18
Seaweed, 8, 275, 292
Seaweed Soup, 277
Seeds, 23
Semolina flour, 200
Serranos, 239
Sesame oil, 50
Sesame seeds, 14
Benne Wafers, 140–41
Shakers, 71
Shiitake
Shiitake Sauce, 66
Tangerine-perfumed Crepes with Shiitake
Mushrooms and Juice, 309–10
Two-Chile Lentil and Shiitake Chili, 237–
38
Shopping for food, 6–7
Shortening, 1, 5
Side dishes
Midwest and Heartland, 144, 165–69
Northeast, 20, 48–53
Pacific Coast, 272, 292–99
the South, 88, 110–14
the West, 212, 232–35
Sixties Reunion, A, 271, 287–92
Slaw
Sweet-sour-hot, 294
Tofu Sandwiches with Barbecue Sauce and
Tangy, 128–30
Slumps, 82
Smoke flavoring, 134

Snow Peas
Couscous with Pistachios, Blood Oranges, and,
301–2
Sodium, 1, 4, 9, 17
Sofrito, 69
Sommerville, Annie, 275
Soufflés, 91
Low-fat Chocolate Raspberry, 286–87
Souffléd Grits with Red Peppers, 123–24
Soup(s)
Bisque of Fresh Peas, 115
Carrot, with Matzo Balls, 172–73
Chilled Blueberry, 55–56
Chilled Yogurt, with Cucumbers, Tomatoes,
and Dill, 149–50
Cold Beet, with Dill, 56–57
Cold Swirled Tomato and Spinach, 298–99
Egg Lemon, with Endive and Orzo, 57–58
Fresh Corn Chowder, 169
Garlic-Spiked Potato, 58
Green and Red Gumbo, 101–2
Hot and Sour, 24, 54–55
Italian Summer Vegetable, 53–54
Lemon-scented Black Bean, 95–96
Midwest and Heartland, 144, 169–73
Minted Garlic Tortilla, 223
noodle, 296
Northeast, 20, 53–58
Pacific Coast, 272, 277, 296–99
Peach and Chardonnay, with Roasted Plums,
325–27
Potato, with Pickle and Horseradish, 170
Pozole, 236–37
Quinoa, Barley, and Brown Mushroom, 235–
36
Seaweed, 277
the South, 88, 115–16
Sweet Potato–Peanut, 116
the West, 212, 235–38
White Bean and Yellow Pea, 171
Winter Vegetable, with Blue Cheese Crou-
tons, 227–28
Won ton, 297–98
Sources and Resources (list), 329–34
Sourdough, 215
starter, 265–66
Whole Wheat Sourdough Bread, 264–65

South (the), 87–142
Southwestern Breakfast for Four, 211, 216- 20
Soybean oil, 199
Soy foods, healing powers of, 4
Soy sauce, 112, 134, 189, 197, 289, 295
Spices, 13–14, 18, 23, 159, 160, 162
    sources of, 333
    in southern cooking, 92
Spinach, 275
    Artichoke and Spinach Frittata, 102–3
    Cold Swirled Tomato and Spinach Soup, 298–99
    Fragrant, 162–63
    Quinoa and Couscous with, 303–4
    Whole Cabbage Stuffed with, and Wild Rice, 194–96
Spinach cream, 299
Spoonbread, 92
    White Cornmeal and Grits, 110–11
Squanto (Tisquantum), 33
Squash, 2, 28, 36, 227
    chayote, 112
    Gratin of String Beans and Yellow, 135
    Savory Stuffed Mirlitons, 112–13
    Steamed, and Peppers and Fennel with Gremolata, 290–91
Starbucks (co.), 321, 322
Starter, 264, 265–66
Stock, vegetable, 9, 17
Strawberries
    Light Strawberry Ice Cream, 109–10
    Strawberry Grunt, 81–82
String beans
    Black Walnut and String Bean Spread with Pita Bread, 165–66
    Gratin of, and Yellow Squash, 135
    Potato and String Bean Salad with Roasted Garlic Dressing, 315–16
    Tarragon-Scented String Bean Salad, Shaker Style, 71–72
Stroll Down Devon Avenue, A, 143, 158–65
Strudel dough, 284
Stuffing
    "Unstuffing" with Carrot-Miso Gravy, 197–98
Sturgis Pretzel House, 78
Succotash
    Two-Corn, 48–49

Sugar, 8
Sunflower seeds
    Broccoli, Raisin, and Sunflower Seed Salad, 154
Sushi, 292–93
Sweet potatoes, 92, 117
    Jerk Sweet Potato Slices with Vidalia Onion Conserve, 96–97
    Sweet Potato–Peanut Soup, 116
    Sweet Potato–Pecan Bread with Sherried Fig Spread, 139–40
Sweets and Sours (Platter), 25–27

Tabbouleh, 147
    Toasted Almond, 188–89
Tarragon vinegar, 71, 72, 73
Tarts
    Chanterelle-Filbert, with Phyllo Crust, 284–85
Taste of the Tropics, A, 87, 92–99
Tea, 277
Techniques, 10–18
Teff, 216, 227
Thanksgiving, 19, 33–41
Thousand Island dressing, 68
Thyme, 13
Tillinghast, Pat, 84
Tofu (bean curd), 4, 6, 7, 15–16, 24, 148, 199, 275, 287
    barbecued, 3
    -Mushroom Burgers, 288–89
    Orange-scented Tofu Carrot Cake, 291–92
    Pan-fried, with Pico de Gallo and Green Peppers, 245–46
    Spice-crusted, with Green and Red Tomatoes, 130–31
    Tofu Sandwiches with Barbecue Sauce and Tangy Slaw, 128–30
Tomatillos, 2, 242, 243, 245
    Bean Burritos with Tomatillo Sauce, 242–43
Tomatoes, 2, 8, 16, 91, 92, 275
    Bruschetta with, and Basil, 42–43
    Cherry, Stuffed with Hummus, 166–67
    Chilled Yogurt Soup with Cucumbers and, and Dill, 149–50
    Cold Swirled Tomato and Spinach Soup, 298–99

green, 130
Layered Buckwheat-Ricotta Crepes with Tomato-Chive Salsa, 246–48
Open-face Cheddar and Farmstand Tomato Sandwiches, 177
Pasta Torte with Goat Cheese and, and Olives, 106–7
peeling, 128
Spice-crusted Tofu with Green and Red, 130–31
tomato soup, 299
Warm Bean and Tomato Salad with Honey-Mustard Dressing, 185–86
Tomatoes, dried, 216, 276
Artichoke Pizza with, and Pine Nuts, 300–1
Buckwheat Focaccia with, 320–21
Tomato Butter, 263
Tortillas, 215, 243, 244, 254
corn, 261–62
flour, 259–60
Minted Garlic Tortilla Soup, 223
salad in, 307
whole wheat, 260–61
Tostadas
Black Bean, 307–8
Tower, Jeremiah, 275
Trail mix, 215
Trail Mix Truffles, 267–68
Trans fats, 5
Tropp, Barbara, 275
Tschirky, Oscar, 49
Turnip greens, 134
Turnips, 67
Tuskegee Institute, 117
Tzimmes, 193

U.S. Food and Drug Administration, 203

Vegetable oil cooking spray, 18
Vegetable oils, 5, 6, 8
Vegetable Packets, 276–77, 278–79
Vegetable stock, 9, 17
Vegetables, 2, 5
Grilled, with Lemon Sage Polenta, 311–12
Grilled Medley of Garden, 108–9
healing powers of, 4–5
Mu Shu, in a Chinese Pancake, 304–6

Simmered, with Buckwheat Noodles, 296–97
in southern cooking, 92
Stir-fry Primavera, 313–14
Vegetarian aware, 1
Vegetarian Cooking Under Pressure (Sass), 119
Vegetarian Times (magazine), 329
Vegetarianism, 1–9
information about, 329
muscular, 203
Vidalia onions
Jerk Sweet Potato Slices with Vidalia Onion Conserve, 96–97
Slow-roasted, with Collard Greens, 110, 133–34
Vinaigrette(s), 108–9, 178
basil, 156
cranberry, 168
Vinegar(s)
cranberry, 168–69
herbal, 73
tarragon, 71, 72, 73
Vitamin A, 4, 11
Vitamin B$_{12}$, 3
Vitamin C, 1, 4–5, 134
Vitamin D, 3, 4, 11
Vitamin E, 1, 4–5, 14, 18
Vitamins, 4, 5

Walnuts, 302
see also Black walnuts
Brown Rice, Fruit, and Walnut Salad, 289–90
Wasabi, 276, 292, 296
Washington, Booker T., 117
Waters, Alice, 275
Wax Orchards, 286
Wehani rice, 289
West (the), 211–69
Wheat, 147, 148, 200, 216
Wheat germ, 18
Braided Egg Bread (Challah) with, 75–76
Wild rice, 2, 148, 186, 216
Whole Cabbage Stuffed with Spinach and, 194–96
Wines, 105, 276
Bordeaux, 100, 283
Burgundy, 42, 149, 227
Cabernet Sauvignon, 93

Wines (*cont'd*)
  champagne, 100, 216, 227, 277, 283
  Chardonnay, 25, 33, 149, 221, 227, 283, 325
  Chenin Blanc, 106
  Chianti, 42, 288
  dessert, 42
  Gewurztraminer, 93
  Merlot, 42, 106, 221, 288
  Pinot Noir, 100, 106, 159, 221, 288
  Rhine-style, 153
  Riesling, 25, 93, 227, 283
  rosé, 33

Sauvignon Blanc, 25, 106, 159
Won ton Soup, 297–98

Yogurt, 18, 162
  Chilled Yogurt Soup with Cucumbers, Tomatoes, and Dill, 149–50
  Peach and Nectarine Compote with Mango-Ginger Frozen, 84–85

Zucchini
  and Carrot, and Potato Pancakes, 151–52
  and Celery Sticks with Blue Cheese Dip, 52–53